Marketing, Rhetoric, and Control

Marketing, Rhetoric, and Control investigates the tensions that surround the place of persuasion (and, more broadly, control) in marketing. Persuasion has variously been seen as an embarrassment to the discipline, a target for anti-marketing sentiment, the source of marketing's value in the modern organisation, a mysterious black box inside the otherwise rational and logical endeavour of enterprise, and a rather insignificant part of the marketing programme. This book argues that this multifarious reputation for persuasion within marketing stems from the influence of two quite oppositional paradigms—the scientific and the magico-rhetorical—that ebb and flow across the discourses of its discipline and practice.

Constructing an interface between original, challenging close readings of texts from the beginnings of the Western rhetorical tradition and an examination of the ways in which marketing has set about describing itself, this text argues for a Sophistic interpretation of marketing. From this perspective, marketing is understood as providing intermediary services to facilitate the continuing exchange of attention and regard between firm/client and stakeholders. It seeks to manage and direct this exchange through an appreciation of the changing rational and irrational motivations of the firm and stakeholders, using these as resources for the construction of both planned and improvised persuasive interactions in agonistic (or competitive) environments.

This book is aimed primarily at researchers and academics working in the fields of marketing, marketing communications, and the related disciplines of marketing theory, critical marketing, and digital marketing. It will also be of value to marketing academics in business schools, including those working in the areas of media and communication studies who have an interest in commercial and corporate communication, brand use of interactive media, and communication theory.

Chris Miles is a Senior Lecturer in Marketing and Communication at Bournemouth University, UK.

Routledge Studies in Marketing

This series welcomes proposals for original research projects that are either single or multi-authored or an edited collection from both established and emerging scholars working on any aspect of marketing theory and practice and provides an outlet for studies dealing with elements of marketing theory, thought, pedagogy and practice.

It aims to reflect the evolving role of marketing and bring together the most innovative work across all aspects of the marketing 'mix'—from product development, consumer behaviour, marketing analysis, branding, and customer relationships, to sustainability, ethics and the new opportunities and challenges presented by digital and online marketing.

Available titles in this series:

Marketing, Rhetoric, and Control
The Magical Foundations of Marketing Theory
Chris Miles

Marketing, Rhetoric, and Control

The Magical Foundations of Marketing Theory

Chris Miles

Routledge
Taylor & Francis Group

LONDON AND NEW YORK

First published 2018 by Routledge

2 Park Square, Milton Park, Abingdon, Oxon, OX14 4RN
605 Third Avenue, New York, NY 10017

Routledge is an imprint of the Taylor & Francis Group, an informa business

First issued in paperback 2020

Library of Congress Cataloging-in-Publication Data
A catalog record for this book has been requested

ISBN: 978-1-138-66727-3 (hbk)
ISBN: 978-0-367-73478-7 (pbk)

Typeset in Sabon
by Apex CoVantage, LLC

For Şebnem

Contents

Acknowledgements

I would like to thank a number of people who have made the conception and writing of this book an easier process. Both Nicholas O'Shaughnessy and Yasmin Ibrahim encouraged my research on rhetoric and marketing from an early stage and acted as sympathetic, influential sounding boards at the start of this project. I am very grateful for the sterling support that I have received in my work from Janice Denegri-Knott in her capacity as Head of Research for the Department of Corporate and Marketing Communication at Bournemouth University and also as the Head of the Promotional Cultures and Communication Centre there. Other colleagues at Bournemouth University, particularly Rutherford and David Alder, have also been very generous in listening to my ramblings and offering sage advice (most of which I have flatly ignored in the interest of consistent cantankerousness). Tomas Nilsson has been an enthusing conversational partner for much of the writing of this book and his commitment to the rhetorical nature of marketing and management work is energizing. Finally, I would like to thank my wife, Şebnem, to whom this book is dedicated, for always supporting me, inspiring me, keeping me sane, and helping me to remember the magic power of language every day.

Introduction

In this study, I investigate the tensions that surround the place of persuasion (and, more broadly, control) in marketing. Persuasion has variously been seen as an embarrassment to the discipline, a target for anti-marketing sentiment, the source of marketing's value in the modern organisation, a mysterious black box inside the otherwise rational and logical endeavour of enterprise, and a rather insignificant part of the marketing programme. I will argue that this multifarious reputation for persuasion within marketing stems from the influence of two quite oppositional paradigms—the scientific and the magico-rhetorical—that ebb and flow across the discourses of its discipline and practice.

The scientific endeavour can be characterised as an effort to strip human investigation, and subsequent practice, of any confounding subjective influence, to objectively lay bare the workings of the natural world without becoming ensnared in the illusions of ideology, religion, myth, and received wisdom. Fundamental to all of these harbingers of error is that they are embedded in language. The careless use of language has been seen as the enemy of the objective discovery of truth since the birth of the modern scientific method (Stark, 2009). The early experimentalists of the Royal Society, for example, sought to eradicate figurative language and cultivate a plainness of style that focused not upon "The Artiface of Words, but a bare knowledge of things" (Sprat, cited in Longaker, 2015, p. 16). This attitude has also suffused much of the intellectual history of economics, commerce and management, where the patina of objective, 'scientific' discourse is important in persuading actors of the unbiased, incontrovertible logic of theories, policies and decisions (McCloskey, 1985; Miller, 1990; Greatbatch and Clark, 2005). Yet, as my own language here implies, the valorising of a plain and factual style, shorn of rhetorical figuration and emotional appeals, is itself a clear rhetorical strategy. Persuasive language does not have to appear florid and overflowing with figuration—it can instead adopt an empirical tone, relying upon the rhetoric of tables and matrices, to seduce readers into believing that the 'logic of science' is operating across its discourse. When academic and practitioner voices speak of banishing persuasion and rhetoric, then, they are often simply taking the opportunity to implement a particular rhetorical strategy of their own, a strategy which at many level is concerned with the manufacturing and maintenance of control.

In order to examine the place of persuasion within marketing theory, one inevitably will have to explore the relationship that the discipline has with scientific discourse (and scientific methodology as a discourse strategy). Yet, as I have already indicated, there is another discourse paradigm that has just as much influence over the development and self-construction of the marketing discipline—the magical worldview. Here, language is something that can enchant, cast a glamour, control from afar, and influence without recourse to logic or facts. Knowing the right set of words (the appropriate incantation) can give you power over others and reduce the confusion of everyday life. Such a power is naturally attractive to us all—but marketing practitioners, who deal constantly with the effort to find the right combination of words to invoke their brand's benefit as effectively as possible are perhaps closer than any other contemporary profession to the allure of the magical paradigm of language. Marketing theorists, who seek to formalise and explain the practice to themselves, their students, and (hopefully) professionals, are inevitably exposed to the assumptions of magical influence that I will show are common across the discipline. They might react to these assumptions, try to exorcise them, construct their theories in order to leave no room for them—but they inevitably become open to infection by them just as they are at the mercy of the assumptions of scientific discourse.

I intend to show that at the root of both the scientific and magical paradigms of language is the same basic concern—control. Marketing is obsessed with control—it is its very lifeblood. Accordingly, it should come as no surprise that marketing theory and practice constantly flip-flop between scientific and magical approaches to language. However, the relationship between the two is not a simple binary one, and it is the tradition of rhetoric which gives important clues as to how they bind together. The study and practice of rhetoric (the classical art of persuasion) has similarly been entwined within variegated constructions of rationality and irrationality throughout its theory and practice. I will demonstrate that marketing is an institutionalised contemporary manifestation of the rhetorical enterprise, particularly as the Sophists conceived of it, and as such can greatly profit from a careful consideration of the history of its mother discipline and the way in which society has at turns embraced and demonised it. This is particularly important at this stage of marketing's evolution. Concerns regarding marketing's authenticity, transparency, manipulative intentions, and effectiveness are rife both within and without the discipline. Marketing academics, with varying degrees of alarmist language, worry about the future of both the academic discipline and the profession (Thomas, 2006; Merlo, 2011; Varey, 2013; Clark et al., 2013; Verhoef and Leeflang, 2009) while report after report demonstrates the crisis of trust that brands face online due to annoying and intrusive control-oriented marketing practices (Daly, 2016). Theories (or proto-theories) such as the Service-Dominant logic (Vargo and Lusch, 2004) can be seen as attempts to re-define marketing in the face of such threats, yet they do this at the cost of making marketing less and less relevant. What is needed, instead, is an honest approach to the centrality of control to the marketing enterprise, one which can bring nuance and insight to the consideration of control rather than simply trying to act as if it is not (or should not be) there. This is what this study attempts to do by making a case for understanding marketing as a Sophistic enterprise, one which is focused upon the control (or management) of attention (or what I will call regard) through a persuasive, interactive engagement with stakeholders in an agonistic (i.e. competitive) environment. In order to argue this case, the reader must be taken through a number of stages and exposed to some quite diverse areas of scholarship and practice. I will now outline the course of the argument that I will be developing over the next nine chapters.

Synopsis

The first part of the book establishes the extent to which rhetoric has already figured as an object of marketing scholarship. In order to do this, and to prepare the reader of the development of my argument in later chapters, I start with an overview of the history of Western rhetoric. What writing there has been to date on the place of rhetoric within marketing practice and theory has tended to have to skimp heavily when supplying the historical and developmental context to rhetoric. This acts as a disadvantage for the further acceptance of rhetorical perspectives in the discipline because it leaves most readers with only a cursory understanding of what rhetoric really is and how much depth there exists in the scholarship that has grown up around it for more than two thousand years. If all we know of rhetoric is that Aristotle said that there were three different types of persuasive argument (*ethos*, *logos*, and *pathos*) and that it also has something (though we might not be sure what) to do with metaphors and figures of speech, then it is not surprising that we might not appreciate how much insight rhetoric can give us into the whole gamut of marketing thought. While there are many worthy primers of rhetoric available to the interested reader (Conley, 1990; Murphy et al., 2014; Kennedy, 1994; Smith, 2003; to name but a few), there are none that seek to summarise the story of the discipline for a marketing audience. Consequently, I will endeavour to lay out the important aspects of the study and practice of rhetoric as they will relate to my later, more involved, arguments regarding control, scientism, and magical thinking. Those readers who are already familiar with the rhetorical tradition are urged to jump straight to Chapter 2. It is here that I review the different ways in which marketing scholars have already engaged with aspects of rhetoric. For in linking rhetoric and marketing I am thankfully not starting *ab initio*. Even before Tonks' (2002) clarion call for rhetoric to have a "central location in making sense of marketing management" (p. 806) there had been a growing weight of research investigating the part that traditional rhetorical approaches to persuasion could have in explaining the power of textual and visual tactics in advertising and public relations (Bush and Boller, 1991; McQuarrie and Mick, 1992, 1996, 1999; Scott, 1994; Stern, 1988, 1990; Tom and Eves, 1999). This tradition has continued and broadened in recent years, with scholars such as Brown (2002, 2004, 2005, 2010), Hackley (2001, 2003) and myself (Miles, 2013, 2014a, 2014b) using rhetorical framings to discuss the ways in which marketing speaks about itself and how academics and practitioners use discourse to construct various aspects of what it means to be doing marketing. Chapter 2, therefore, brings us 'up to date' with the small but significant 'rhetorical turn' in marketing.

If, so far, marketing scholarship has not been overly receptive to arguments that it should be interpreted as an instantiation of rhetoric it is worth investigating just how it is that marketing does actually see itself. Chapter 3, therefore, begins by examining the foundation myths of marketing, looking at where scholars think the discipline comes from and how it has been thought to have developed in its formative years. Central to this examination is a consideration of the way that marketing has sought to define itself as a science and the sometimes quite vociferous debates that have flared up around this issue, particularly between those promoting a 'relativistic' interpretation of marketing truth and those supporting a far more empirical, 'realist' one. These debates are important for the stage that they set for my later analysis of the Sophistic character of the marketing enterprise, but they can also be analysed as attempts to run away from considering marketing's true nature as a discipline of rhetorical control. This leads me directly to a discussion of the centrality of control in any consideration of marketing practice and theory. I start this discussion by tracing an alternative history of marketing in what Beniger (1986) has called the "crisis of control" (p. 219) accompanying the Industrial Revolution. I will argue that modern marketing developed as a technology of control designed to stimulate and direct consumer demand and that these origins have continued to direct its evolution, despite the manifold extensions and re-focussings that the practice and discipline have undergone in the following decades. Marketing's ability to control consumption is dependent also upon the intermediary position of the marketing practitioner. The description of marketers as 'middlemen', though common in the late nineteenth and early twentieth century has largely fallen by the wayside. However, I will argue that the phrase holds an important key to the way in which the modern profession can be seen as reflecting a truly ancient dynamic. This is a cue for our first return to Plato and his dealings with early marketers (or retailers and traders) in order to worry away at the origins of this middle position of the marketer. Marketing historians have often reached for Plato when they have wished to underscore the esteemed history of the discipline, and I will consider the rhetorical ramifications for such an appeal. This will also serve as context for my oppositional reading of Plato's description of marketing middle men which occurs in Chapter 4. Chapter 3 finishes with a consideration of marketing scholarship's unquenchable desire to increase its scope as far as possible and relates this to the issue of exchange, a concept which has been repeatedly put forward as the one motif which can unify all marketing thought.

Chapter 4 builds upon the discussion of exchange that finishes the previous chapter and uses it to present an initial conception of how marketing can be considered an instantiation of the rhetorical discipline. I begin by exploring the ramifications of understanding marketing as an attempt to control the flow of value. I adopt the idea of the marketer as an intermediary but also return to Plato's discussion of the origins of the marketer in order to provide a detailed, Sophistic, oppositional reading of how the *urmarketer* functions in society. This allows me to offer an initial definition of marketing as rhetoric, a definition which is then qualified, expanded upon, and altered over the course of the chapter and its examination of the ways in which Plato deals with the infecting, liminal, dangerous presence of marketing in his ideal city-states. The chapter culminates with an argument, following Lanham (2006), for basing an understanding of marketing as rhetoric upon the provision of services to facilitate the exchange of attention.

Having argued for the broadly rhetorical nature of marketing, in Chapter 5 I make the case for considering marketing as particularly Sophistic. Once again, I return to Plato and the issue of the middle position of the marketer and demonstrate how that philosopher treated the Sophists in a very similar way—as infecting, dangerous outsiders who threatened the balance of society and the morals of those who composed it. On this basis I examine the legacy of Sophism, asking what made it unique as a rhetorical approach and what made it so threatening to Plato and Aristotle. This leads to a discussion of the way in which marketers are seen in modern society, and how the sorts of accusations and negative sentiment that are routinely thrown at marketing are similar to the ways in which Plato and his philosophical descendants saw both the marketers of their time and the Sophists. I argue that the reason for this similarity comes down to the fact that marketers (both ancient and modern) and Sophists were both performing very similar roles in society based upon controlling attention and the appreciation of value. Finally, I consider the question of why, if the links between rhetoric and marketing are so clear, has there been so little effort made by scholars of rhetoric to engage with marketing?

Much of Chapters 4 and 5 is concerned with the consequences of millennia of public and scholarly unease with marketing and rhetoric, with attempts to control others for commercial, political, or personal gain. A lot of this unease comes from the ways in which rhetoric and marketing remind people of magic. Magic is also about controlling people and things, destiny and luck. And it has a significant part to play in the practice of early rhetoric, particularly Sophistic rhetoric. There are, also, very close connections between marketing and magic, both in terms of the ways that consumers think of products and consumption and the ways that scholars outside marketing have occasionally attempted to explain its power and purpose. The next three chapters of the book deal with how magic, rhetoric, and marketing come together. Firstly, Chapter 6 reviews the Western scholarly engagement with magic, the way that it has been defined around attempts at control, and the importance of language in our understandings of what it is. This then allows us to move on in Chapter 7 to a detailed consideration of how the Sophistic approach to language was one based upon a consideration of the magical power of speech. This chapter argues that the deep roots of early rhetoric in ritual and magical performative language constituted a significant part of the threat seen by Plato and Aristotle in the Sophists' teachings and public demonstrations. Consequently, much of the systematisation of rhetoric, its bureaucratisation, can be seen as a series of attempts to expunge magic (as conveyed in ritual patternings, highly figurative language, vivid imagery) from public disputation. Although the 'magical' aspect of rhetoric never truly disappeared, authorities concerned with managing political, legal, and ceremonial disputation and declamation have often tended to take serious measures to keep it on the outside of the establishment. I argue that the practice of marketing can be seen as the last refuge of the magical roots of magic, and it marks, ironically, a (qualified) triumph after many millennia of marginalisation of this tradition. Chapter 8 then considers a number of instances in non-marketing and marketing scholarship where marketing or consumption have been identified with magic or sorcery. Examining the work of Williams (1980), Williamson (2002) and Jhally (1989), amongst a number of others, I argue that scholars working outside the marketing academy have often used the accusation of magical practice against marketing as a way of damning it, or publicly shaming it and the capitalist system that they argue utilises it to spread a glamour in front of the reality of the production and consumption process. As a counter to this, I also examine the consumer culture theory literature that seeks to uncover the magical thinking behind consumption experiences. I argue that as insightful as it is, this strand of marketing scholarship turns away from any real engagement with the magical nature of marketing itself, rhetorically positioning the consumer as the only agent in the creation of consumption magic. While it, therefore, recognises the continuing importance of magic in the modern market, it tells only half of the story. Instead, if we examine the relationship between magic, rhetoric, and marketing, we can fully appreciate the position of the marketer as both magician and rhetor.

The final chapter of the book, Chapter 9, returns to the establishment of a Sophistic understanding of marketing, and works towards presenting an improved version of the definition of marketing originally presented in Chapter 4. The chapter revisits and deepens major themes from the previous chapters in order to arrive at a more rounded conception of marketing as rhetoric. It considers the value of relativism, improvisation, magical thinking, and an agonistic perspective in understanding what makes marketing powerful, desirable, and unique. It also argues that, without a recognition of the centrality of control to what marketing does, a full understanding of marketing's place in society will be always out of reach.

References

Beniger, J. (1986). *The Control Revolution: Technological and Economic Origins of the Information Society*. London: Harvard University Press.

Brown, S. (2002). The Spectre of Kotlerism: A Literary Appreciation. *European Management Journal*, 20(2), 129–146.

Brown, S. (2004). Writing Marketing: The Clause that Refreshes. *Journal of Marketing Management*, 20(3–4), 321–342.

Brown, S. (2005). *Writing Marketing: Literary Lessons From Academic Authorities*. London: Sage.

Brown, S. (2010). Where the Wild Brands Are: Some Thoughts on Anthropomorphic Marketing. *The Marketing Review*, 10(3), 209–224.

Bush, A., and Boller, G. (1991). Rethinking the Role of Television Advertising During Health Crises: A Rhetorical Analysis of the Federal AIDS Campaigns. *Journal of Advertising*, 20(1), 28–37.

Clark, T., Key, T. M., Hodis, M., and Rajaratnam, D. (2013). The Intellectual Ecology of Mainstream Marketing Research: An Inquiry Into the Place of Marketing in the Family of Business Disciplines. *Journal of the Academy of Marketing Science*, 42(3), 223–241.

Conley, T. (1990). *Rhetoric in the European Tradition*. White Plains, NY: Longman.

Daly, C. (2016). *Keep Social Honest Research: Why Transparency Is Key for Brands to Help Build Trust With Consumers on Social Media*. Chartered Institute of Marketing Website. https://exchange.cim.co.uk/editorial/keep- social-honest-research/ [Accessed June 24, 2016].

Greatbatch, D., and Clark, T. (2005). *Management Speak: Why We Listen to What Management Gurus Tell Us*. New York: Routledge.

Hackley, C. (2001). *Marketing and Social Construction: Exploring the Rhetorics of Managed Consumption*. London: Routledge.

Hackley, C. (2003). 'We Are All Customers Now . . .' Rhetorical Strategy and Ideological Control in Marketing Management Texts. *Journal of Management Studies*, 40(5), 1325–1352.

Jhally, S. (1989). Advertising as Religion: The Dialectic of Technology and Magic. In L. Angus and S. Jhally (Eds.), *Cultural Politics in Contemporary America*. New York: Routledge, 217–229.

Kennedy, G. (1994). *A New History of Classical Rhetoric*. Princeton, NJ: Princeton University Press.

Lanham, R. (2006). *The Economics of Attention: Style and Substance in the Age of Information*. Chicago: University of Chicago Press.

Longaker, M. (2015). *Rhetorical Style and Bourgeois Virtue*. University Park, PA: The Pennsylvania State University Press.

McCloskey, D. (1985). *The Rhetoric of Economics*. Madison: University of Wisconsin Press.

McQuarrie, E. F., and Mick, D. G. (1992). On Resonance: A Critical Pluralistic Inquiry Into Advertising Rhetoric. *Journal of Consumer Research*, 19(2), 180–197.

McQuarrie, E. F., and Mick, D. G. (1996). Figures of Rhetoric in Advertising Language. *Journal of Consumer Research*, 22(4), 424–438.

McQuarrie, E. F., and Mick, D. G. (1999). Visual Rhetoric in Advertising: Text-interpretive, Experimental, and Reader-response Analyses. *Journal of Consumer Research*, 26(1), 37–54.

Merlo, O. (2011). The Influence of Marketing From a Power Perspective. *European Journal of Marketing*, 45(7/8), 1152–1171.

Miles, C. (2013). Persuasion, Marketing Communication, and the Metaphor of Magic. *European Journal of Marketing*, 47(11/12), 2002–2019.

Miles, C. (2014a). Rhetoric and the Foundation of the Service-Dominant Logic. *Journal of Organizational Change Management*, 27(5), 744–755.

Miles, C. (2014b). The Rhetoric of Managed Contagion: Metaphor and Agency in the Discourse of Viral Marketing. *Marketing Theory*, 14(1), 3–18.

Miller, C. (1990). The Rhetoric of Decision Science, or Herbert A. Simon Says. In Herbert W. Simons (Ed.), *The Rhetorical Turn*. Chicago: The University of Chicago Press, 162–184.

Murphy, J., Katula, R., and Hoppmann, M. (2014). *A Synoptic History of Classical Rhetoric*. London: Routledge.

Scott, L. M. (1994). Images in Advertising: The Need for a Theory of Visual Rhetoric. *Journal of Consumer Research*, 21(2), 252–273.

Smith, C. (2003). *Rhetoric and Human Consciousness: A History*. Prospect Heights, IL: Waveland Press.

Stark, R. (2009). *Rhetoric, Science, and Magic in Seventeenth-Century England*. Washington, DC: Catholic University of America Press.

Stern, B. (1988). Medieval Allegory: Roots of Advertising Strategy for the Mass Market. *Journal of Marketing*, 52(3), 84–94.

Stern, B. (1990). Other-speak: Classical Allegory and Contemporary Advertising. *Journal of Advertising*, 19(3), 14–26.

Thomas, M. J. (2006). The Malpractice of Marketing Management. *Marketing Intelligence & Planning*, 24(2), 96–101.

Tom, G., and Eves, A. (1999). The Use of Rhetorical Devices in Advertising. *Journal of Advertising Research*, 39(4), 39–43.

Tonks, D. (2002). Marketing as Cooking: The Return of the Sophists. *Journal of Marketing Management*, 18(7–8), 803–822.

Varey, R. (2013). Marketing in the Flourishing Society Megatrend. *Journal of Macromarketing*, 33(4), 354–368.

Vargo, S. L., and Lusch, R. F. (2004). Evolving to a New Dominant Logic for Marketing. *Journal of Marketing*, 68(1), 1–17.

Verhoef, P. C., and Leeflang, P. S. H. (2009). Understanding the Marketing Department's Influence Within the Firm. *Journal of Marketing*, 73(2), 14–37.

Williams, R. (1980). *Problems in Materialism and Culture*. London: Verso.

Williamson, J. (2002). *Decoding Advertisements: Ideology and Meaning in Advertising*. London: Marion Boyars.

1 A History of Rhetoric for Marketers

This chapter provides a grounding in the history of rhetoric so that the reader can later be brought to an understanding of exactly how modern marketing (both its theory and practice) represents the most sophisticated, influential, and articulated flourishing of the rhetorical tradition. The fact that, by and large, both marketing and modern rhetorical studies do not recognise this connection can be argued to be a, rather ironic, function of marketing's own rhetorical success. In order to lay out the case for this position, we will initially have to concern ourselves with definitions of rhetoric and an overview of its history. In looking at how rhetoric has evolved over time we can develop some appreciation of how its practice, purpose, and public status have altered in response to changes in society and culture. In particular, I wish to emphasise the ways that rhetoric has been expected to be used professionally—for what purposes and by whom has rhetoric been employed?

In constructing this history, I have tried to write it from the perspective of the key concepts that develop around the art of persuasion. While this means that I will inevitably have to cover some historical material, to give an idea of how certain concepts became popular or unpopular and to trace the evolution of the discipline, I will be trying to present this historical material in a way that is grounded as much as possible in considerations of the main rhetorical concepts that will be important for the reader's full appreciation of the later arguments that I will be constructing regarding the relationship between marketing and rhetoric. The marketing scholarship on rhetoric, which I will be examining in detail in Chapter 2, has generally not attempted to provide readers with an understanding of the historical development of rhetoric. Journal articles tend to quickly fill in some sense of Aristotle's legacy in the systematisation of rhetoric and then move on to the more important business of finding rhetoric in marketing communication executions or interpreting marketing writing in the light of narrow definitions. It is, therefore, important in a book that intends to argue that marketing *is* fundamentally and completely rhetorical that a wider, more detailed overview of the long development of thinking around Western rhetoric is provided for the reader. What follows, however, is just that—an overview designed to sketch out some aspects of the evolution of the field and provide the interested reader with some jumping off points for their own further reading. The reader who is well versed in the rhetorical tradition might skip ahead to Chapter 2, where I examine the ways in which this tradition has been applied in marketing scholarship.

Western rhetoric was born in ancient Greece, though the exact nature of its origins is shrouded in obscurity and argument (perhaps not unfittingly). The discipline does have its oft-repeated foundation myth, however, and this identifies the inventors of rhetoric as Corax and Tisias, who are alleged to have authored a treatise on the art of public speaking around 476 BCE in the city-state of Syracuse (in what we now call Sicily). Syracuse had recently transformed from a tyranny to a democracy and, as a result, many private citizens found that they had to represent themselves in claims to recover land that the earlier tyrants had stolen from them (Kennedy, 1994; Murphy et al., 2014). Corax and Tisias, so the story goes, sought to take advantage of the great demand for instruction in persuasive discourse that attended this flourishing of litigation. This timely exploitation of a marketing niche brought them to produce the first codification of the *techne* (or art) of persuasive oratory (though this work is now lost to us). Tisias was the pupil of Corax, and it is this relationship that provides the frame for perhaps the most famous story regarding the Sicilian pair to come down to us. It is said that Corax sued Tisias for unpaid tuition fees. Corax's argument was that Tisias will inevitably pay, for if he won then the court must judge his education to be successful and thus worthy of payment, whereas if he lost the court would force Tisias to pay anyway. Of course, Tisias used exactly the same argument to argue for his own success—the court could not expect him to pay if he lost to Corax for that would prove that Corax's own teaching was useless. The court is thought to have given up and walked away from the whole mess.

The move towards democracy in Athens meant that similar opportunities were available in the significantly larger and more influential market there. The courts of Athens in the fifth century BCE were boisterous affairs. With no judges or lawyers, prosecuting and defending parties had to convince a jury of at least 201 members (often significantly more) of the truth of their arguments. This meant that everything hinged upon the effectiveness of speeches and, as a consequence, the demand for custom-written addresses to the court provided by a *logographos* was intense. At the same time, political decisions in Athens were made in a similar way. Radical democracy meant that any Athenian citizen could speak in the assembly, but in practice the power to influence the assembly lay in the hands of effective speakers who "represented the views of shifting factions within the state" (Kennedy, 1994, p. 16). Such speakers, sometimes called demagogues, could stir the assembly to ill-considered decisions that often might go against the long-term interests of the city-state.

The Sophists and the Birth of Rhetoric

It is in this environment that the thinkers we now know as the Sophists flourished (their name coming from the Greek for 'wise', *sophos*). Murphy et al. (2014) note that "while the term applied originally to any wise person, it soon came to denote those who engaged in the art of rhetoric in the courts, the legislature, and/or the public forum" (p. 28). Sophists might earn their living from the teaching of argumentation, the writing of speeches for others, or from the public display of their oratorical skills. Now, all three of these vocational directions will lead at some point to the Sophist having to construct an effective argument for a case that might be called (to use Aristotle's terminology) the weaker. So, a speechwriter will compose a plea for a client whose case might be full of holes, a teacher might build an exemplary argument for a patently absurd case in order to teach the use of particular tropes and strategies, and an orator who lives on the generosity of the crowd will sometimes seek to display his admirable skills in ways that are greatly entertaining precisely because they clearly make the weaker case the stronger. Modern marketers are, of course, familiar with the pressures; sometimes the realities of the profession mean that marketing skills are used to valorise a shoddy product or weak brand. Your campaign can still win a Cleo even if it is for a nutritionally suspect soft drink that others are convinced contributes to teen obesity levels. Indeed, in the same way that modern marketing is routinely lambasted for being at the root of a host of social ills (Critser, 2003; Chomsky, 2012; Klein, 2009; Malkan, 2007; Moss, 2013; Schlosser, 2002), the Sophists attracted a reputation for a dangerous lack of consideration towards the truth and for being concerned with victory in argument at any cost (called *eristic* argument). The nature of Sophistic argument and how it relates to what will later flower into the discipline of rhetoric is important to my thesis linking rhetoric and marketing, so I will spend a little time delineating the principal perspectives that surround it and we will return to it in later sections.

Much of the way that Sophistic practice is now understood has come down to us from the discourse of those who have sought to attack it. In particular, the works of Plato and Aristotle have powerfully influenced later understanding of the Sophists, tainting them with the "stigma of deception" (Tindale, 2004, p. 40). Platonic dialogues such as *Euthydemus*, *Gorgias*, *Hippias Major*, and *Protagoras* characterise their eponymous Sophists as unconcerned with objective or ultimate truth (*aletheia*), instead focused upon the importance of opinion (*doxa*) and how it can be swayed by appeal to an audience's sense of what is most likely or probable (*eikos*). For Plato, such an approach is diametrically opposed to his own project of finding the truth of the *good life* because it leads to a mercenary style of relativism. The root of Sophistic *eikos* can be found in Protagoras 'measure maxim'. Protagoras (484–411 BCE), along with Gorgias, is the most famous of the Sophists and was the first to settle in Athens. His 'measure maxim' asserts that "man is the measure of all things, of things that are as to how they are, and of things that are not as to how they are not" (quoted in Murphy et al., 2014, p. 31). The meaning here is that man cannot perceive the truth behind appearances; all we can do is to pay attention to our own subjective experiences, to the way that things seem to us. Consequently, it follows that in deciding upon any issue we should ask ourselves 'what is the more probable'? In doing so, each of us will look upon our own experience and make a judgement. Such a position was not just antithetical to Plato, of course. Many aspects of Athenian culture assumed the existence of absolute truths and the "rampant individualism" (ibid.) displayed in the teaching of the Sophists (almost every one of them *metics*, or foreign-born immigrants to Athens) generated much anxiety in the city-state while at the same time contributing "to a more pluralistic and tolerant society than would exist at any other time in Greece" (Smith, 2003, p. 47).

One of the most obvious methodological differences between the Sophists and Plato is the former's focus on public argument, often instantiated in lengthy speeches, which contrasts with the latter's belief in "interior reasoning" (Tindale, 2010, p. 33). Disputing in public meant that Sophists relied upon the audience. This meant, from Plato's perspective, that they cared "not for truth but only for persuading their audience" (ibid.). The Socratic *elenchus* (the question and answer pattern Plato has Socrates use in the dialogues) is far better suited to intimate argumentation between a few friends. It is also more adapted to the hunting down of small detail around specialised aspects of topics. The long speeches that were the Sophists' tool in trade were primarily concerned with portraying the bigger picture, the wide sweep of a topic, in order to win over a large audience. Perhaps the most famous example of the power of Sophistic speech-making is Gorgias' *Encomium to Helen*. Gorgias represents the final important element in Sophistic style and that is the power of poetic oratory. The *Encomium* provides four reasons why Helen should be considered blameless in the events surrounding her kidnapping by Paris. By Gorgias' time, Helen's part in the horror of the Trojan War had been much mulled over by generations of poets, playwrights, and philosophers and one's view of her guilt or innocence was a litmus test for where one stood "in the emerging Greek sense of morality" (Murphy et al., 2014, p. 233). The *Encomium* is famous for two reasons. Firstly, it is a clear application of Gorgias' poetic style to argumentative purposes—Gorgias plays with patterns of length, rhyme, and sound throughout the piece to great effect. Secondly, it contains a description of how Gorgias saw the operation of persuasion through the power of words that has become canonical in regard to the practice of rhetoric. In the *Encomium* Gorgias considers four reasons as to why Helen voyaged to Troy (abandoning Sparta and her husband, Menelaus). The third possibility, and the one that he spends the most time considering, is that "speech persuaded her, and deceived her soul" (ibid., p. 234). For Gorgias, speech (*logos*) "is a powerful lord" that can alter the "opinion of the soul" as if by the arts of witchcraft or magic". The persuader is therefore a "user of force" and can rely upon the power of speech as having "the same effect on the condition of the soul as the application of drugs to the state of bodies" (ibid.). As Conley (1990) remarks, this means that "the relationship between speaker and audience is, so to speak, 'asymmetric' as it is the speaker who casts a spell over the audience and not the other way around" (p. 6). In addition, we should note that Gorgias' *Encomium* is itself an example of the power of *logos* to bewitch—it "both pays homage to the power of *logos* to create impressions and at the same time uses it to do so" (Tindale, 2004, p. 47). It advertises the power of which it speaks through its continuing power to enchant even in the twenty-first century.

I will be giving the Sophists significantly more attention in later stages of this study. Their legacy is, I will argue, central to a nuanced understanding of the rhetorical and magical nature of marketing. For now, though, we need to move on to consider the way in which competing and later Greek philosophers reacted to Sophistic rhetoric by constructing a systematised, bounded approach to persuasive argumentation that sought to cleanse public discourse of some of the more apparently irrational and dangerous aspects of Sophistic practice.

Plato and Anti-Rhetoric

It is no wonder that, despite their moral relativism and sceptical perspectives, Sophists such as Gorgias, Protagoras, Antiphon and Isocrates had such tremendous influence over the education of Athenian youth. Their emphasis on the cultivation of effective, persuasive speech had great practical value in the radical democracy of Athens. They were also very much part of the market—the sold their skills as teachers, speechwriters, speech-makers, and authors of teaching texts. Plato, who spent so much time across his dialogues attempting to ridicule and undermine the Sophist tradition, was certainly not a speech-maker. For him, the end of discourse was the philosophical discovery of absolute truth. The fact that we now use the word 'sophistry' in an entirely pejorative way to describe deceptive, fallacious arguments is in no little degree due to the influential early characterisations of Sophistic discourse provided by Plato. The speech-making of the Sophists was seen by Plato as trapped in the material world, the world of appearance and opinion, and as such was incapable of reaching the absolute truth that lies behind the senses. Plato "established dichotomies that the Sophists rejected: inquiry is preferred to persuasion; reason is preferred to emotion; one-on-one communication is preferred to mass persuasion" (Smith, 2003, p. 57). We shall see these tensions repeat themselves throughout the current study—they are not ancient matters far removed from our modern lives but instead sit at the heart of contemporary marketing thinking (as well as public reactions to it).

Plato was suspicious of rhetoric and poetry precisely because he was suspicious of *the audience*. Unlike the Sophists, who thrived upon the challenges of an audience-led civic life in democratic Athens, Plato was no supporter of the crowd. His conception of the ideal state as outlined in *the Laws* and *the Republic* has the public audience "slotted into well-defined positions and not allowed to defy the philosopher king" (Smith, 2003, p. 59). If rhetoric was to be used, then it was to be restricted to ensuring the "consent of the governed by the governors" (ibid.). For Plato, the fact that Sophists were willing to teach all citizens the means of securing adherence to their position was not only a reckless and irresponsible abandonment of intellectual duty but it was also based upon an incorrect understanding of what the duty of a citizen should be. Perhaps one of the most fundamental problems that Plato had with the Sophist approach to *logos* is that it fosters a power asymmetry in discourse. This might be ironic in a broader sense, when we consider that Plato envisaged a state where each citizen had an allotted place and was led to knowledge of absolute truth (and hence the *good life*) by the forces of the philosopher king. However, in regard to the methodology of argumentation, Plato's position is quite clearly concerned with equality between disputants. In *Gorgias*, Plato argues that the rhetor is successful only because he is talking to those who are ignorant of the matters in hand. While it might be true, as his interlocutor Gorgias contends, that a good rhetor could persuade a patient to accept a course of treatment far more effectively than a doctor might, this is only because the patient is ignorant and therefore will be swayed by the language tricks of the rhetor. Conversely, the rhetor has no power to convince the doctor regarding medical topics. The Sophist takes advantage of the ignorance of his audience, while the philosopher (i.e. one schooled in the methodology of Socrates) seeks to lead his interlocutor through a dialectic that will uncover for both of them the real truth. Similarly, in the *Phaedrus* Plato describes the way in which Sophistic *logos* can seduce the young (represented by the titular character) by aping the tricks of the Sophistic rhetor Lysias and bewitching Phaedrus with his speech on love only to point out that he has been successful through a use of linguistic and argumentative manipulation. As an antidote to this, Plato has Socrates expound upon the *real* art of rhetoric—by which, of course, he means a *philosophical rhetoric* that is anchored in, and convinces because of, the true knowledge of that which the rhetor speaks.

Perhaps the biggest irony regarding Plato's position on rhetoric is that, while ridiculing the Sophists' reliance upon the persuasive power of *logos*, he is such a masterful user of these techniques himself. Indeed, while Plato clearly has many important issues with Sophism, there is one area in which their methodology remains fundamental to Plato's project. As Corey (2015) notes, the Sophists are adept at producing wonder, "of awakening interlocutors from their dogmatic slumber" (p. 231). While he might disagree with the Sophist approach to truth, Plato recognises that words have to be used in order to bring an audience, even if it is an intimate audience, to a realization that their common-sense views of the world need to be questioned, that what they thought to be true might not really make any sense. And it is this realization that can be "the starting point for philosophy" (ibid.).

Aristotle and the Art of Rhetoric

Plato's Academy continued to exist and be influential in Athens (and so in Greek scholarship) for hundreds of years after his death. The Sophists left no comparable institution behind and their works have been largely lost to history. Consequently, Plato's handling of the Sophists has (until comparatively recently) tended to be the one that has formed the accepted interpretation of the Sophists and their early approaches to rhetoric. However, in regard to the broader subject of rhetoric itself it certainly cannot be said that Plato's view carried the day. His pupil, Aristotle, had a much more enthusiastic and nuanced understanding of the importance of rhetoric recognising it as an art "crucial for human survival" (Smith, 2003, p. 71). His work, *On Rhetoric*, quietly restores much of the Sophist thinking on the use of arguments of probability in persuasive civic discourse as well as powerfully establishing the contingent nature of argumentation. It also does an awful lot more, acting as a nexus (and testing ground) for much of Aristotle's previous thinking on logic, psychology, civic duty, and morality. As a consequence, the work is a considerably complex one and in its taxonomic structure it is less clear and all-encompassing than many of Aristotle's other works. As Murphy et al. (2014) note, this suggests that "rhetoric deals with human inter-relationships involving so many variables that not even an Aristotle can devise a 'system' to describe it scientifically" (p. 62). Despite this complexity, *On Rhetoric* has served directly or indirectly as the model for mainstream Western rhetorical studies to this day. It contains a number of concepts and distinctions that will be essential to my later arguments and expositions, so I will introduce these now.

The Genres (Eide) of Rhetoric

While rhetoric is the "detection of the persuasive aspects of each matter" (Aristotle, 1991, p. 70) and its "technical competence is not connected with any special, delimited kind of matter (p. 74), Aristotle makes it clear that there are three main areas of life in which rhetoric plays a fundamental part: the law courts (forensic rhetoric), political assemblies (deliberative rhetoric), and ceremonies (epideictic rhetoric). Each of these environments calls for a particular genre of rhetoric, with each genre having its own objective and temporal emphasis. So, forensic rhetoric focuses on the past (what has happened) and tries to prosecute or defend, deliberative rhetoric tries to urge or deter and is concerned with the future (what shall be done), while epideictic rhetoric (sometimes translated as rhetoric of 'display', or 'demonstrative' rhetoric) focuses on the present and attempts to praise or blame. As we shall see later, this typology is perhaps a little artificial—much political argument has always focused on what the opposition has done in the past, for example. However, I should note here that the inclusion of epideictic rhetoric is important for us as marketers as it covers the persuasion of an audience who are considering the *worth* of someone or something. Aristotle was concerned to describe rhetoric as a *techne*—a body of knowledge that has clear bounds and clear applications. Plato had argued that rhetoric was no such thing as it had no knowledge in and of itself but rather depended upon the *lack of knowledge* in its audience. Aristotle's consideration of the types of rhetoric is part of his argument that the discipline has clear bounds of concern, and strategies for approaching the engineering of how an audience should value something are very much within those bounds. As I will elaborate upon below, when considering the relationship between rhetoric and marketing, the place of epideictic discourse is central.

The Proofs

Another way in which Aristotle frames rhetoric as a *techne* is through the establishment of the proofs as the basic concerns of the art of rhetoric. There are certain kinds of proof which are not to be contained within the art and these are the ones "that are not contrived by us" and therefore require no invention on our behalf, only exploitation. Examples of these proofs are witness statements, confessions under torture, contract agreements, etc. The proofs that are the concern of rhetoric are the "artistic" proofs, which are "furnished through the speech" (ibid.). These can be divided into three types: proofs that "reside in the character of the speaker" (*ethos*), proofs that are dependent upon "a certain disposition of the audience" (*pathos*), and proofs which are located "in the speech itself" (*logos*). The three forms of rhetorical proof are not meant to be mutually exclusive and a speech might use all three with each coming to the fore at various moments.

The Primacy of the Audience

The three artistic proofs clearly highlight the way in which Aristotle's conception of rhetoric is based upon an interactive relationship with the audience. Arguments from *ethos* work because a speaker has discerned what personal qualities a particular audience will value and therefore makes an effort to demonstrate (or simply claim the ownership) of such qualities in their speech. The same *ethos* arguments will not work for every audience—for some audiences, in some situations, making a point of your Harvard degree at the start of your speech might make your words appear more trustworthy, while for other audiences in other situations it might instead cast suspicion on your motivations or your character. Similarly, arguments from *pathos* depend upon a careful reading of a particular audience to determine which emotions its members might be more easily led to and, from those, which emotions would be more useful in generating a sympathetic reception to the rest of your argument. Much of *On Rhetoric* is devoted to a description of different emotions, their antecedents, and the rhetorical uses that they can be put to when addressing different groups of people. For Aristotle, rhetorical persuasiveness is contingent upon a careful, strategic consideration of the audience to be addressed. His rhetoric is a 'market-oriented' one, we might say. Certainly, *On Rhetoric* plainly elevates audience research and insight to an essential component of the rhetorical enterprise. Related to this is the topic of *kairos* (often translated as 'timeliness'), which is an idea that informs much Sophistic rhetoric. As Kinneavy and Eskin (2000) note, Aristotle's understanding of rhetoric places a high regard on "situational context" (p. 439), on knowing what type of argument, what metaphor, what stylistic device is appropriate at a particular moment. This almost improvisatory aspect of rhetoric is something that I will return to in later discussions of interactivity and marketing strategy.

The Tools of Rhetorical Argumentation

As well as decisions regarding the appropriate choice of rhetorical genres and proofs, the successful speaker must master the effective use of what Conley (1990) calls the "instruments of demonstration" (p. 15)—the *enthymeme* and the *example*. These are the substance of the proofs of *logos* and, given that they are used to demonstrate, or appear to demonstrate, they establish the link between rhetoric and the more formal *dialectic*. So, the *enthymeme* is the rhetorical equivalent of a deductive *syllogism*, while the example (or *paradigm*) is the rhetorical version of logical induction. Importantly, both rhetorical instruments work on what the audience knows (or will accept) as probable or likely. The syllogism is a way to universal truth, whereas the enthymeme is a way to a particular audience's acceptance of what is likely. In form, the enthymeme is a truncated syllogism because it relies upon the audience to supply one of the premises. The speaker, therefore, does not have to set out all the premises but can compress his logic, taking advantage of the 'common sense' of the audience to fill the gaps. The most compressed form of enthymeme is the *maxim* that is really the conclusion from a syllogism without any accompanying premises. Aristotle warned that maxims work persuasively only if the speaker judges the prejudices of the audience well—but when they do work they can build a strong rapport with the audience due to the evident sharing of 'common sense' that they demonstrate. *On Rhetoric* provides a long list of common lines of enthymemetic argument, or *topoi*, so that speakers could pick and choose the most appropriate for their particular purposes. Aristotle also demonstrates a number of fallacious enthymemes that should be avoided by those who wish to succeed in rhetoric and which should be attacked if apparent in an interlocutor's arguments.

The Place of Style

The last two sections of *On Rhetoric* deal with style and composition. As we have seen, these are topics which were much valued in Sophist rhetorical education, although Aristotle's treatment of them is quite individual. For a start, Aristotle comments that if he were simply writing about what is *appropriate* in rhetoric he would leave the subject of style well alone, "but since the entire enterprise connected with rhetoric has to do with opinion, we must carry out the study of style not in that it is appropriate but in that it is necessary" (Aristotle, 1991, p. 216). It is necessary "because of the baseness of the audience" (p. 217). People are moved by words and their patterning and as the aim of rhetoric is to move an audience towards a particular acceptance of a position, it makes sense to study this adjunct to argumentation. One can certainly detect in Aristotle something that looks like embarrassment here, and he is at pains to make it clear that the sort of style he is talking about is certainly not the artificial, overly poetic one that Plato ridiculed in the Sophists. For Aristotle, style must be always appropriate and clear, giving the "impression of speaking not artificially but naturally" (p. 218). At the same time, one of the purposes of style is to draw attention to the speech, to make it "sound exotic; for men are admirers of what is distant, and what is admired is pleasant" (ibid.). The principal stylistic figure that Aristotle expounds upon in *On Rhetoric* is the metaphor, which is useful to the persuasiveness of a speech because, as well as bringing "clarity, pleasantness, and unfamiliarity" (p. 219), it serves to make the "inanimate animate" and infuse vividness and actuality into the terms of an argument. In general, across all the figures and patterns that Aristotle discusses, his key advice is the use of proportion and appropriateness. Word and figure choice should be a strategic matter of balance—one's metaphors must be clear but unfamiliar, one's words must be exotic yet simple, one's rhythm should be pleasing to the ear yet restrained. It is not hard to feel the cautionary spectre of Gorgias being invoked through such admonishments. Certainly, later authors (particularly of the Roman school) will pay a lot more attention to the myriad detail of stylistic figurations than Aristotle does. This also applies to the subject of speech organization. Aristotle initially states that the only structure a speech really needs to have is a presentation (where one states the subject matter) and a proof (where one demonstrates it). However, as if seemingly embarrassed by this excessive simplicity in the face of so many other teachers of rhetoric making of organization such a complicated and involved topic, Aristotle concedes that, although "these [divisions] are the proper ones", "the maximum number are introduction, presentation, proof, and epilogue" (p. 246). We will consider the matter of rhetorical organization in a little more depth when discussing Cicero.

The Influence of Aristotle

Aristotle's *On Rhetoric* is today a fixture of many introductory speech and writing units on US university curricula, helping to ensure that the distinctions between *ethos*, *logos*, and *pathos*, as well as concepts such as the enthymeme and the three genres serve, as a foundation for the consideration of persuasive speech and writing in the English-speaking world (Gaines, 2000). However, the text itself has not enjoyed an unbroken tenure as the epitome of rhetorical system-making across the centuries. Conley (1990) states that "the *Rhetoric* failed to exercise much influence in the centuries after Aristotle's death" (p. 17), having mostly indirect impact upon the works of Cicero and Quintilian during the Roman period which became so influential into the Middle Ages and the Renaissance. Smith (2003), however, notes that "most of the theory that comes after him extends what Aristotle had to say; in very few cases are wholly new conceptualizations developed" (p. 106). The translation of *On Rhetoric* into Latin in the thirteenth century did little to immediately spark a return to Aristotelian fundamentals, despite enthusiastic recommendation from Roger Bacon. It was only with the sixteenth century that debate around the ideas in Aristotle's text began to make it central to the European understanding of speech and persuasion.

Isocrates and the Improving Power of Logos

Before moving on to discuss the rhetoric of the Roman era, we should briefly consider the figure of Isocrates, who ran his school at the same time as Aristotle set up his own Lyceum. Isocrates can best be seen as Aristotle's main competitor in the provision of education in Athens. He believed in a balanced approach to education, the *paideia*, and his inclusion of gymnastics, science, philosophy, mathematics, and rhetoric in his curriculum has served as an influential model for general education ever since. For Isocrates, the act of rhetoric was "the final phase of a total process of personal growth and development" (Murphy et al., 2014, p. 52). Learning how to speak more effectively in public is something that for Isocrates will significantly aid in a man's social standing and his own character, for "the stronger a person desires to persuade hearers, the more he will work to be honourable and good and to have a good reputation among the citizens" (quoted in Kennedy, 1994, p. 47). This improving power of rhetoric was encouraged by Isocrates through the study and copying of speeches that he had composed on virtuous subjects. He reasoned that the more one considered and argued for the virtues, the more one would become virtuous. Chief amongst the virtuous topics that Isocrates composed essays upon was the cause of Panhellenism, an idea which offered to bring together all of the Greek feuding city-states. Isocrates locates the practice of persuasive *logos* firmly within a frame of idealised civic duty. In this sense, Conley (1990) argues that he "tried to bridge the gap between morality and technical skill that had been created by his sophistic predecessors and Plato alike" (p. 18). Alongside his general impact upon the development of education, Isocrates' teachings had a definite influence upon the early Roman conception of rhetoric, particularly through his focus on *kairos*, his ornate style, and impressive use of amplifications (or *makrologia*, where sentences are prolonged in various ways in order to underline the importance of particular words).

Stasis and the Orator-Leader

Roman rhetoric is characterised by the presentation of "highly specific, pragmatic systems" of oration (Murphy et al., 2014, p. 111). In this sense, it is influenced by the tradition of rhetorical handbooks that flourished throughout the times of Plato and Aristotle. Most of these handbooks have not survived, though a few of the more influential, such as the *Rhetorica ad Alexandrum*, have. However, their decidedly practical orientation formed the model for the works of Cicero and Quintilian as well as the anonymous *Rhetorica ad Herennium*, which became the first work to attempt to create an exhaustive listing of the rhetorical figures and which became the basis of rhetorical education well into the sixteenth century.

It is interesting to note that, as Athens turned from being a radical democracy towards more tyrannical forms of government, so the necessity for public displays of deliberative (political) rhetoric diminished. In the Hellenistic period, it was in the law courts that most rhetoric happened and, as was natural given the move away from democracy, the arbiter who was to be persuaded became not a large group of citizens but a very small number of judges. Not surprisingly, therefore, the next significant innovation in rhetoric comes from a re-consideration of the demands of forensic rhetoric. Hermagoras' theory of *stasis* (c. 150 BCE) had a great effect upon the early Roman rhetoricians, particularly Cicero, with whom the term is most closely associated in modern times, and the author of the *Rhetorica ad Herennium*.

Stasis, meaning 'stance', refers in rhetorical theory to "the stand taken by a speaker toward an opponent" (Kennedy, 1994, p. 98) and concerns the ability to locate the "relevant points at issue in a dispute and to discover the applicable arguments drawn from the appropriate 'places" (Conley, 1990, p. 32). Stasis theory essentially comes down to walking through a series of questions to determine what is the best defence in any particular case. These questions relate to issues of fact, definition, justification, quality (including mitigating circumstances), jurisdiction, and procedure (Smith, 2003; Murphy et al., 2014).

Any fan of modern police procedurals or court room dramas will be familiar with the arguments that result from a consideration of the stasis system; "as the records of his ankle tracker clearly show, my client was in Texas at the time of the murder in New York" (an issue of fact), "yes, my client stabbed the deceased but she did it in the heat of the moment and therefore this is not a malicious, premeditated murder" (and issue of definition), "while it is true that Dr. White administered the fatal dose of morphine to the President, he did this in order to save the whole country from entering an unjust and illegal war that would have claimed the lives of thousands of our armed forces personnel" (an issue of justification), "my client ran the red light, it is true, but having just failed his PhD viva he was in no fit mental state to consider the rules of the road and he throws himself upon your mercy" (an issue of quality), "my client is a sovereign citizen of the Oceanic state of Linux and does not recognise the authority of this court in matters relating to taxation" (an issue of jurisdiction), "my client was not read her Miranda rights at the time of arrest and so was held illegally" (an issue of procedure).

A subtle mastery of the stasis system provided a speaker with the reliable means to *invent* effective arguments in forensic environments but could also be used to effect in deliberative and epideictic situations. Cicero was known for his careful use of stasis both in his early career as a lawyer and in his later life in the Roman Senate. His *De Inventione*, an early and incomplete work, though one that was to have a great influence in the teaching of rhetoric, contains a thorough consideration of the system. The *Rhetorica ad Herennium* provides us with a more complete picture of early Roman approaches to rhetoric, however, providing a large amount of discussion and advice on style, delivery, memory, and arrangement as well as the topic of invention under which stasis falls. Certainly, in comparison to the texts that remain to us from the Greeks, the *Rhetorica ad Herennium* portrays a far more integrated and systematised approach to the subject. There is little sense that the text is constructed in opposition to any other prevailing opinion on the discipline; it is not an adversarial document. Style and delivery are given as much emphasis as the instruments of argument and the *topoi*. In many ways, we can see the *Rhetorica* as a pragmatic fusion of the best of Greek thinking on the subject—elements of Aristotle mix with elements of the Sophists and Isocrates. While this made of rhetoric something that was far easier to transmit—a comparatively unproblematic, self-contained system with clear applications and procedures—it did rather paper over some of the epistemological and ontological tensions that had been present in the art from its inception, tensions which would continue to appear down through the centuries.

Under the influence of Cicero and Quintilian, rhetoric became seen as the essential skill of the virtuous citizen. In a similar manner to Isocrates, Cicero held that an orator would become virtuous through the necessity of learning as much as there was to learn about the matters they would speak upon. As well as being knowledgeable about their subjects, of course, they need to be knowledgeable about those whose opinions they seek to lead—they "must have a scent for an audience, for what people are feeling, thinking, waiting for, wishing" (quoted in Smith, 2003, p. 129). Very importantly, the rhetor must seek to embody a moral authority (*auctoritas*) that would aid them in their persuasive endeavours. The notion of this authority was based upon Aristotle's conception of *ethos* but became in Cicero's work a far more substantial matter. In *De Oratore*, Cicero explained how *auctoritas* was generated through *gravitas*, a word we still use today, of course, to refer to someone's impressive dignity but which for Cicero reflected a worthy public persona built up through one's family connections, one's educational history, one's record of civic duty, and one's reputation for wise advice. All of these elements contributed to who you were, or who you were perceived to be, and this could have a tremendous impact upon how your audience would judge you and your arguments. In this way, the serious study of rhetoric must inevitably touch almost every aspect of a person's inner and outer life. Those who wished to lead in Roman life, to be able to navigate the vicissitudes of the law courts and political assemblies, must cultivate a virtuous persona with the *gravitas*, and hence the authority, to persuade. Placing rhetoric at the heart of such a general moral education was something that typified the general Roman approach to oratory and we see it forming the foundations of Quintilian's later depiction of the rhetor as the "good man, skilled in speaking" (quoted in Smith, 2003, p. 130).

Another instance of peculiarly Roman elaboration upon a Greek rhetorical concept can be seen in the matter of *decorum*. As we have seen, *kairos* defined the idea of the right rhetorical moment, "adapting to rhetorical circumstances and exigencies, which include the orientations of both speaker and listeners, the moment, the place, and so forth" (Sipiora, 2002, p. 4). It was a central idea to Greek rhetoricians, no matter their other disagreements with each other. In Roman rhetoric, *kairos* developed into the ideas of propriety and *decorum*. Perhaps naturally, given the thinking that influenced the emphasis on *auctoritas* and *gravitas*, Roman understanding of oratorial propriety centred around fulfilling the expectations of the audience. Argument forms and figures should be chosen with respect to their suitability for a particular audience—they should attract attention and give pleasure but at the same time not overly stimulate or tax the hearer. In Cicero's famous analogy, the forms and ornaments of a speech should all be necessary to its function, just as all the parts of a ship are necessary to its sailing—there should be no superfluous use of words, patterns, or imagery. *Decorum* represents the rationalisation, the systematisation, of style, then, and as part of this process the Romans began to catalogue as many rhetorical figures (*ornatus*) as could be found. Use of *ornatus* also tended to determine how far a speaker embodied either the Asiatic or the Attic styles. The Asiatic, or grand style, was "impetuous and ornate" (Kennedy, 1994, p. 96) and was often contrasted unfavourably by Roman writers such as Cicero and Quintilian with the plain, sober style of Atticism (which looked to early classical Greek oratory for its models). Indeed, Cicero at one point even calls Asiatic oratory "fat and greasy" (quoted in Kennedy, 1994, p. 96). However, what actually drew the ire of such Roman rhetorical theorists was the exclusive use of either style. Their advice was that a speaker should know when to adopt the grand style, when to speak plainly, and when to tread the middle ground, and it was the exercise of such judgement that typified the mastery of *decorum*.

The flowering of the Asiatic style (influenced by the practices of orators from Asia Minor) is generally located within what is called the 'Second Sophistic', a phase of Roman oratory that sits at the heart of the Imperial period (Smith, 2003). Imperial Rome saw the genre of epideictic rhetoric gain ascendance, perhaps because the arenas of the law courts and political assemblies had become less democratic and the opportunities for forensic and deliberative rhetoric less common. However, as Smith (2003) points out, the rhetoric of praise and blame can have significant deliberative aspects and it was often used in the Second Sophistic to praise behaviour or values that a speaker wished to bring to the attention of the Emperor in the hopes of influencing his policy and decisions. However, of particular interest for us is an anonymous work (previously attributed to Longinus) written at this time, *On the Sublime*, which raises the use of *ornatus* and the generation of *decorum* to an extreme level of importance. The author of this text is concerned with understanding the type of speech that *transports* the audience. This is something of a higher order than just the generation of appropriate emotion in an audience. When the sublime is achieved in a speech, its power is irresistible, bringing the audience almost to the point of madness (de Romilly, 1975). The author advises the rhetor who desires to attain such effects to portray noble ideals in their speech and to use careful and decorous word patternings. Words, when arranged appropriately, can have the same effect as a magic charm upon the audience. So, while we see here clear evidence of a move back towards the sort of emotive, inspiring power that an eloquent, Gorgian style might focus upon, it is reined tightly in by a Roman focus on decorum, balance, and noble intent. This is a dynamic which I will come to discuss in more depth when I consider marketing as a particularly Sophistic instantiation of rhetoric in later chapters.

Arrangement and the Faculties of Rhetoric

Before leaving our discussion of Roman rhetoric, it will be worthwhile to briefly outline the way in which the Latin authors approached the broad categorisation of the discipline. In particular, a consideration of the superstructure found in the *Rhetorica ad Herennium* allows us to appreciate the way in which this highly influential text understood the strategic planning behind the duties of the orator. A quick discussion will serve to highlight the range of skills that the successful orator was expected to master.

The *Rhetorica ad Herennium* starts by listing the faculties that the orator should possess (often referred to as the 'canons' of rhetoric)—invention, arrangement, style, memory, and delivery (Anonymous [trans. Caplan] 1954). Invention covers "the devising of matter, true or plausible that would make the case convincing" (ibid., p. 9) and therefore relates to the creative construction of proofs (of *logos*, *ethos*, and *pathos*). Arrangement is then concerned with how these proofs are organised to best effect, "making clear the place to which each thing is to be assigned" (ibid.) The *Rhetorica* promotes a six-part arrangement scheme consisting of introduction (designed to catch the attention and empathy of the audience), narration (or the statement of facts), division (which makes "clear what matters are agreed upon and what are contested"), proof (where the main arguments and their corroboration are presented), refutation (wherein we destroy our opponent's arguments), and finally the conclusion (where the speaker summarises their case and makes a final appeal to the emotions of the audience). Style relates to the effective choice of words and sentences to clothe the proofs. The *Rhetorica* devotes its whole final book to a discussion of style, which the author explains is determined by the qualities of "taste, artistic composition, and distinction" (ibid., p. 269). Memory, of course, is an essential skill for the orator (made somewhat redundant in contemporary scenarios by the magic of the auto-prompt) and the *Rhetorica* provides instruction on how to train the imagination to construct images and "backgrounds" which can serve as mnemonics for all aspects of a speech. The final faculty, delivery, is accorded considerable significance by the author, who affirms that it has "exceptionally great usefulness" (p. 189) and that its mastery "is a very important requisite for speaking" (p. 191). Chiefly, delivery covers the study of voice quality and movement and how these elements are used in order to support the organisational stages of the speech and the strategies of invention that have been chosen.

Roman orators, then, had much to busy themselves with. Rigorous training across all five faculties was necessary for a student to master the discipline and both an opponent and the audience would pick upon weakness in any of them easily. Considered generally, however, the faculties of rhetoric provided the essential tools for successful public life. The cultivation of invention brought the early science of decision-making away from the rarefied field of philosophical dialectic and into 'real life', with all its messy concerns with reputation, opportunism, emotions, and what was probable (rather than true). The study of arrangement taught the rhetor how to take arguments and organise them clearly and effectively, mindfully leading the audience through a series of progressively convincing stages designed to secure their adherence to a way of thinking about something or someone. A knowledge of style led to a command of the power of language, a power that allowed a rhetor to buttress any argument they might make with word choices and patterns that would help put the audience in a receptive mood or frame of mind. The study of delivery educated the physical side of the student, providing them with conscious control over the associations that tone of voice and gestures (body language) could invoke in their audience. While it has become fashionable in modern education to avoid reliance upon memorisation and even to ridicule its cultivation, a cursory glance through the intellectual histories of any civilisation will make it plain just how important the training of the memory has been in establishing and transmitting intellectual culture (Carruthers, 2008; Yates, 2001; Olick and Robbins, 1998). Memory training of the form developed in the Western rhetorical tradition functions as a form of personal knowledge management, allowing the user to build and sort intellectual resources and form connections and categorisations amongst them all within the confines of their own mind.

So, the faculties covered everything that a citizen would need to function in the political and legal milieu. We must also not forget that at the root of faculties such as invention and style is the necessity of researching the appropriate information so that arguments can be chosen wisely and formed persuasively for particular audiences. The centrality of knowledge (of the audience, of the laws, of the political expediencies of the time) to the successful pursuit of the rhetorical faculties cannot be overstated and the way in which this closely mirrors the central place of market research in the market orientation demonstrates the fundamental similarity between the two enterprises.

Rhetoric and Religious Persuasion

The place of rhetoric in the Christian establishment of the Middle Ages is an important topic for us as it demonstrates the way in which the nature of the discipline shifts according to its political and cultural environment. Many figures in the early years of the church came from a background where the Greco-Roman educational system, which afforded such an important place to rhetoric, was still influential. As Conley (1990) remarks, "virtually all the early Fathers were converts who had studied and, in many cases, taught, rhetoric" (p. 63). Many of their audiences were also people who had been acculturated to Greco-Roman rhetorical practices and would thus respond well to this tradition of oratory and persuasion. In addition, it is worth remembering that Judaism, and the Christianity and Islam that sprang from it, "are speech-based religions to a much greater extent than Greco-Roman paganism" (Kennedy, 1994, p. 257). Early Judaism had its own system of rhetoric that relied strongly on "proclamation based upon the divine authority of the speaker" (ibid), but also contained structures of logical reasoning as well as a highly developed use of metaphor and allegory. Through its instantiation in the books of the Old Testament (as well as some of the New Testament such as the gospel of Mark) this tradition would influence the evolving rhetorical practice of Christianity alongside the conventions of Greco-Roman oratory.

At the same time, the political and social position of early Christianity had its own influence upon the formation of its rhetorical approach. The persecution that the Christians faced from pagan leaders and communities led to a significant emphasis upon the genre of the 'apologetic', in which Christians such as Justin Martyr, Tatian, and Tertullian would defend and explain their faith "against slanders heaped upon it by its opponents" (ibid. p. 259).

The Church Fathers were faced with a number of persuasive challenges; defending the reputation of their persecuted faith, converting pagans to the faith, establishing doctrinal unity within that faith, and, perhaps most importantly, establishing a discipline of interpretation which could help to explain the corpus of texts chosen as the Old and New Testament. However, classical rhetoric was ostensibly seen as corrupting because of its associations with pagan cultures and institutions and many early Christian writers ironically found themselves echoing Plato's sentiments when they asserted that rhetoric could not help uncover the truth. Smith (2003) recounts the tale of Jerome, who converted to Christianity after an early life being trained in the Ciceronian tradition in Rome. One night Jerome dreamed that he had ascended to heaven and stood outside its gates awaiting entry. However, he is turned away because he is judged to have spent his life as an advocate of Cicero rather than Christ. After that day, the chastened Jerome "pledged never to read pagan works again" (p. 158) and argued vociferously for Christians to rely solely upon the truth of divine revelation in their lives. Yet such attitudes were largely short-lived and were entirely overturned in the work of Augustine, the most influential of the Christian writers on rhetoric.

Although Augustine was born to a Christian mother, he did not himself become a Christian until he was thirty. His early years were instead spent training to become a lawyer in the law courts of Carthage. As a part of this education he became intimately familiar with the works of Cicero and the larger Greco-Roman rhetorical tradition but, at the same time, he also began to explore the many religions that thrived in the environment around him. Giving up his attempts at a legal career, he began to teach rhetoric and finally moved to Rome in search of better students and better prospects. He thrived in this milieu and was awarded the chair of rhetoric at Milan (Kennedy, 1994). However, over time, Augustine found himself being drawn closer and closer to a consideration of Christianity, aided by his friendship with Ambrose, the bishop of Milan, and he resigned his teaching post and converted in 387 CE, eventually becoming the bishop of Hippo. Augustine's work, *De Doctrina Christiana*, contains much instruction upon the place of rhetoric in Christian education and is heavily indebted to his Ciceronian background. From Augustine's perspective, however, certain long-standing tenets of rhetorical theory were superfluous to what the discipline was to be used for by the church. Consequently, the division between the three genres was collapsed as there was only need for one—the genre of preaching (later to be called *homiletics*).

Eloquence of style was something Augustine connected with the status of the speaker—the writings of the church fathers and the scriptures were to be imitated because they embodied the form of eloquence that Christians should uphold. But, importantly, eloquence of style is something which allows the preacher to "sway the mind so as to subdue the will" (Book 4, ch. 13). This is in keeping with Cicero's *dictum* that the purpose of rhetoric is to teach, to delight, and to move, though the end result for Augustine is always the hearer's appreciation of the truth of God's word. This brought out a strong distinction between the Christian rhetor and the pagan orator for while much Greco-Roman speech-making had been designed to aggrandise the speaker and win them applause, Augustine reminded his readers that the only motivation for effective, persuasive, speaking was the communication of "the truths which deliver us from eternal misery and bring us to eternal happiness" (Book 4, ch. 18).

Alongside the development of ecclesiastical rhetoric as a tool of persuasive preaching, Augustine also helped in the establishment of a Christian tradition of *hermeneutics* which sought to provide a system of Biblical interpretation which could help unlock a proper understanding of the sometimes contradictory or confusing, and often highly allegorical, scriptures. Preachers needed to be able to work out the meaning of scripture for themselves before they could use it to enlighten their audiences. They therefore needed to be skilled interpreters who would be able to light upon the truth of a passage perhaps entirely couched in figurative language and then invent the most effective way of explaining it to an audience lacking in their own educational background. Christian hermeneutics took advantage of the considerable amount of Greco-Roman studies on metaphor, allegory, and symbolism that came out of the rhetorical and poetic traditions.

The influence of Augustine saw to it that the study and practice of rhetoric had a place in the Christian educational system, and this position was to remain reasonably secure well into the late Renaissance. Rhetoric became a tool of religious persuasion, helping to convert, assuage, educate, and (to use Augustine's own term) subdue a vast variety of audiences. However, Medieval scholars extended a facet of Augustine's teaching on rhetoric in a way that had some powerful consequences.

As we have seen, attention to the peculiarity of any given audience was an important component in classical rhetoric. It influenced the concepts of *kairos* and *decorum*, was fundamental to the reasoning behind Aristotle's discussion of ethos and pathos, and is ever-present in discussion of the effective choice of stylistic figures. Augustine developed this mindfulness of the audience in a direction that had not been previously considered, however. He wrote that the stylistic genres (sublime, temperate, and calm—corresponding with the grand, the middle and the plain of the Ciceronian tradition) were suited to particular audiences. The temperate style, where ornamentation produces a beauty of expression, is of use to cause adherence in an audience who are "vain of their eloquence" and who will therefore react well to the aesthetic nature of such a speech. The sublime, or grand, style is best suited to an audience of those who know the truth of a message already but resist it through the pressures of custom, society, or fear, whereas the calm style is to be used to instruct those who are ignorant of the truth. As Smith (2003) notes, later Medieval writers greatly amplified the letter and spirit of such distinctions and "argued that different types of discourse should be used with different types of audience: demonstration for scholars of the same faith, dialectic for the intelligent of other faiths, and rhetoric for the masses" (p. 187). This unwarranted compartmentalisation, such a characteristic of the Medieval scholastic mindset (Vickers, 1999), meant that rhetoric slowly began to lose its place at the centre of education, becoming instead a specialised tool not generally suited to application in intellectual discourse. Instead, the Scholastics moved logic to the fore, influenced by their study of Plato and Aristotelian texts such as the *Organon*. While humanists such as Roger Bacon wrote against the diminishing of rhetoric by those scholars unfamiliar with its full history and true worth, it was generally the case that the associations between ignorance and rhetoric meant that it became a somewhat moribund and fragmented area of study in the Medieval period (Smith, 2003; Vickers, 1999). An interest in stasis theory was maintained as teachers found it a useful introduction to the broader study of the (more worthy) dialectic (Kennedy, 1994), while hermeneutics, homiletics, and the study of effective letter writing meant that isolated strands of the Classical rhetorical tradition found niches in which to survive, if not significantly develop.

Renaissance Rhetoric

The re-discovery of many Classical texts that did so much to feed the flames of the humanist movement of the Renaissance had a tremendous impact on the resurgence of interest in rhetoric during this time. Renaissance human-ism was largely a reaction to the extreme abstraction of Medieval Scho-lasticism, which became perceived as unaesthetic and disconnected from the realities of everyday life. Humanism looked back beyond the church fathers to a conception of civic life that was fundamentally Ciceronian, where eloquence of expression was a mark of virtue and an essential tool in making one's way through an uncertain public life (Conley, 1990). As Mack (2013) puts it, "rhetoric and the renaissance are inextricably linked" (p. 2). Language (particularly Latin but increasingly also Greek) became something that should be studied deeply so that its total resources could be mastered. These resources would then be the key to both a more powerful and effective functioning within public life but also a fuller understand-ing of all the other Classical texts of science, history, and law which were also being discovered. Classical rhetoric, particularly as presented in the full versions of Quintilian's *Institutes*, Cicero's *De Oratore*, and Aristotle's *On Rhetoric* that became available during the Renaissance, offered a complex, thorough, but eminently practical means of approaching the study of effec-tive language use. Rhetoric gradually become an important complement to the study of dialectic instead of just a small backwater of the grand frame-work of Scholastic logic. As a result of this re-balancing between the two forms of argument there also emerged a willingness to think more critically about the supposed differences between the them, "prompting new thinking about both subjects" (Mack, 2013, p. 311).

Renaissance rhetoricians such as Agricola and Melanchthon also rehabili-tated the place of emotion in rhetoric, returning to Aristotle's treatment of it in *On Rhetoric*, particularly the way in which the rhetor needs to carefully consider the connections between the characteristics of a specific audience, the particular arguments that need to be conveyed, and the ways in which different emotion can influence different types of decisions.

The learning of rhetorical figures and tropes became a staple of the Euro-pean school room. Pupils were expected to first memorise all of the con-siderable number of figures collected by such figures as Susenbrotus (who listed 132 of them), then be able to identify them in any piece of Classical writing that they were presented with, and then finally master the art of composing with the figures themselves (Vickers, 1999). The creation of a commonplace book was taught as an aid to this process of memorisation and identification, with pupils being directed to collect examples of figures and quotations from worthy sources which would provide them with a fecund storehouse to base their own compositions upon as well as providing useful authority for their arguments. The commonplace book was part of the more general programme of *copia* (or 'abundance') that was introduced in Erasmus' eponymous work, a treatise that soon found its way to the heart of European rhetoric education. The idea of *copia* was to be able to construct impressive writing through the artful use of lexical, phrasal, and source variety. Rather than just sticking to the same old tired expressions, the mastery of *copia* allows a writer to use original turns of phrase, convey subtle meaning, and present themselves and their ideas within a vivid and powerful framework of reference. As an illustration of how the techniques can be applied, Erasmus provides 195 variations on the phrase "your letter pleased me greatly" (Mack, 2013)! Erasmus' *De Copia* was an immensely rich textbook that embodied a fascination with, and joy of, the possibilities of impressive (and so persuasive) linguistic communication.

Perhaps inevitably, the sheer abundance of rhetorical material that found its way into the hands of scholars and teachers prompted many calls for the simplification and systematisation of the discipline. These calls finally found substance in the educational reforms of Peter Ramus in the middle of the sixteenth century (Conley, 1990). Ramus is often accused of radically diminishing the scope of rhetoric, particularly through his transfer of invention and arrangement away from rhetoric and into the realm of logic. This left only embellishment through figures and stylistics of voice and gesture (Smith, 2003). However, Ramus was clear that dialectic should be studied alongside rhetoric and, as Mack (2013) notes, this meant that although the technical provenance of invention and arrangement might have shifted in Ramist schooling, nevertheless students were effectively furnished with all of the traditional areas of rhetorical knowledge. As a result, although his approach is predominantly dialectical, Ramus "is strongly committed to the broad syllabus of rhetoric: invention, organization, style, and delivery" (ibid., p. 146).

The Protestant Sermon

The rise of Protestantism saw the practice of rhetoric drawn squarely into the realm of religious discourse once more. Both John Calvin and Martin Luther were talented rhetors in their own right and also were adamant regarding the importance of rhetorical training in the formation of new priests (Vickers, 1999). It was certainly the case, however, that their models were not the Classical texts beloved of the humanists. Instead, Protestant rhetors swung the pendulum back to a consideration of scripture and the church fathers as the source of rhetorical instruction. At the same time, the emphasis that Protestantism placed upon religious instruction in the vernacular, both directly in the pulpit and via the programmatic translation of the Bible, meant that the influence of vernacular style and language usage began to make its way into widespread rhetorical practice.[1] The Protestant sermon, delivered in the vernacular, could often became a rhetorical tour de force designed to seize the emotions of the congregation and make as vivid as possible the errors of their ways and the dire consequences of those errors.

Of course, such vituperative rhetoric was also directed at the opponents of the Protestant movement. The Catholic establishment, for its part, sought to define itself in a number of ways. Outside of the 'inartistic proofs' of warfare, torture, imprisonment, and battery, the battle between Protestant and Counter-reformation forces also took place within the realm of rhetoric. The Jesuits, and their mission to "teach the young and convert the heathens" (according to its original 1540 charter, quoted in Conley, 1990, p. 152), were the Catholic bulwark against the rising Protestant tide, sweeping "out across Europe to seek and destroy the arguments of [Luther's] followers" (Smith, 2003, p. 220). The founder of the Society of Jesus, Ignatius Loyola, was just as adamant as the Protestant leaders in giving rhetorical training a central place in their educational endeavours. For the Jesuits, written and oral eloquence were vital tools in seeking and maintaining adherence to the Catholic worldview. The number of rhetorical textbooks written by Jesuits, and the number of editions they went through, was so large "that it is difficult to arrive at any precise estimate of the total number of such books and of the extent of Jesuit influence" other than to say that the numbers "were gigantic and the influence correspondingly great" (Conley, 1990, p. 153). Jesuit authors such as Cypriano Soares and Nicholas Caussin based their work upon a generally conservative use of Aristotle, Cicero, and Quintilian. Of note, however, is the strong emphasis put upon emotion as a persuasive force across both Jesuit and Reformation rhetorical writings. This perhaps reflects the legacy of the Renaissance in general, where rhetoric was returned to a far more practical discipline (Vickers, 1999). The battle for the souls of Reformation and Counter-reformation Europe was a battle very much waged through the "arousal and orientation of emotion" (Conley, 1990, p. 155). Rhetoric became a vital tool in learning "anew how to make powerful speeches on behalf of new religions, in defense of old religions, and for political gain" (Smith, 2003, p. 233). It is perhaps understandable, then, that in the nascent science and political philosophy of the seventeenth century the power of rhetorical language began to be treated with caution. The Enlightenment was born amidst fervent religious and political discord that for many called into question established traditions and assumptions. Examining the place that language played in furthering such discord led many thinkers to attempt to place clear bounds upon its persuasive force, or at least to bring to public attention the dangers that rhetoric might hold for those involved in empirical, rational investigation into the natural and social worlds.

Science, the Plain Style, and the Enlightenment

Concerns regarding the way in which language can potentially obscure the truth are common in early scientific discourse as well as the philosophy of the

Enlightenment. Some of these concerns might well originate in the growth of the alternative communicative and ratiocinative language of mathematics. So, for example, Galileo had already declared in 1623 that the "grand book" of the universe is "written in the language of mathematics, and its characters are triangles, circles, and other geometrical figures, without which it is humanly impossible to understand a single word of it" (quoted in Stark, 2009, p. 95, n. 18). Additionally, new approaches to the rational investigation of the world such as Francis Bacon's *Novum Organum* (published in 1620) and Descartes' *Discourse on the Method* (printed in 1637) had begun to promote a clarity and simplicity of language, as well as a distrust of the 'idols' of tradition, which was often at distinct odds with contemporary rhetorical approaches to communication. The language of "enthusiasm", namely the religious reliance on a torrent of stylistically powerful words to bully an audience into a passionate resonance with an orator's vision of the truth, was seen by the protagonists of the Enlightenment as the enemy of rational enquiry and the cause of uncertainty and chaos in public and private life.

Perhaps the most concerted attack upon the deleterious effects of rhetoric was to be found in the movement for plain speech in the early years of the Royal Society. Directly influenced by Bacon's writings, the Royal Society was established in 1660 as a meeting place for those thinkers interested in the new experimental, 'scientific' approaches to natural philosophy. Many of those associated with the founding of the Society were staunch in their mistrust of the stylistically complex and obscurantist writing of the old guard natural philosophers of the previous generations, particularly such occult writers as Agrippa and Paracelsus (Stark, 2009). Propagandists for the Society, such as Thomas Sprat, published tirades against the use of extravagantly figured, Latinate language in philosophical discourse, urging for the adoption of a "close, naked, natural way of speaking" which would bring to scientific discussion a "near Mathematical plainness" (quoted in Conley, 1990, p. 169). Rhetorical figures were seen by Spratt as dangerous, even evil, as they "give the mind a motion too changeable, and bewitching, to consist with right practice" (quoted in Stark, 2009, p. 49). The Royal Society attempted to promote a new form of rhetoric, then, one shorn of its "bewitching" potential. This attempt is born of the strong assumption that certain ways of using rhetoric can lead audiences to error and can be used by authors and orators to deceive—to "insinuate wrong ideas, move the passions, and thereby mislead the judgement" as John Locke wrote in his own condemnation of the "artificial and figurative application of words" (quoted in Stark, 2009, p. 54). For many language reformers of the Enlightenment such as Locke, Spratt, John Dryden, and Joseph Glanvill, rhetoric was a tool that could be used by those inspired by the devil in order to befuddle, enchant, inflame, and lead astray. While these thinkers were great promoters of the new experimentalist perspective, which was based upon a rational, sceptical approach to the natural world, they were also still part of the religious world of their time; their desire for rational language was built upon a fear of the irrational, magical influence of "bewitching" rhetoric.

The strong tension between magic, rhetoric, and science is at the core of the current study's perspective on marketing, and it is something that we will explore in more depth in Chapters 3 and 4. For now, however, it is sufficient to note the important part that the suspicion of rhetorical influence had in the early development of the scientific view of language and communication.

Rhetoric, Elocution, and Belles Lettres

The Enlightenment desire for a balanced language that communicated in a pleasing, but rational, manner was to have a definite influence upon the teaching of rhetoric in the seventeenth and eighteenth centuries. At the same time, increasing opportunities and demand for social mobility in European society meant that the need to be able to impress with one's spoken and written language was becoming of larger public interest. In particular, the issue of "taste" in expression became an important focal point for the theories of rhetoric that evolved out of (and, in some senses, as a reaction to) the plain language reforms as well as the wider culture of salon and club discourse that marked the Enlightenment. For example, Adam Smith, known to us now as the founder of free market economic theory, spent more than a decade lecturing on rhetoric in Edinburgh and his popularity as a source on the subject was greatly aided by the opinion that "his pronunciation and his style were much superior to what could, at that time, be acquired in Scotland only" (as his anonymous obituary in the *Gentleman's Magazine* states, quoted in Smith, 2001, p. 7). Social aspiration, making one's way in the world, demanded effective and appropriate communication skills and it was to rhetoric, and its recent flourishing into the scene of *belles lettres*, that Europe looked to provide instruction and inspiration. It is no coincidence that much of the great work done on rhetoric in Britain during the eighteenth and nineteenth centuries sprang from the Celtic fringes and the North of England. As Conley (1990) notes, the curricula at Trinity Dublin, Edinburgh University, and Marischal College in Aberdeen were designed to help students overcome the "serious cultural handicaps" of being born and brought up outside the influence of London. The teaching of rhetoric in these places was therefore designed to provide students with the ability to generate persuasive ethos through eloquent speech and writing.

Allied to the rise of rhetoric as a tool of social power was the eighteenth-century British explosion in the art of elocution. While delivery, the performance aspect of oration, had usually been something that writers on rhetoric had paid at least some attention to, it had become somewhat side-lined in the Medieval and Renaissance period. However, the part played by gesture and voice in the successful delivery of affecting, persuasive speech began to occupy a number of educators and theorists in the latter years of the Enlightenment. Michel La Faucher's 1657 study on the use of pronunciation and gesture in public speaking was translated into English in 1727 and is generally considered to have been the seed for the Elocutionary movement in Britain (Conley, 1990). Later English manuals, such as the Irish actor John Sheridan's *A Course of Lectures on Elocution* (published in 1762) began to move on from such physical minutiae as instructing the reader upon the correct use of the eyebrows when marking their words as sarcastic, to include a broader cultural project of establishing a standardised 'English' speech for all to educate themselves in. Sheridan held that the correct model of English pronunciation was to be found at court, and that deviation from this model was bound to lead to the judgement that the speaker was not worthy of attention or elevation.

The principles behind the Elocutionary Movement became mainstays of the Victorian approach to the proper mastery of English and were also enthusiastically taken up in the United Sates. Yet, by the early twentieth century elocution had largely become an embarrassment, something to be suspicious of or ridiculed (Sloane, 2013). Indeed, most people's exposure to the idea of elocution nowadays comes directly from Shaw's mockery of it in his 1913 *Pygmalion* or that play's vivid film adaptation as *My Fair Lady*. The value and ethos of regional and 'class' accents have become a lot more complex in contemporary English (across all its international manifestations), and though they still remain an object of strategic persona construction an English public figure eager to appear approachable and sympathetic might be more concerned with making their vowels a little more Estuary English rather than Received Pronunciation (which is not to downplay the continuing role that negative stereotyping plays in the reception of regional accents). Indeed, while the motivations of the Elocutionary Movement seem to be at clear odds with the cult of 'authenticity' that has apparently taken over Western popular culture (Barker and Taylor, 2007; Gilmore and Pine, 2007; Banet-Weiser, 2012), it is precisely because of the desire to be seen as authentic that a return to considerations of 'proper' delivery has occurred—even though the definition of 'proper' might have radically shifted.

Movements such as those promoting Elocution and belles lettres (in both its Continental and British manifestations) tended to be guided by concerns of aesthetics and taste. Hugh Blair, the preeminent British proponent of belles lettres, saw taste as "ultimately founded on a certain natural and instinctive sensibility to beauty" (quoted in Smith, 2003, p. 257) and as such must reflect the universal components of beauty, namely order, proportion, and harmony. The influence of the sublime was quite apparent in Blair's approach, and a tasteful piece of writing should activate an appreciation of the sublime in its audience, moving it "to new levels of conviction born of appeals to the imagination and the affections". *Logos* becomes dominated by appeals to *pathos* and, to a lesser extent *ethos*, here. This unbalancing of the traditional rhetorical faculties and proofs in some sense reflects the gradual fragmentation of rhetoric as a discipline over the eighteenth, nineteenth, and twentieth centuries. We can see this also, at the other extreme, with the attempts by Richard Whately to centre the study of rhetoric around *logos* and a far deeper and nuanced consideration of logical proof than had been popular for many centuries. For Whately, the Elocutionary Movement was far too concerned with *the speaker* when what should be given the weight of attention was the argument and its presentation. Though Whately did write on delivery (it constitutes Part Four of his popular *Elements of Rhetoric*, first published in 1828), he believed that rather than concentrating on imitating all the gestural and tonal minutiae beloved of the Elocutionary Movement, which would only lead to a stilted, mechanical performance, a speaker should instead let the argument that they are making move them naturally. Whately's *Elements of Rhetoric* had an important influence on the way that the teaching of rhetoric was transformed into the teaching of composition, and it is to this that we will now turn.

Rhetoric and Composition

Today, in Britain, rhetoric is rarely to be found on the school curriculum or in the university lecture theatre. Students of Latin or Greek might come across it tangentially and those studying for a degree in English Literature might be introduced to it as an arcane precursor to literary criticism or as a means of further understanding some of the Renaissance texts they are reading but the concerted study of rhetoric and its history has largely disappeared from formal education. In the US, things are rather different, and this is primarily due to the importance of forensics and debate teams in high school and freshman composition classes at universities. As Conley (1990) points out, rhetoric appears to have become transformed into the study of composition in the US largely through the tremendous influence of one book, John Mitchell Bonnell's *Manual of the Art of Composition*, published in 1867. Bonnell argued that the proper province of rhetoric was composition, not delivery or elocution. This approach resonated with developments in US higher education after the Civil War, which saw the establishment of state universities and a far less elitist conception of the purpose of university education. Students needed to be prepared for "a fruitful occupation and individual self-realization" (Conley, 1990, p. 248). One of the most essential tools on the road to professional and individual success in the world was universally considered to be the ability to write clearly and correctly and so to communicate effectively. Consequently, no matter their major of choice, university students began to be drilled in the rhetoric of composition. The effects of this change in emphasis continue to this day, with rhetoric scholars in US universities afforded their position due to the continued place in the curriculum of composition courses that service the broad student population. While for many years this might have meant that the teaching of rhetoric in the US was hampered by unrealistic expectations and functionalist orientations, it nevertheless has assured a continuing presence for the discipline (or a subset of it) in the everyday life of higher education in the US. It is not surprising, also, to find that so much of the work advancing and evolving the study and application of rhetoric in the twentieth century came from US-based academics. The composition focus in US rhetorical studies of the nineteenth and early twentieth centuries was greatly indebted to the work of Alexander Bain, a Scottish scholar who applied Continental empirical psychology to rhetorical theory, bringing a scientific basis to the pursuit of effective communication. As Smith (2003) notes, Bain's introduction of the vocabulary of psychology into rhetorical studies is a line that leads quite directly to the rhetorical conception of Kenneth Burke, the doyen of twentieth-century US rhetoric.

Contemporary Rhetoric and the 'Rhetorical Turn'

The significance of language in constructing the way we view and understand the world is one of the major scholarly obsessions of the twentieth century, running throughout modernism, structuralism, postmodernism, deconstruction, and constructivism, as well as being fundamental to debates in the philosophies of mind and language, socio- and psycholinguistics, sociology, and anthropology. It is not my intention, and I certainly do not have the ability, to review the extremely fecund and variegated literature generated in the twentieth century on the power of language. Instead, in the final part of this historical review of the discipline of rhetoric, I will remain focused upon those ideas and authors that have most influenced the understanding of rhetoric in the last 100 years. Principal among those authors who have advanced rhetorical theory in the twentieth century are I. A. Richards and Kenneth Burke, and I will endeavour to summarise the nature of their contributions. Additionally, I will review the broad *rhetorical turn* (Simons, 1990a) that has placed scientific discourse under the lens of rhetorical interpretation. I would direct the reader eager for further detail and explication regarding the major figures of twentieth-century rhetorical theory to Foss et al.'s (2002) classic overview in *Contemporary Perspectives on Rhetoric*.

I. A. Richards

The traumatic events of the First World War, the horrors of the trenches, the gargantuan loss of life, caused many thinkers and artists to reflect upon the ability of language to represent such realities and even wonder about the part that language might have played in the generation of such events. Mass media advertising and public relations had been used by governments with great efficiency both before and during WW1 in order to manufacture consent and emotional support for military actions (Ewen, 1996).

Distrust regarding the ways in which language might be made to manipulate and distort perception and thought became a haunting leitmotif through much Western literature and philosophy of the 1920s and 30s. I. A. Richards' work can be seen as springing from a fundamentally optimistic urge to produce a series of frameworks that would eradicate the ambiguity and misunderstanding that so much language use appeared to suffer from. His most important work from our perspective, *The Philosophy of Rhetoric* (1965), seeks to establish a 'new rhetoric' that is motivated by the desire to eliminate misunderstanding. Richards characterised traditional Western rhetoric as fundamentally "combative" in nature, concerned with persuasion, winning and dominating. While persuasion was certainly a part of rhetoric, for Richards, it was only a very small part of what the discipline should be about. What was needed for the new century was a rhetoric focused on fostering agreement and understanding, a method of inquiring into the workings of all discourse so that we might become as aware as possible as to how language acts upon us and the world around us. Central to Richards' new rhetoric is the notion of context. Meaning is produced through context, which is formed of clusters of memories and associations. When one member of a cluster is re-experienced, then all the other constituents of a cluster are recalled and contribute to the understanding of that experience. So, for example, the word 'flame' might, for Person X, refer to a cluster of associations such as death, pain, helplessness, choking smoke, etc. Such a context will mean that every time Person X experiences the word 'flame', their understanding of the word is informed by this negative, alarming cluster of memories. Yet Person Y might have a very different context for 'flame', one that involves references of warm nights, conviviality, friendship, the canopy of stars. For this person, the word 'flame' (Richards describes words as *symbols*) has a positive context with a very different meaning. In both cases, the *referent*, the actual thing to which the word refers, is the same, but the referenced context is different. From the perspective of Richards' Context Theorem of Meaning, effective communication with one person, let alone a mass audience, is therefore a hazardous enterprise. If I address an audience that includes both Person X and Person Y, and I use the phrase "the flame of enthusiasm", the meaning I might intend by using this metaphor is going to be created quite differently by these two people. If context is based upon personal experience and can therefore shift radically from person to person, how can we ever hope to arrive at true agreement?

For Richards, a true rhetoric for modern times would train us in navigating the minefields of personal context, aiding us in seeking out those common contexts that might be relied upon as foundations for agreement and heightening our sensitivities to meanings that are not shared and which therefore risk being transformed into misunderstandings. The building blocks of this new rhetoric were *words* rather than the *patterns* that traditional rhetoric had mostly tended to concern itself with, for it was our attitudes to words that needed the most drastic overhauling in Richards' estimation. We all tend to suffer from what he dubbed the *Proper Meaning Superstition*, the assumption that what a word means for me is what it means for you and everyone else. The idiosyncrasies of personal context will mean that we can rarely rely upon such an assumption. Only "long and varied acquaintance-ship, close familiarity, lives whose circumstances have often corresponded", producing "an exceptional fund of common experience", (Richards, 1924, p. 178) will provide the sort of shared context that might be able to avoid constant misunderstanding. Given that such relationships do not charac-terise those found in the majority of our communication environments, the new rhetoric sought to inculcate a variety of techniques to foster aware-ness of that lack of shared common context. So, a communicator should always attempt to provide careful definitions of terms, which should start from shared contexts and work out to the unfamiliar. Also of importance is an appreciation of the *interinanimation* of words, the way that they work with each other in a "literary context" (by which Richards means the phrases, sentences and paragraphs within which they are situated). Rather more unusually, Richards also established a series of specialised quotation marks, or superscripts, which were designed to wrap around key words in order to indicate to readers particular messages about their context. Finally, Richards focused upon the metaphor as the principal tool for encourag-ing mutual understanding. In a pre-echo of later linguistic theories which see the metaphor as residing at the core of human communication (Lakoff and Johnson, 2003), Richards describes human thought as fundamentally metaphoric and sees the metaphor as a tremendously compact way of giv-ing an audience the shared context for a word that they might otherwise lack. In contrast to much traditional rhetoric, instead of seeing the use of metaphor as something "special and exceptional in the use of language", Richards sees it as the "omnipresent principle of all its free action" (1965, p. 90). Consequently, he encouraged a "command of the interpretation of metaphor" in order to help us more fully understand that "control of the world that we make for ourselves to live in" (p. 135). As part of his analysis of the modes of metaphor, he introduced the distinction between the *tenor* and the *vehicle*, the former being the "underlying idea or principal subject" of the metaphor and the latter being the borrowed resemblance which is designed to invoke the tenor. Richards argues that while metaphor is deeply helpful in our communicative efforts, misunderstandings or misperceptions of the relationships between tenor and vehicle in our omnipresent use of metaphor in common speech can profoundly influence the "the ways we envisage all our most important problems" (p. 134). Richards, therefore, moves the study of metaphor to the heart of the new rhetoric.

Kenneth Burke

Kenneth Burke's writing covers a vast array of subjects from literature, eco-nomics, anthropology, and politics to religion, linguistics, and rhetoric. While there has been almost as much criticism of his involved, neologism-heavy style as there has been praise for his insight and the value of his theoris-ing (see Foss et al., 2002) it is undoubted that for the discipline of rhetoric,

Burke's work has been seminal in the twentieth century. He sought to do both a "job of reclamation" (Burke, 1969, p. xiii) on rhetoric, snatching back much of the range of rhetorical motivations that had been built over by sociology, psychoanalysis, and anthropology, and also to extend the "traditional bounds" of the discipline beyond just persuasion and into wider realm of *identification*. In a similar way to Richards, Burke sees the study, or the philosophy, of rhetoric as a way to consider how "individuals are at odds with one another, or become identified with groups more or less at odds with one another" (p. 22). It becomes, therefore, a therapeutic or remedial discipline. The basic *function* of rhetoric, however, is "the use of words by human agents to form attitudes or to induce actions in other human agents" (p. 41). Our rhetorical use of words is rooted in the symbolic, and so Burke further glosses rhetoric by describing it as "the use of language as a symbolic means of inducing cooperation in beings that by nature respond to symbols" (p. 43). Furthermore, the rhetorical use of symbols revolves around how they might communicate *identification*. You can induce cooperation in an audience if you can convince them of your identification with them—"you persuade a man only insofar as you can talk his language by speech, gesture, tonality, order, image, attitude, idea, *identifying* your ways with his" (p. 55). This is at the root of Burke's important insight that successful rhetoric is an interactive relationship between rhetor and audience, for while the rhetor seeks to change the audience's opinion on one matter they will have to demonstrate identification with that audience in other matters, they must "yield to that audience's opinions" (p. 56). From this perspective rhetoric does not quite constitute the dominating, domineering *suppression* of the audience that it is sometimes characterised as representing. While Burke is certainly not eliding the 'strife' that is central to the enterprise of rhetoric the depiction of a rhetor who must change while seeking change has much of value that I will come back to later in this work. Certainly, its intimations of reciprocity are taken up in later feminist and postmodern rhetorics discussed below.

The importance of identification in Burke's thinking on rhetoric is also linked to its "ironic counterpart, division" (p. 23). For while we may seek to persuade by identifying ourselves with the audience, this is usually at the expense of dividing ourselves from some other audience—in drawing a mark around ourselves and our listeners we necessarily draw a mark that bounds us from others. Connected to Burke's thinking about division is the important place that hierarchy has in his thinking about rhetoric. For Burke, "the hierarchic principle itself is inevitable in systematic thought" (p. 141) and *rhetorical situations* revolve around attempts by the rhetor to transform hierarchical difference into identity or to reverse hierarchical order. Hierarchy here does not simply refer to social order but to the whole principle of *gradation*, and so covers such wider tropes as growth, evolution, and spiritual development (and the reversal of all such processes).

As with Richards' reconception of rhetoric, Burke's work radically broadens the discipline away from what had become the comparatively narrow confines of elocution and effective composition within which it had mostly operated in the late nineteenth century. At the same time, it is fair to say that Burke's emphasis is predominantly on a conception of rhetoric as critique or analysis. Indeed, the methodology that he uses to arrive at his insights is the close reading of a truly vast variety of philosophical, literary, religious, and political texts (from Diderot's *Neveu de Rameau* and Shakespeare's *Venus and Adonis* to Kierkegaard's *Fear and Trembling* and Veblen's *Theory of the Leisure Class*). He presses these texts for the rhetorical motivations that they can betray and in doing so constructs a general theory of rhetorical motives that the reader can then apply to their own reading of texts (whether those be anchored in canonical cultural discourses, the pronouncements of our leaders and revolutionaries, or the ephemeral conversations of the everyday). Like Richards, Burke saw the development of a competence in uncovering the rhetorical motives in discourse as a means to build a better, more harmonious, society. The cultivation of critical awareness via mastery of Burke's tools allows us to look upon the "mystery of the hierarchic" that is "forever with us" and "scrutinize its range of entrancements, both with dismay and in delight" (p. 333).

The shift in rhetoric from the creative, or generative, towards the analytical is a marked one in the evolution of the discipline in the twentieth century. It is, of course, not a complete shift. Firstly, as already discussed, the training of students in both debating and written composition retains the generative focus of traditional Western rhetoric. Secondly, there is a serious argument to be made for the generative nature of much rhetorical criticism of the past 100 years. So, while the teachers of composition and forensics guide or instruct their pupils in the creation of persuasive communication, their own research is usually focused on rhetorically *reading* chosen collections of the myriad artefacts and discourses that our societies have historically produced (or are in the process of producing). Yet these readings often exhibit (and are the conduit for) the rhetorical scholar's skill and mastery of the persuasive strategies of the rhetorical discipline, strategies which are designed to win over a specialised audience of their peers, reviewers, and tenure committees. In this sense, though, all academic discourse, whether penned by rhetorical scholars or not, must engage in the particular rhetorical structures that construct it, and this is something that I will turn to in more depth when I discuss the 'rhetorical turn'. Before I do so, however, it is worth briefly examining the origins of twentieth-century rhetorical analysis.

Neo-Aristotelianism

The publication in 1925 of Herbert Wichelns' essay 'The Literary Criticism of Oratory' marks the clear birth of rhetorical criticism. Wichelns sought to make a convincing case for the critical study of oratory, while at the same time strategically differentiating rhetorical criticism from the literary criticism that was dominant throughout departments of English language and literature. In this sense, Wichelns' essay not only kickstarted the practice of rhetorical criticism but also aided in the establishment of Speech (and later Communication) as viable academic departments in North American universities (Foss, 2004). In seeking to draw the bounds of rhetorical criticism, Wichelns emphasised the "practical nature of the rhetorical art: It was concerned, he wrote, not with permanence or beauty but with effect" (Zarefsky, 2006, p. 383). The critical study of oratory should therefore attempt to uncover the elements that drove that effect. In drawing up his influential early list of these elements, Wichelns went straight back to Aristotle and directed his readers to explore the speaker's background, the nature of the particular audience (their background and expectations), the types of proof utilised by the speaker, the topics that the speaker made reference to, the arrangement and delivery of the speech, the style adopted by the speaker, and all the other major variables of the Aristotelian conception of rhetoric. Wichelns provided a template, then, a "magisterial method" (King, 2006, p. 365), for all those who wished to align themselves with this new, practical, civically oriented critical focus and disciplinary opportunity. It was a template grounded in worthy Classical precedent but designed to be applied to the study of effective public address—an incarnation of rhetorical scholarship which would be able to engage fruitfully with the recent political history of the United Sates as well as the immediate political environment that was beginning to be dominated by the power of radio.

So successful was Wichelns' essay that, by the 1960s, as one US rhetorical scholar puts it, "for forty years, the method had been viewed as our final declaration of independence from the other language arts, and it had provided a sense of disciplinary unity and common enterprise for the discipline" (King, 2006, p. 366). Yet, success had also engendered stagnation. While Wichelns had originally underlined the critical component in his analysis of oratory, many who took up his call began to focus on the (often highly specious) measurement of effect rather than the critical exploration of the elements leading to it (Zarefsky, 2006). Because the method was designed to examine public address, scholars generally ignored the vast amount of written discourse around the topic areas they investigated. Their focus was exceedingly narrow—generally historical speeches made by eminent (white) men. As Foss (2004) points out, if a scholar has to study the details of a speaker's life and background, as well as the nature of the audience for a particular speech, then it is likely that such information would have been archived only for famous people, those thought worthy of such attention by the arbiters of their time. Rhetorical criticism thus took on a monocultural focus that would inevitably restrict its evolution. Dissatisfaction with the neo-Aristotelian approach of rhetorical criticism gathered force and variety through the 1960s and eventually led to a concerted tearing away of its methodological straitjacket and the flourishing of the discipline across a number of different approaches.

The Break with Neo-Aristotelianism

In the same way that Wichelns' essay had provided the catalyst for the formation of the neo-Aristotelian approach of rhetorical criticism, so another work crystallised the dissatisfactions and suspicions regarding what the field had become and sounded the clarion call for an explosion of new directions. Black's (1965) *Rhetorical Criticism* (dedicated to his former teacher Wichelns) sought to rescue the discipline from its moribund and increasingly irrelevant state, calling for it to shake off the strictures of the Aristotelian paradigm and vastly broaden its scope and concerns. A way of thinking about public persuasion that was rooted in the concerns and ideologies, let alone the social and political institutions, of ancient Athens and Rome was necessarily inappropriate for the sophisticated, *critical* investigation of contemporary public discourse. More importantly, Black argued against the neo-Aristotelian focus on a single piece of public address and the way that its immediate audience had received it. Rather, he wished to investigate the "universe" of large rhetorical discourses, assuming "the single discourse to be part of a historic process of argument [. . . that . . .] has never really ended, but has instead passed into new phases" (p. 177). He demonstrated how investigations into the "cluster of opinions" (p. 168) held by audiences and how they interact with the "argumentative synthesis" (p. 173) to be found in suasive discourse are able to uncover the reasons for shifting identifications between rhetor and audience, at the same time making the benefit of expanding the arena of rhetorical criticism out from single instances of public address to considerations of all forms of public discourse (whether spoken or written). Black's (1965) text also argued forcefully against the emphasis upon rational appeals that had tended to suffuse the neo-Aristotelian programme and which had thus left it weak in effectively critiquing persuasion attempts based on emotional or 'irrational' rhetorical strategies.

Once the cracks had begun to appear in the edifice of traditional rhetorical criticism, it was not long before it began to crumble. While neo-Aristotelianism would remain dominant in the teaching of rhetorical criticism for some time to come, by the early 1970s scholarship in the area had clearly begun to abandon it, embracing instead a plurality of approaches such as (Burke-inspired) cluster criticism, genre criticism, feminist criticism, narrative criticism, metaphor criticism, and (again, Burke-inspired) Pentadic criticism (Foss, 2004). Slowly, these differing approaches have become a collection of "tools for listening to discourses in specific ways" (Condit, 2006, p. 370). The contemporary landscape of rhetorical criticism offers a wonderful richness of investigative stances that are turned towards such diverse discourses as the version history of the *Internationale* (Cloud and Feyh, 2015), Soviet-era posters (Haskins and Zappen, 2010), late-colonial New Spain *casta paintings* (Olson, 2009), and Mia and Ronan Farrow's 2014 Twitter campaign against Woody Allen (Salek, 2016). In stark contrast to the established, historically mainstream public speeches that were the subject of neo-Aristotelian analyses, such explorations apply their various methodologies to uncovering rhetorics which might suppress or express (or perhaps both) subaltern voices, the Other, or hitherto elided perspectives. In other words, there has been a fundamental re-imagining of what constitutes civic discourse.

Outside of the Speech and Communication departments, however, there has also been a significant re-imagining of rhetoric in the last quarter of the twentieth century, and it is to this that I will turn in the final part of my review of the history of Western rhetoric.

The Rhetorical Turn

The *rhetorical turn* is a phrase that springs from Richard Rorty's address to the 1984 Iowa Symposium on the Rhetoric of the Human Sciences and was coined to distinguish the work of the assembled scholars from the two preceding movements (the *linguistic turn* and the *interpretive turn*) that had attempted to "reconceive inquiry in the human sciences" (Simons, 1990a, p. vii). What distinguishes the *rhetorical turn*, or more properly, the *rhetoric of inquiry*, from earlier attempts to reframe the practice and philosophy of science, is that "it rejects the notion that there can be a single and autonomous set of rules for inquiry—rules standing apart from actual practices [. . .] it differs from other postmodern accounts of science in appreciating the importance of *rhetoric*—the quality of speaking and writing, the interplay of media and messages, the judgement of evidence and arguments" (Nelson et al., 1987, p. ix). In other words, the way that scientists inquire about the world is inextricably bound up with the way that they talk and write about it. The Iowa Symposium gathered a large collection of scholars from a wide variety of disciplines to talk about the significance of rhetoric in the theory and practice of biology, psychology, mathematics, economics, political science, legal studies, and history, as well as broadly considering its place in the social and 'hard' sciences.

While not originating the rhetorical turn, the Iowa Symposium was an opportunity to gather together scholars who had already been applying a rhetorical perspective to their own disciplines in order to help outline the broader case for a rhetoric of inquiry that might hold their work together in a 'movement'. Simons (1990b) argues that the rhetorical turn is a consequence of general epistemological uncertainty in an age "in which the philosophical moorings of inquiry have been found none too secure" (p. 2). It has become clear, he continues, that "what gets called *fact* or *logic* is symbolically mediated if not symbolically (i.e. socially) constructed" (ibid.). The authors represented at the Iowa Symposium (and the follow-up conference at Temple University two years later) all share this approach to their respective disciplines. They focus upon the ways in which particular terminologies inside disciplines become proposed, accepted, adopted, and then treated as inviolable, limiting the search for knowledge and invention that a discipline might otherwise be founded upon. They also look at the way in which disciplinary discourses can be used to control debate within the field and determine what questions get asked and how they get investigated. There is also much concern with the way in which the mantle of science is used to guarantee certainty and authority when these might not be warranted. So, Davis and Hersh (1987) explore the nature of *rhetorical mathematics*, which they distinguish from either pure or applied mathematics by noting that "no practical results issue from rhetorical mathematics—except publications, reports, and grant proposals" (p. 55). In other words, what Davis and Hirsh focus on with this term is the use of mathematics to rhetorically afford a sense of scientific certainty and seriousness to otherwise vague, ambiguous, or uncertain ideas. The patina of mathematics might be used in psychology, sociology, economics and "other branches of the so-called behavioural sciences" (p. 57) in order to produce superficially impressive models that rely more upon the "high prestige accorded to mathematics by twentieth-century North America" and "academic gamesmanship" (p. 58) than they do any real mathematical understanding. Yet, rather than simply pointing at the disciplinary Others beyond their field's boundaries, Davis and Hirsh also examine the rhetoric *within* mathematics. They note initially that the *truth* of mathematics is, of course, "considered to be established by means which are the antithesis of rhetoric" (p. 59), namely, the careful (mathematically) logical steps that proceed from hypothesis to conclusion. This view of how mathematics is done is, they argue, "absolutely false" (p. 61). A published mathematics paper will only ever present a part of the evidence that has convinced the editors to stand behind it. There is much that is deemed "routine" or "inessential" and so is left out of the actual paper, forming an "unstated background" which only certain readers will be able to supply. Additionally, as all formal proofs are necessarily incomplete, it needs an exceptionally high familiarity with a particular specialism to be able to understand when any particular incomplete proof will be "convincing and acceptable to qualified professionals" (ibid.). Davis and Hirsh then go on to examine the weaknesses of the refereeing and editorial process which tend to naturally favour established methods and authors. Continuing on to consider the treatment of a paper after publication, the authors then outline the way in which the (really quite small) community of discourse can be blind to major logical flaws in well-received mathematical treatise. In conclusion, they say, mathematical argument is "a human interchange based on shared meanings, not all of which are verbal or formulaic" (p. 67) and our confidence in its conclusions is not "fundamentally different in kind form our confidence in our judgement of the realities of ordinary daily life" (p. 68).

I have described the outline of Davis and Hirsh's (1987) presentation at the Iowa Symposium in some detail because it represents, perhaps, the epitome of much work included under the banner of the rhetoric of inquiry. It takes a discipline which outsiders have a deep respect for in terms of its objectivity and rationality and then proceeds to undermine the case for that objectivity and rationality, exposing these judgements as part of a myth around the discipline that outsiders have fallen prey to and which they might even have utilised in a cargo-cult manner in their own work. So, Campbell (1987) introduces us to the tremendous use of persuasive language and rhetorical strategies in Charles Darwin's work, designed to accommodate his message "to the professional and lay audiences whose support was necessary for his acceptance" (p. 69) and an understanding of which may still serve as a "bridge uniting science and culture" (p. 84). Rosaldo (1987) explains the disciplinary rhetoric of anthropology which seeks to imbue with objectivity a very particular form of "distanced normalizing discourse" (p. 105) that is in many senses as far from the lived experience of the ethnographic narrator (let alone her subjects) as one might get, yet is signalled by the discipline as "the one and only legitimate form for telling the literal truth about other people's lifeways" (p. 106). Bazerman (1987) examines the ways in which the *APA Publication Manual* "embeds rhetorical assumptions" (p. 125) about what it is to do science, arguing that "in adopting a scientific style of communication, the humans sciences neither escape rhetoric nor eliminate the possibility of rhetorical choice" (ibid.). And a final example in a very rich line-up might be Klamer's (1987) essay examining "economics as an art of persuasion" (p. 164), in particular looking at the "metaphorical quality of economic discourse" (p. 180) in order to argue a case for economists to be "more modest in their pretensions concerning economics as a discipline and more uncomfortable with economics as an intellectual discourse" (p. 181–2).

The rhetorical nature of economics is something that has been heavily investigated by McCloskey (1983, 1985, 1995), and her work has obvious ramifications for marketing, given that the discipline is often keen to point to its apparent roots in economics as a way of underlining its 'scientific' and rational status. McCloskey is not interested in simply proving that economics is 'not scientific'. Such a claim would make little sense, anyway, if one recognises that science (good, useful, healthy science) is constructed from metaphors and persuasive discourse much of the time. Rather, her argument is that economists would be capable of so much more if they were more consistently reflexive about the language that they did their economics in—"the temper of argument among economists would improve if they recognised on what grounds they were arguing" (1983, p. 482), and they will then "find it less easy to dismiss contrary arguments on merely methodological grounds" (ibid.). Economists, McCloskey contends, "claim to be arguing on grounds of certain limited matters of statistical inference, on grounds of positive economics, operationalism, behaviorism, and other positivistic enthusiasms of the 1930s and 1940s", yet in their "actual scientific work they argue about the aptness of economic metaphors, the relevance of historical precedents, the persuasiveness of introspections, the power of authority, the charm of symmetry, the claims of morality" (ibid.). Her careful uncoverings of the myriad rhetorical gambits common in everyday economic science as well as in the hallowed tomes of the greats is motivated by the desire to improve a discipline she values so highly—a creative, generative, healing motivation.

McCloskey's lessons are central to the way in which I will be approaching the exploration of the rhetorical nature of marketing, a discipline which has been riven by profound scholarly disagreements around its 'scientific' status and its relationship with scientific 'truth'.

While the 'rhetorical turn' has certainly produced a significant and variegated body of work covering the hard and social sciences, the extent of its influence on the academic discipline of marketing has so far been comparatively small. The next chapter reviews the various ways in which marketing scholars have engaged with the rhetorical tradition

Note

1. Certainly, the use of rhetorical training in the vernacular European languages was not something that was entirely the result of the Protestant Reformation. For example, Mack (2013) includes an overview of the way in which discussions of rhetoric were included in sixteenth-century 'courtesy books', manuals which sought to instruct the reader in polite conversation and the manners of a courtier and which were usually published in the vernacular (vide Casiglione's *The Book of the Courtier*). This is to say nothing of the native rhetorical traditions of day-to-day conversational gambits, oral storytelling, folk traditions of public address, etc.

References

Anonymous (trans. H. Caplan). (1954). *Rhetorica ad Herennium*. London: Loeb Classical Library.

Aristotle (trans. H. C. Lawson-Tancred). (1991). *The Art of Rhetoric*. London: Penguin Books.

Banet-Weiser, S. (2012). *AuthenticTM: The Politics of Ambivalence in a Brand Culture*. New York: New York University Press.

Barker, H., and Taylor, Y. (2007). *Faking It: The Quest for Authenticity in Popular Music*. London: W. W. Norton & Company.

Bazerman, C. (1987). Codifying the Social Scientific Style: The APA Publication Manual as a Behaviorist Rhetoric. In J. Nelson, A. Megill, and D. McCloskey (Eds.), *The Rhetoric of the Human Sciences: Language and Argument in Scholarship and Public Affairs*. Madison: University of Wisconsin Press, 125–144.

Black, E. (1965). *Rhetorical Criticism: A Study in Method*. New York: Macmillan.

Burke, K. (1969). *A Rhetoric of Motives*. Berkeley, CA: University of California Press.

Campbell, J. (1987). Charles Darwin: Rhetorician of Science. In J. Nelson, A. Megill, and D. McCloskey (Eds.), *The Rhetoric of the Human Sciences: Language and Argument in Scholarship and Public Affairs*. Madison: University of Wisconsin Press, 69–86.

Carruthers, M. (2008). *The Book of Memory: A Study of Memory in Medieval Culture*. Cambridge: Cambridge University Press.

Chomsky, N. (2012). *How the World Works*. London: Hamish Hamilton.

Cloud, D., and Feyh, K. (2015). Reason in Revolt: Emotional Fidelity and Working Class Standpoint in the 'Internationale'. *Rhetoric Society Quarterly*, 45(4), 300–323.

Condit, C. M. (2006). Contemporary Rhetorical Criticism: Diverse Bodies Learning New Languages. *Rhetoric Review*, 25(4), 368–373.

Conley, T. (1990). *Rhetoric in the European Tradition*. White Plains, NY: Longman.

Corey, D. (2015). *The Sophists in Plato's Dialogues*. Albany, NY: State University of New York Press.

Critser, G. (2003). *Fat Land: How Americans Became the Fattest People in the World*. London: Penguin.

Davis, P., and Hersh, R. (1987). Rhetoric and Mathematics. In J. Nelson, A. Megill, and D. McCloskey (Eds.), *The Rhetoric of the Human Sciences: Language and Argument in Scholarship and Public Affairs*. Madison: University of Wisconsin Press, 53–68.

de Romilly, J. (1975). *Magic and Rhetoric in Ancient Greece*. Cambridge, MA: Harvard University Press.

Ewen, S. (1996). *PR! A Social History of Spin*. New York: Basic Books.

Foss, S. (2004). *Rhetorical Criticism: Exploration and Practice*. Long Grove, IL: Waveland Press.

Foss, S., Foss, K., and Trapp, R. (2002). *Contemporary Perspectives on Rhetoric*. Long Grove, IL: Waveland Press.

Gaines, R. (2000). Aristotle's Rhetoric and the Contemporary Arts of Practical Discourse. In A. Gross and A. Walzer (Eds.), *Rereading Aristotle's Rhetoric*. Carbondale: Southern Illinois University Press.

Gilmore, J., and Pine, B. (2007). *Authenticity: What Consumers Really Want*. Boston: Harvard Business School Press.

Haskins, E., and Zappen, J. (2010). Totalitarian Visual 'Monologue': Reading Soviet Posters With Bakhtin. *Rhetoric Society Quarterly*, 40(4), 326–359.

Kennedy, G. (1994). *A New History of Classical Rhetoric*. Princeton, NJ: Princeton University Press.

King, A. (2006). The State of Rhetorical Criticism. *Rhetoric Review*, 25(4), 365–369.

Kinneavy, J., and Eskin, C. (2000). Kairos in Aristotle's Rhetoric. *Written Communication*, 17(3), 432–444.

Klamer, A. (1987). As If Economists and Their Subject Were Rational. In J. Nelson, A. Megill, and D. McCloskey (Eds.), *The Rhetoric of the Human Sciences: Language and Argument in Scholarship and Public Affairs*. Madison: University of Wisconsin Press, 163–183.

Klein, N. (2009). *No Logo*. New York: Picador.

Lakoff, G., and Johnson, M. (2003). *Metaphors We Live By*. London: University of Chicago Press.

Mack, P. (2013). *A History of Renaissance Rhetoric 1380–1620*. Oxford: Oxford University Press.

Malkan, S. (2007). *Not Just a Pretty Face: The Ugly Side of the Beauty Industry*. Gabriola Island, Canada: New Society Publishers.

McCloskey, D. (1983). The Rhetoric of Economics. *Journal of Economic Literature*, 21(2), 481–517.

McCloskey, D. (1985). *The Rhetoric of Economics*. Madison: University of Wisconsin Press.

McCloskey, D. (1995). Metaphors Economists Live By. *Social Research*, 62(2), 215–237.

Moss, M. (2013). *Salt, Sugar, Fat: How the Food Giants Hooked Us*. London: WH Allen.

Murphy, J., Katula, R., and Hoppmann, M. (2014). *A Synoptic History of Classical Rhetoric*. London: Routledge.

Nelson, J., Megill, A., and McCloskey, D. (Eds.). (1987). *The Rhetoric of the Human Sciences: Language and Argument in Scholarship and Public Affairs*. Madison: University of Wisconsin Press.

Olick, J., and Robbins, J. (1998). Social Memory Studies: From 'Collective Memory' to the Historical Sociology of Mnemonic Practices. *Annual Review of Sociology*, 24, 105–140.

Olson, C. (2009). Casta Painting and the Rhetorical Body. *Rhetoric Society Quarterly*, 39(4), 307–330.

Richards, I. A. (1924). *Principles of Literary Criticism*. London: Routledge and Kegan Paul.

Richards, I. A. (1965). *The Philosophy of Rhetoric*. Oxford: Oxford University Press.

Rosaldo, R. (1987). Where Objectivity Lies: The Rhetoric of Anthropology. In J. Nelson, A. Megill, and D. McCloskey (Eds.), *The Rhetoric of the Human Sciences: Language and Argument in Scholarship and Public Affairs*. Madison: University of Wisconsin Press, 87–110.

Salek, T. (2016). The Rhetorical Form of Mia and Ronan Farrow's 2014 Online Firestorm Against #WOODYALLEN. *Communication, Culture & Critique*, 9(3), 477–494.

Schlosser, E. (2002). *Fast Food Nation: What the All-American Meal Is Doing to the World*. London: Penguin.

Simons, H. (Ed.). (1990a). *The Rhetorical Turn: Invention and Persuasion in the Conduct of Inquiry*. Chicago: University of Chicago Press.

Simons, H. (1990b). The Rhetoric of Inquiry as an Intellectual Movement. In H. Simons (Ed.), *The Rhetorical Turn: Invention and Persuasion in the Conduct of Inquiry*. Chicago: University of Chicago Press, 1–31.

Sipiora, P. (2002). Introduction: The Ancient Concept of Kairos. In P. Sipiora and J. Baumlin (Eds.), *Rhetoric and Kairos: Essays in History, Theory, and Praxis*. Albany, NY: State University of New York Press, 1–22.

Sloane, T. O. (2013). From Elocution to New Criticism: An Episode in the History of Rhetoric. *Rhetorica: A Journal of the History of Rhetoric*, 31(3), 297–330.

Smith, A. (2001). (ed. J. C. Bryce). *Lectures on Rhetoric and Belles Lettres*. Oxford: Clarendon Press.

Smith, C. (2003). *Rhetoric and Human Consciousness: A History*. Prospect Heights, IL: Waveland Press.

Stark, R. (2009). *Rhetoric, Science, and Magic in Seventeenth-Century England*. Washington, DC: Catholic University of America Press.

Tindale, C. (2004). *Rhetorical Argumentation: Principles of Theory and Practice*. London: Sage.

Tindale, C. (2010). *Reason's Dark Champions: Constructive Strategies of Sophistic Argument*. Columbia, SC: University of South Carolina Press.

Vickers, B. (1999). *In Defence of Rhetoric*. Oxford: Clarendon Press.

Yates, F. (2001). *The Art of Memory*. Chicago: University of Chicago Press.

Zarefsky, D. (2006). Reflections on Rhetorical Criticism. *Rhetoric Review*, 25(4), 383–387.

2 Marketing Scholarship and Rhetoric

The extant marketing literature that recruits one or more aspects of the rhetorical tradition as framework, point of comparison, or theoretical foundation can be divided into three main areas. Firstly, there is research that has looked at marketing communication practices in order to identify the use of traditional rhetorical tools and techniques (most commonly the 'figures of speech'). Secondly, there is research that has looked at marketing scholarship for evidence of rhetorical strategies—treating the academic marketing word as persuasive communication. Finally, there is a small amount of research that has sought (like the current work) to argue that marketing is *entirely* a rhetorical enterprise. I will consider each of these research streams in turn and then finally consider how they can help us refine the conception of Sophistic marketing as I have been constructing it.

Rhetorical Practices in Marketing Communication

The first concerted attempt to investigate the ways in which advertising makes use of rhetorical figures would appear to be Durand's (1987) classificatory framework collected in Umiker-Sebeok's (1987) edited collection of essays on marketing and semiotics. Although published in English in the late 1980s, Durand's piece was based upon work that he conducted in the 1960s while working at Publicis and studying with Roland Barthes at the École Pratique des Hautes Études. He published this work in French journals throughout the 1970s. Predictably, Durand's way of conceptualising the rhetorical figures had little to do with the extant rhetorical tradition and a lot to do with the classificatory tropes of structuralism. Consequently, his categorisation focuses around grouping figures found in advertising into groupings of similar pattern ("figures of suppression", "figures of addition", etc.). There is very little sense that these figures are performing a persuasive function—instead, Durand considers them rhetorical because they embody a transformation from a simple proposition to a figurative one. The word 'rhetoric' has been largely stripped of its historical context, and "rhetorical operations" (p. 295) become processes of visual arrangement with largely obscured motivations.

Semiotics and structuralism provide the background for the next step in the exploration of rhetorical techniques in advertising output. Edward F. McQuarrie and Glen Mick had both been mining the vein of semiotic analysis of advertising in work throughout the mid and late 1980s (Mick, 1986, 1987, 1988; McQuarrie, 1989). Their early 1990s collaboration (McQuarrie and Mick, 1992) takes the cue from Durand's work of adopting a semiotic approach to rhetorical figures in advertising language, in this case focusing on what the authors term "resonance" or "wordplay in the presence of a relevant pictorial" (p. 80). While they do employ a semiotic conceptual framework and this naturally influences their choice of vocabulary, they do make it clear that "resonance" is "but one example of a family of literary devices termed 'rhetorical figures'" (p. 83). However, their understanding of what 'rhetorical' might mean is, as with Durand, largely absent of any historically contextualised sense of rhetoric as a tradition of persuasive communication. Instead, their identification of rhetoric with "literary devices" demonstrates their grounding of the subject within an *aesthetic* tradition. Nevertheless, from this beginning McQuarrie and Mick, together with Barbara Phillips, have evolved a body of research that has moved towards a more 'rhetorical' exploration of the use of rhetorical figures in marketing communication (McQuarrie and Mick, 1996, 1999, 2003, 2009; McQuarrie and Phillips (eds.), 2007; Phillips and McQuarrie, 2002, 2004, 2009, 2010). So, McQuarrie and Mick (1996) start off their attempt to classify the figures of speech used in advertising executions by locating them very much within the historic tradition of rhetoric, the "primary repository of Western thinking about persuasion" (p. 424). The time is ripe, they argue, for "rhetorical phenomena" to be "grasped and integrated into consumer research" (ibid.). They also note that previous attempts to classify the ways in which the figures have been used in advertising have focused "on outcomes other than persuasion" p. 425). Instead of simply framing the rhetorical figures as 'literary devices", we see a clear appreciation by McQuarrie and Mick of their place within a persuasive tradition. They do continue to classify rhetorical figures under the general rubric of "aesthetic objects" (p. 426)—but it is plain that this is done in order to explain their persuasive impact. All aesthetic objects, they maintain, "provide a means for making the familiar strange", for deviating from audience expectations. When an advertiser uses a rhetorical figure, then, they are motivated by an attempt to generate "what consumer researchers might have called incongruity" (ibid.). The rhetorical figure attracts attention and causes the audience to think about the advertisement. They also maintain their earlier aesthetic perspective when noting that "incongruity (i.e. deviation) can produce a pleasurable degree of arousal" (p. 427). Finally, the authors observe that deviation can aid memorability in an audience. McQuarrie and Mick's (1996) typology of figures is thus based upon a continuum of deviation—all figures deviate from expectations but some types of figure deviate more strongly than others.

Certainly, McQuarrie and Mick's 1996 article marks the true start of a research stream which investigates the persuasive motivations for using certain types of rhetorical figures over others in marketing communications material. It is noticeable, however, that there is still very little contextualisation of the rhetorical figures within the larger rhetorical tradition. There is no discussion of how such stylistic devices function alongside other aspects of rhetorical practice—or even the suggestion that there might be other aspects *to* rhetorical practice. This pattern continues in later work and is echoed in the punning title of McQuarrie and Phillips' (2007) edited collection on "new directions in advertising rhetoric"—"Go Figure!". Other researchers have taken up this approach and there are now many studies which use empirical research to test the effectiveness of rhetorical figures in marketing communication executions (Tom and Eves, 1999; Stathakopoulos et al., 2008; Kronrod and Danziger, 2013; Fox et al., 2015; Theodorakis et al., 2015). There also continue to be researchers who seek to create more sophisticated or more efficient typologies to that advanced by McQuarrie and Mick (1996)—this includes work involving McQuarrie himself, such as Phillips and McQuarrie (2004), which explicates a typology specifically adapted for visual rhetorical figures in advertising, as well as work by scholars seeking to tie a classification of rhetorical tropes to various theories of persuasion drawn from the psychological literature (i.e. McGuire, 2000).

Linda Scott's (1994) study on "the need for a theory of visual rhetoric" to conceptualise the use of imagery in advertising has been strongly influential in this research stream. Scott's work is, however, particular in its appreciation of the broadly rhetorical nature of the entire advertising process, its non-reliance on a heavily semiotic or structuralist perspective from which to consider rhetoric, and a sophisticated understanding of the breadth of the rhetorical tradition. This means that her theory of visual rhetoric does not focus around constructing another typology of rhetorical figures—instead, she uses three of the traditional canons of rhetoric (invention, arrangement, and delivery) in order to organise our understanding of how images work as persuasive arguments within an advert. Indeed, Scott intends this suggested framework to begin to "unite other work towards an encompassing rhetorical theory for advertisements" (1994, p. 271) that might then be able to integrate the sort of narrow focus on stylistic figures with considerations of other aspects of rhetorical strategy and practice. Scott herself, for example, explores the way in which advertising imagery can generate and amplify the *ethos* of products and brands. Similarly, in an earlier piece on the rhetorical use of music in advertising (Scott, 1990), musical style is explicitly linked to ethos, as she argues that "the viewer interprets the stylistic choices as a sign indicative of the character or intent of the communicator" (p. 227). Scott's small but highly constructive body of work on rhetoric in advertising serves as an important model for constructing an approach to marketing as *essentially* rhetorical. It is indicative that although the 1994 paper is well cited, its closing call for a "rhetorical theory of advertising images" (p. 271) has largely remained unanswered. Work has certainly continued on researching the effectiveness of rhetorical figures in advertising but this has stopped short of any theory seeking to integrate the conclusions of the various quantitative and qualitative studies into a larger understanding of how advertising imagery, and even advertising in general, works rhetorically. O'Shaughnessy and O'Shaughnessy (2004) do make it clear from the beginning of their book-length treatment of persuasion in advertising that the profession is one fundamentally tied to the tradition of rhetoric. They state that "in persuasion, everything depends on how things are put, that is on rhetoric" (p. 32) and they also contextualise much of their discussion of modern psychological approaches to rhetoric with reference to, and consideration of, traditional rhetorical explanations and techniques. So, for example, they discuss Aristotle's three artistic proofs (*ethos*, *logos*, and *pathos*) when explaining their argument that "emotional appeals are as relevant as rational appeals" (p. 45) and also underline the heavy rhetorical use of metaphor in modern political marketing. Yet, despite their careful connecting of advertising and rhetoric, O'Shaughnessy and O'Shaughnessy (2004) spend more time elucidating the intricacies of such modern psychological theories of persuasion as the Elaboration Likelihood Model and reversal theory, and even psychoanalysis. This situation is remedied somewhat in O'Shaughnessy's (2004) study of propaganda, his explication of which rests upon the "essential trinity" of "rhetoric, myth, and symbolism" (p. 66) and contains much analysis of a variety of rhetorical strategies and tactics (both classical and modern). However, although his chapter on determining an exact meaning for the term makes it clear that any definition of propaganda "must remain open ended since there can be no closure when a concept comes laden with so much historical baggage" (p. 13), it is quite clear that O'Shaughnessy does not make an easy equation between propaganda and marketing (or even political marketing). Rhetoric is central to both advertising and propaganda but in substantively different ways, not least in terms of the other elements with which it has to function; O'Shaughnessy's argument that propaganda uses rhetoric entwined with narrative and myth perhaps might prompt us to ask, when considering marketing as rhetoric, what are the essential elements that interlace with rhetoric in the practice of marketing?

Finally, it is important to recognise marketing scholarship that has contributed to our knowledge of rhetorical constructs in marketing whilst not explicitly identifying itself as doing so. A prime example would be the work of Barbara Stern, particularly her early papers on the use of allegory in advertising (Stern, 1988, 1990). Stern identifies allegory as an aspect of "literary style" (1990, p. 14) and only very indirectly references the rhetorical tradition. However, her definition of allegory is heavily rhetorical in spirit—it is a flexible "persuasive tool" (p. 15), developing in the Middle Ages into an "art form with a persuasive purpose" (Stern, 1988, p. 85). Stern argues convincingly that allegory remains "particularly attractive for advertising purposes" (1990, p. 5) and her articles on the subject provide admirable detail on the rhetorical nature of the form and its practical use for marketing purposes.

Further research that either unknowingly or tangentially contributes to a rhetorical tradition in advertising scholarship would include all those authors who have investigated the place of metaphors in marketing communication. Metaphor can be, and often is, thought of as a poetic, literary device. This is how Stern (1988), for example, describes it looking all the way back to Aristotle's first definition of the term in the *Poetics*. Yet Aristotle also devotes a good part of his discussion of rhetorical style in Book III of *On Rhetoric* to the subject of metaphor. Metaphor has the power to produce "clarity, pleasantness, and unfamiliarity" (Aristotle, 1991, p. 219) in an audience and therefore it can arrest attention and charm the understanding. Aristotle proceeds to go into much detail regarding the principal practical challenge of the metaphor—how to find the most *appropriate* one for a particular occasion and audience.

There is, then, a long tradition of rhetorical research into how and why metaphors persuade. In marketing scholarship, this tradition has continued and metaphor is often included in the sorts of research into rhetorical figures in advertising already discussed above. However, there is also a body of scholarship in the marketing literature that has examined metaphor divorced from a sense of its place in the rhetorical tradition. This work, nevertheless, contributes to any argument for (and understanding of) the rhetorical basis of marketing communications practice. Morgan and Reichert (1999), for example, investigate metaphor comprehension in advertisements while avoiding any reference to the metaphor as a rhetorical device—their frame of reference is drawn largely from psychology and so they do not conceive of the metaphor as an example of rhetoric's presence in advertising practice but rather as a linguistic pattern whose effectiveness at the transmission of meaning can be interrogated by statistics. Another illustration of the sideways contribution to the 'advertising as rhetoric' research stream is Hirschman's (2007) "anthropological construal of metaphor" (p. 227) in the marketplace. While not entirely ignoring metaphor's place in rhetorical stylistics, Hirschman makes an interesting point when she notes that the extant marketing research on metaphor draws from two main traditions: one "grounded in literary theory and linguistics" and the other springing from "symbolic anthropology [and] grounded in cultural images, especially visual and musical, used to transfer meaning between the human and natural worlds" (p. 228). She does mention the rhetorical use of metaphor as being included within that "literary theory of metaphor" (ibid.) but that is the extent of her recognition of the persuasive function of metaphor within marketing. Instead, Hirschman seeks to portray the way in which brands are "mere hitchhikers" upon the "much more powerful force" of "cultural metaphor" (p. 245). Brands are ephemeral, whereas it is the "metaphor that lives on" (ibid.). This reflects her position that advertising is not a "meaning maker" but a "preeminent meaning USER" (p. 244). So, metaphors are never generated by marketing—rather, to be affective/effective marketing must "be grounded in shared metaphoric understandings, which are deemed culturally appropriate for a particular consumption context" (ibid.). It is, perhaps, indicative of the fact that the rhetorical tradition remains alien to so many scholars that Hischman's point was made more than 2,000 years ago by Aristotle himself. For, although rhetoric is often mischaracterised as an art which exerts entirely external control over the audience (and this, as we shall see, is one of the fears of rhetoric which has often linked it with 'magical' manipulation) what power the rhetor wields comes entirely from within the audience in the sense that rhetorical strategies rely upon what an audience will agree with, what they already (think they) know, what they will resonate with. A rhetor must consider the "agreed premises or received opinions" (Aristotle, 1991, p. 77) of her audience when constructing a persuasive argument for them just as she must also consider what imagery and phrasing that audience will consider to be beautiful and wise when choosing metaphors. Once more, we should remind ourselves of Protagoras' summation that "man is the measure of all things".

This leads us to perhaps the most intriguing instance of a piece of marketing research that makes no mention of rhetoric (or even persuasion) and yet which exhibits *deeply* rhetorical thinking. Zaltman and Coulter (1995) introduce the Zaltman Metaphor Elicitation Technique, "a patented research tool designed to (1) surface the mental models that drive consumer thinking and behaviour, and (2) characterize these models in actionable ways using consumers' metaphors" (p. 36). The authors make heavy use of Lakoff and Johnson's (2003) argument that metaphor is central to the way in which humans think about the world. As Lakoff (1993) argues, "the locus of metaphor is not in language at all, but in the way we conceptualise one mental domain in terms of another" (p. 203). As a consequence, "everyday abstract concepts like time, states, change, causation, and purpose all turn out to be metaphorical" (ibid.). Of course, this puts metaphor at the centre of human cognition, not just rhetorical style! Nevertheless, the use that Zaltman and Coulter (1995) make of this position is entirely rhetorical in motivation for, as they conclude, "it is only through their metaphors that we can understand consumer thinking and behavior and thus learn how to develop and market goods and services successfully" (p. 38). If we can uncover the metaphors that consumers use in their thinking about the world, then we will have the keys to talk to them effectively (persuasively) about how our products fit into that world. As I have already argued above, Aristotle's *On Rhetoric* makes it clear that rhetoric is about the audience—the rhetor must always consider the disposition of the audience but also they must try to construct their persuasive gambits from elements that are familiar and acceptable to the audience. In the case of devices such as metaphor, although much of the arresting charm of such figures is to be found in their unfamiliarity, their exoticness, nevertheless, the rhetor must walk a very careful line. Metaphors must be unfamiliar enough to attract but also clear and fitting enough to be easily understood and processed by the audience. The rhetor must therefore consider carefully that the metaphor she constructs reflects a truth that is easily recognised by her audience. At the same time, Aristotle advises against using constructions that are too unfamiliar, too unnatural. In general, then, consideration of the audience is the central guarantee of rhetorical success— if you want to persuade a group of people you must first find out what they believe, what they value, how they speak to each other and themselves, and what they will consider to be just on the right side of unfamiliar enough to be led to recognition of commonality. Zaltman and Coulter's (1995) technique is thus an insightful extension of the rhetorical tradition, aiding marketing rhetors in a deep consideration of the disposition of their audience (through an uncovering of their metaphor maps) and then also helping them to utilise this research to create more effective (i.e. persuasive) marketing material for that audience. The technique's end-users are "copy developers, creative staffs, product-design teams, strategic planning groups" (1995, p. 40) and others who create or contribute to persuasive marketing messaging. The absence in the ZMET literature of any framing which references rhetoric or even persuasive communication is, perhaps, either a function of the authors' desire to (rhetorically) position the approach as modern and 'scientific' or, once again, unfamiliarity with the rhetorical tradition. In any case, the ZMET technique fits perfectly within an understanding of marketing as rhetoric.

Marketing Writing as Rhetorical Practice

Metaphors are a good place to begin a consideration of marketing scholarship that has sought to explore the rhetorical nature of marketing writing. Again it is worth distinguishing between those researchers who explicitly use a rhetorical frame to investigate the persuasive strategies in marketing writing and those who instead either adopt a broader 'literary' perspective or who anchor their analysis in some other tradition while nevertheless advancing rhetorical readings of marketing discourse. As we have seen with Zaltman and Coulter (1995), the work of Lakoff and Johnson (1980, 2003) and Lakoff (1987, 1993) has provided researchers with a cognitive linguistics paradigm to discuss the hold that metaphor has upon our minds. This means that scholars can seek to address the way in which marketing thought uses metaphors without having to engage with either the poetic or rhetorical traditions around metaphor (both, of course, originating in Aristotle's work). After all, Lakoff (1993) argues that metaphor is not just part of aesthetic and persuasive expression but is fundamental to our everyday understanding of the world and informs "much of ordinary everyday language" (p. 203). Accordingly, marketing scholars who notice the central place of metaphors in the construction of marketing theory and discourse do not have to situate their analysis in rhetoric but can instead make use of Lakoff's perspective. This makes sense—in rhetoric, metaphors are stylistic devices that aid persuasion attempts, in Lakoff's theory of *conceptual metaphor*, "as soon as one gets away from concrete physical experience [. . .] metaphorical understanding is the norm" (p. 205). Looking at the metaphors that lie at the centre of everyday marketing language, therefore, should provide us with insight into the way in which marketers think about marketing. So, for example, that familiar phrase, 'target audience', is one that most of the time we do not stop to consider, it is an everyday metaphor that we have come to overlook yet which influences the way in which we, as marketers, view and treat consumers. The research that inspired Lakoff's perspective is Reddy's (1979) essay on what he calls the "the conduit metaphor". Reddy provides a convincing case that the metaphors that fill our everyday speech have a tremendous power to set the frames by which we perceive the world. He does this by demonstrating how English discourse about communication is pregnant with metaphors of containment, as if meaning is contained in language and then transported directly to receiving minds. This is, of course, a tremendously popular way of thinking about communication in marketing and therefore has quite a deleterious effect upon how marketers understand their communication role and their relationship to consumers (Varey, 2000, 2002, 2008; Miles, 2010).

Research into the conceptual metaphors at the roots of marketing theory and practice thus seeks to uncover their framing implications. Cornelissen (2003), for example, examines the metaphors that inform the concepts of corporate identity and relationship marketing from a perspective informed by philosophical and linguistic theories on metaphor in order to evaluate how helpful these metaphors are in helping us understand the field of marketing. So, Cornelissen is concerned to outline "a method whereby metaphors can be evaluated and used in a reasonably systematic, directed, and thoughtful manner" (2003, p. 21). As interesting as this is, it does rather ignore the power of marketing metaphors as persuasive constructions, designed to facilitate the adoption of particular marketing perspectives by publics whom various marketing scholars, authors, and thought leaders might be trying to seek support form. The "organisation is identity" metaphor that Cornelissen evaluates as "offering little heuristic value for researching and understanding the complexity of individuals and actions composing organizations" (p. 222) might nevertheless remain a powerful and persuasive one for buttressing the necessity for certain consultancy services, for example. So, the metaphor works rhetorically even if it might be judge to have "little heuristic value" for market researchers. Indeed, one might say that the less heuristic value a metaphor has for a market researcher the more interesting it becomes from a rhetorical perspective. Capelli and Jolibert (2009) take a similar approach to Cornelissen (2003, 2006) in their analysis of the "validity of metaphor" (p. 1079) in marketing discourse. Again, the rhetorical motivation for metaphor is largely ignored and the researchers focus on whether particular popular marketing metaphors (in this case, the product lifecycle and brand personality) have "validity". Metaphors are judged according to whether they accurately reflect the reality of corporate and marketing prac- tice rather than how they might be working to advance a particular posi- tion persuasively. This research stream appears to have a clear normative intention to expose metaphors that do not reflect reality accurately enough, which do not "advance theory by generating novel insights or by clarifying existing interpretations of organizations" (Cornelissen and Kafouros, 2008, p. 376). This position seems somewhat redolent of that taken by the Royal Society in its search for plain language in scientific discourse, and it certainly seems unwilling to admit that rhetorical motivations might be present in marketing management thinking and discourse. Nevertheless, such scholar- ship does at least obliquely point to the power of discourse choices to effect the way that we think about our profession and discipline.

It is perhaps worth pointing out that Reddy's (1979) work that forms the basis of the "conceptual metaphor" approach that much of this research is embedded in is quite normative in its perspective. So, Reddy (1979) argues that the conduit metaphor is the source of much of the English-speaking world's inability to "improve our communication" (p. 285), that it produces a "frame conflict [that] has considerable impact on our social and cultural problems" (ibid.). His argument, therefore, is that we need to change the metaphors that we use to talk about communication in order to move con- structively forward. This normative attitude is certainly echoed in much of the marketing scholarship above that has engaged with metaphor in market- ing discourse. Lakoff's work is actually far less normative and motivated by an attempt to highlight and explain the way in which metaphors reflect and reproduce our mental categorisations of the world.

There is even *overtly* rhetorical scholarship examining the use of met- aphors in marketing discourse which continues this normative theme. O'Malley et al. (2008) consider the rhetorical nature of the relationship marketing metaphor, for example. Interestingly, unlike Cornelissen (2003), they judge the metaphor at the heart of relationship marketing to be "harm- ful for theory and practice in marketing" (p. 177). However, at the same time, they acknowledge its "powerful rhetorical function", which has helped its adoption and continued popularity amongst marketers. Despite this rec- ognition of the persuasive power of marketing metaphors, O'Malley et al. (2008) appear to share Cornelissen's discomfort with situations when "the explanatory potential of the metaphor has been extended beyond its lim- its" (p. 179). So, while recognising the role that rhetoric plays in marketing discourse, O'Malley et al. (2008) gently frame it as a problem, something which taints its *explanatory* mission.

Only when one regards marketing scholars who adopt a clearly social constructionist agenda does one begin to come across research that does not necessarily understand rhetoric as something indicative of weak or errant thinking or which insists on judging metaphors against some yardstick of reality. So, Hackley's (2001) social constructionist investigation into the generation of "mainstream marketing" discourse is subtitled "exploring rhetorics of managed consumption". The author is careful to explain that the rhetoric that he is concerned with analysing should not be thought of as being "counterposed to a reality of which it is a misrepresentation" but instead should be understood as referring to the "ways in which we work up common-sense forms of linguistic usage which order the ways we think and which inform our sense of the everyday, but which cast an ideological light on the ordinary" (p. 11). He notes that marketing discourse is uncomfortable with open discussion of its rhetorical character "labelling all such criticism as criticism of capitalism", despite the fact that such discussion is critical only of "very particular ways of studying and writing about marketing" (ibid.). For, indeed, Hackley is, in the end, concerned with the damage that rhetoric does to marketing scholarship and enquiry—as he states, "marketing rhetoric used unconsciously becomes a powerful tool of dominance for relatively narrow groups of interest" (ibid.). So, while he is certainly not making the assertion that rhetoric is, *qua* rhetoric, destructive or manipulative, he is stating that the types of rhetoric he is focusing on in his work reproduce "relations of power and authority" which generate and maintain a dominant orthodoxy in the discipline. Hackley is, most definitely, thinking about rhetoric as a persuasive force in marketing discourse, something that serves to secure adherence to particular ways of thinking about its nature and practice. The focus of his rhetorical criticism is thus those areas of marketing that are currently in ascendance, in the dominant mainstream position. The alternative perspectives do not call out for rhetorical criticism because the power structures that they might be attempting to construct, reproduce, and amplify are disadvantaged in comparison. Of course, Hackley's critique furthers the cause of those alternative positions because it exemplifies the insights that they can provide. His critique is a rhetorical strategy enmeshed in its own "relations of power and authority". This is certainly the case with much of the 'critical marketing' (Tadajewski, 2010a, 2010b) literature which has engaged with rhetorical and discourse strategies in marketing writing. So, Hackley (2003) examines "managerial marketing rhetoric" in marketing textbooks, for example, and finds that the "bluster" of "extravagant" "militant pro-marketing rhetoric" (p. 1327) has become so normalised that reflective, critical approaches to the topic become forcibly Othered. As Hackley puts it, "marketing writing can be seen itself as a form of marketing, catering for the marketing 'needs' of students, and teachers, of management" (p. 329). Critical marketing scholars may therefore read the rhetorical choices made in marketing texts for what they can tell us about the persuasive goals those texts seek to advance, goals which for the most part, Hackley asserts, are ideological (marketing is "the sole source of human happiness", "exchange value is prior to all others", and whatever marketing does is "benign and beyond question", p. 1326).

Perhaps the scholar who has most determinedly (and entertainingly) examined the rhetorical basis of marketing writing is Stephen Brown (1995, 1999, 2002, 2004, 2005, 2007, 2010, *inter alia*). Yet, Brown has generally not framed his work as rhetorical criticism. Instead, he has focused upon marketing writing as "artistic endeavour" (2005, p. 14) and therefore presents his readings of Kotler, Holbrook, Vargo and Lusch, Levitt, Hunt etc., as examples of literary criticism applied to marketing writing. Brown's argument is that the greats of marketing are great because of their writing not because of any inherent superiority of their research. It is the way that they clothe their thoughts that makes them attractive, powerful, resonant with their audience of fellow scholars, teachers, and students. In other words, he is talking about *rhetorical* style—style that makes an argument more powerful, a position more winning, a rhetor more credible. As we have already seen above, Brown finds the idea that marketing might be called a 'science' a ridiculous position. It is, quite clearly, an art. Its greatest thinkers should therefore be analysed and judged for their artistry. This gives Brown the grounds for bringing the tools of literary criticism to bear upon famous marketing scholars even though what he is actually doing is analysing what stylistic devices and argumentation patterns they use in order to achieve adherence to their positions. If Brown is saying that it is the style that they adopt which provides the energy that drives these scholar's careers, that makes others see them as credible voices, that makes their concepts appear worthy of adoption and reproduction, then he is actually analysing their rhetoric. He is not, in the end, simply 'appreciating' their artistry—he has instead a very powerful point to make about what it takes to win in the agonistic realm of marketing academia. You will find very few literary scholars who concern themselves with 'why Proust is more successful than Balzac amongst 18 to 25 year old middle class shut-ins', or 'why Dorothy Richardson was less successful than Virginia Wolff', or even 'why Calvino's style is better than Svevo's'—such agonistic considerations are generally considered to be too vulgar and commercial for the literary establishment. But Brown's use of the blind of 'literary criticism' is designed to do just such a job—to uncover the stylistics of success in marketing writing. Indeed, his 2005 monograph concludes with the "3Rs of marketing writing" (p. 182), a prescriptive recipe for what makes great marketing writers great: "breadth of reading", a constant overturning ("righting") of received wisdom in the discipline, and a great facility with stylistics ("rhythmatics" as Brown calls it) that manifests in constant wordplay and neologisms even at the expense of readability. These are the instructions for ascendency, the take-away from Brown's fearless explorations of our gurus' outputs, that will allow the budding scholar to carve an impressive, influential career from the unforgiving rock face of marketing academe. Brown certainly peppers his work with references to rhetoric. For example, when discussing Levitt and Holbrook's writing, he remarks upon their "sophistry" (but note the small 's') and then goes on to assert that "after reading these authors' essays, skeptics are left with a sneaking suspicion that sheer style has triumphed over mere content; that rhetorical slight of hand has disguised the perceived shortcomings in the argument" (1999, p. 7).[1] He then proceeds to equate such rhetorical tactics with illusion, trickery, prestidigitation, even (in an interesting code switch) 'thaumaturgy'. From Brown's postmodern perspective, of course, these are not meant to be negative value judgements but they might point to the reason why throughout his oeuvre he has remained uncomfortable with an overt rhetorical framing, preferring to retain the mantle of artistic or literary scholarship. I would hazard that Brown is quite cognisant of the central rhetorical thrust of his work, but in an act of rhetorical strategising, has preferred to present it under the guise of *literary appreciation*. This makes it seem so much less harmful, so much less destructive, less critical. It allows the importation of an approach to marketing discourse that is fundamentally critical while appearing to celebrate. Certainly, this might seem like a sensible course of action when pointing out that the marketing greats have no flesh underneath their stylish rhetorical clothes.

Other critical marketing scholars have also focused on the way in which marketing discourse has functioned to assert and maintain power relations, legitimise or delegitimise various practices and perspectives, and define the limits of practice and theory (Brownlie and Saren, 1992, 1995, 1997; Morgan, 1992; Lowe et al., 2008; Zwick et al., 2008; Shankar et al., 2006; Skålén et al., 2006, 2008; Svensson, 2007; Tadajewski, 2006; Ellis and Hopkinson, 2010). Most of this research originates from discourse analysis and Foucauldian frameworks and so largely bypasses the rhetorical tradition. As Svensson (2007) explains, "it is widely recognized in social sciences today that language use, or discourse, is one of the main engines in the continuous creation and maintenance of 'the organization'" (p. 276), and discourse analysis/critical discourse analysis (*vide* van Dijk, 1993; Fairclough, 2013; Potter, 2005) is a methodology that has arisen within the social sciences to analyse the way in which such language use enforces, reinforces, and reproduces social structures, ideologies, cultural assumptions, power relations, etc. In other words, what van Dijk (1993) has referred to as "focusing on the role of discourse in the (re)production and challenge of dominance", where dominance is defined as "the exercise of social power by elites, institutions or groups, that results in social inequality, including political, cultural, class, ethnic, racial and gender inequality" (p. 249–250). There is, doubtless, a good deal to be written on the relationship between constructions of the rhetorical tradition and the evolution of discourse analysis and critical discourse analysis in the social sciences but this is not the place to start such a project. Suffice it to say that such research streams within marketing buttress the argument that the discipline and profession are full of discourses working strategically to influence. However, what they do not do is argue that marketing discourse is any more full of this than any other discourse. CDA/DA and the Foucauldian perspective that they originate from are used to discover the ways that language aids dominance across all our elites, groups, and institutions—marketing is one of these institutions, but not particularly special. Marketing scholars who adopt these perspectives thus demonstrate how the discourses of marketing, *in similar ways to other discourses*, serve to '(re)produce and challenge' (though mostly the former) dominance. Of course, such analysis might well be surprising and uncomfortable for scholars (and even practitioners) of marketing who consider themselves to be working within an entirely objective, rational, scientific discipline and had never considered the possibility that their discourse was enmeshed within power relations and struggles for dominance. In many ways, we might consider some of the move towards emphasising co-creation and dialogue in contemporary marketing and business strategy theories (relationship marketing, S-D Logic, DART) as an indication that more scholars are recognising the implicit power plays that constitute much of traditional marketing discourse. Or one could simply see it as a rhetorical gambit designed to quell criticism and dissent. I will deal with this important question in more detail in a later chapter.

Fundamentally, it is important to recognise that while the concept of rhetoric might not appear to be *central* to DA/CDA marketing scholarship, in the sense that its legacy and terminology are not heavily used or cited, the classical tradition of rhetoric is an important foundational pillar of the methodologies. Nowhere is this more clear than in the work of Michael Billig (1985, 1996, 1998), a major theorist and staunch defender of Critical Discourse Analysis, who has engaged in great depth with the Sophistic tradition of rhetoric as a part of his construction of a rhetorical approach to social psychology. Billig's work has been influential on other CDA scholars, most notably Potter (2005) who approvingly cites Billig's argument that "rhetoric should not be confined to obviously argumentative or explicitly persuasive communication" (p. 106). This leads Potter to define rhetoric for his purposes in decidedly agonistic terms. For Potter, rhetoric is "discourse used to bolster particular versions of the world and to protect them from criticism" (p. 33). He later refines this to an understanding of rhetoric as "a feature of the antagonistic relationship between versions: how a description counters an alternative description, and how it is organized, in turn, to resist being countered." (p. 108). While there is much to admire in this definition, it is clearly constructed for a particular purpose—for examining disciplinary, professional, and political and cultural discourses to uncover the ways in which positions struggle for dominance, in other words, for investigating "discourse which is constructing versions of the world" (p. 107). Potter develops this further with his distinction between "offensive" and "defensive rhetoric", the former works to "undermine alternative descriptions" whereas the latter is designed to "resist discounting or undermining" (ibid.). Such understandings are tremendously useful for a rhetorical investigation of marketing discourse (*vide* Miles, 2010) but like many contemporary instantiations of rhetorical *criticism*, they make of rhetoric something which is entirely analytic. While Billig's (1996) work certainly has aspects which support a rhetorical approach to communication, in the sense of celebrating the argumentative, agonistic nature of human discourse, in practice most CDA/DA work is predominantly focused upon interpretive, analytical activities. As a consequence, CDA/DA has mostly manifested itself in marketing scholarship as an aid to the exploration of how ideological dominance and governmentality are achieved through mainstream marketing discourse, which means that its understanding of rhetoric is mostly confined to Potter's (2005) "versions of the world" thesis. This is valuable as far as it goes, but does mean that rhetoric, when invoked, is narrowly understood.

In closing this section, I shall discuss marketing research that explicitly adopts rhetorical theory as the principal conceptual framework for exploration of marketing discourse about theory and practice.

Scholarly engagement with marketing practice is gradually becoming an area in which rhetorical analysis is seen to be able to contribute. This might well be a reflection of the way in which rhetorical analysis has been adopted in management and organizational studies. As Hartelius and Browning (2008) state in their review of the area, "recent work by management and organizational researchers draws heavily on rhetorical scholarship" (p. 13). This is not surprising if one considers the practice of modern management to be "based on persuasion" (Bonet and Sauquet, 2010, p. 121) and "even if management sciences usually conceptualize management as activities led by rational arguments and decisions, management constantly involves rhetorical conversations, in which managers use language for achieving their aims" (p. 132). The organizational studies literature has, in particular, embraced the rhetorical stance demonstrating the breadth of uses that it can be put to in considering internal and external organizational persuasive strategies, enabling the identification (and interrogation) of "the multiple, overlapping, and conflicting interests that define the organizational voice" (Boyd and Waymer, 2011, p. 488) (*vide* Cheney, 1983; Alvesson, 1993; Watson, 1995; Zbaracki, 1998; Cheney et al., 2004; Zanoni and Janssens, 2004; Meisenbach and McMillan, 2006; Sillince and Suddaby, 2008; Heath, 2011).

Studies in the marketing realm that have considered marketing practice from a rhetorical perspective are by comparison rare. Nilsson (2010) studies managers as rhetors in the context of change management in a technology company in Sweden. Although this paper came about as a result of Nilsson's work for the company as an external marketing consultant, it does not specifically deal with the rhetoric of marketing practice in the environment. However, Nilsson's work has elsewhere focused more explicitly on marketing (Nilsson, 2006), and his PhD dissertation has been recently published under the subtitle "a study of marketing work in the spirit of contradiction" (Nilsson, 2015). Here, Nilsson examines the practice of those engaged in "marketing work" and concludes that theirs is a "rhetorical business accomplished by sophistic and self-reflexive marketers who argue in, through, and in between volatile *kairotic* encounters commonly known as 'marketing meetings', in which they employ versatile and expansive language, and enact contradictory selves, for persuasive purposes" (p. 180). Marketing practice, Nilsson argues, is a rhetorical practice.

Koskull and Fougère (2011) have performed an explicitly rhetorical analysis of the arguments around the issue of customer orientation deployed by members (including marketing personnel) of a service development project at a bank. They categorise exchanges based upon rhetorical appeals such as Aristotle's three artistic proofs and their research found that arguments relating to *ethos* were the most common. Perhaps more interestingly, they also discovered that, while there was much talk about the necessity for 'knowledge', "when team members referred to 'knowledge' it was almost only in the form of either 'well-known truths', IT-derived 'objective facts' or claims allegedly coming from frontline personnel about informal customer feedback". So, even though the project team had access to significant amounts of information already collected about their customers, they did not use it. Furthermore, they made no effort to acquire any more, even though at the same time "appealing to *ethos* by expressing guilt and frustration for not living up to the customer oriented ideal" (p. 216). Koskull and Fougère (2011), therefore, demonstrate the usefulness of rhetorical analysis in examining the ways in which marketing practice might deviate from the expectations of marketing theory. The authors are careful to note that "service development practice, of course, is not all about rhetoric" (p. 218). They position their adoption of rhetoric to study this particular issue as an extension of the literature on organizational rhetoric and there is no sense in the paper that rhetoric provides anything more than a tool for analysis to be used by researchers.

I have also used rhetorical analysis to examine the intersection between marketing theory and marketing practice (Miles, 2013, 2014b, 2016) as well as to investigate the marketing of marketing theories to academics and practitioners (Miles, 2010, 2014a, 2017). This has often involved adopting a mixture of rhetorical perspectives—(Potter-inspired) CDA/DA-oriented rhetoric-as-version-making, Classical Aristotelian and Sophistic rhetorics, as well as contemporary rhetorical theories such as Foss and Griffin's (1995) "invitational rhetoric". This has allowed me to explore the rhetorical strategies involved in the adoption of contagion metaphors in viral marketing (Miles, 2014b), consider the ways in which concepts such as interactivity (2010), empowerment (2010, 2016) and co-creation (2014a, 2017) have been used by marketing theorists and practitioners to persuasively advance inconsistent or contradictory positions (often in conflict with customer orientation), and also examine the Othering rhetoric used in intellectual critiques of the marketing enterprise (2013). I have also called for a consideration of marketing *as* rhetoric (Miles, 2010, 2013) that goes beyond the adoption of rhetorical analysis as a methodological tool for the examination of marketing theory and practice and seeks to describe marketing as a continuation, evolution, or mutation of the Western rhetorical tradition. Obviously, this is a position present at the very core of the current work, but I will finish this section with a review of the (very few) pieces of scholarship in the marketing literature which have argued for an entirely rhetorical positioning of the marketing profession and discipline.

Marketing as Rhetoric

The first scholars to argue for the rhetorical basis for marketing are Laufer and Paradeise ([1990] 2016). They begin their book length study of "public opinion and media formation in Democratic Societies" by setting out their principal contention, that "marketing is the bureaucratic form of Sophism" (p. 2). They argue that while the negative connotations of both Sophism and marketing have weight (and are based upon "the same accusations, point for point") they also share a "positive definition" which is "essential to an understanding of marketing and, therefore, of contemporary society". The accusations common to Sophism and marketing are summarised by the authors as revolving around the "primary charge" that "they do not tell the truth". They link this, of course, with a relativistic position in general and Protagoras' statement that "man is the measure of all things" specifically. Arguing that the Protagorean perspective means that man's "approval can be won only by influencing perception . . . [. . .] . . . by playing skillfully on his sensations and feelings", they remind us that both "marketing men and Sophists" claim to possess the "knowledge of how to conjure up appearances out of words and to present objects and people in a flattering light" (p. 3). They also note the similar focus on technique; they are pragmatists, uninterested in reflecting upon the "ends for which their services are bought" (p. 3). They are both "indifferent to power" (p. 5), having no interest in challenging "the powers that be" (p. 4). They are both also attacked and dismissed by those who strike a virtuous pose—the Sophists faced derision from philosophers of 'truth' who saw them as mere marketers of technical knowledge (as Plato says in the *Sophist*), while "professors of marketing face opposition from the 'noble' disciplines" (p. 5) who see them as concerned only with the crass, vulgar, and manipulative. And, just as Sophists were mistrusted for their roots in the colonies of Asia Minor, so are marketers in Europe treated with suspicion as outposts of a North American pragmatism and energy "besieging an ageing Europe" (p. 6).

Laufer and Paradeise ([1990] 2016) argue that marketing and Sophism are best thought of as "naive techniques of non-naive power" (p. 18). Not being concerned with the "why" they find refuge solely in the "how" and thus become naive agents of those who are concerned with the Machiavellian pursuit of power. In the modern world ("the empire of rhetoric", p. 148), this meant the "Bureaucrat Prince", whose "only criterion was the pragmatic one of efficiency" and whose "method consisted in the manipulation of opinion in its modern form of marketing".

Laufer and Paradeise ([1990] 2016) equate rhetoric (Sophism) with marketing from the perspective of critical marketing scholars. Their concern is to demonstrate the identity of the two practices/traditions in order to reproduce Plato and Aristotle's critiques of the Sophists but now directed at marketing, all within a large Weberian framework of systems of legitimacy.

It is unclear what exactly the ramifications of this construction are. It seems to make of marketing little more than a technique of manipulation and it is fair to say that there is not much engagement with what marketing actually is (i.e. the richness of its scholarly and/or professional traditions) in the work. While, as is obvious from my arguments in the book you are currently reading, the similarities between Sophism and marketing are tremendously important for a nuanced consideration of marketing's nature, once they have pointed them out, Laufer and Paradeise do little with them (the same is true for a later, rather compressed, piece by Laufer, 2016).

Tonks (2002) is influenced by Laufer and Paradeise's 1990 text but takes a decidedly more celebratory tone. He starts from the position that "persuasion can be seen as a framing concept for marketing in general and marketing management in particular" and argues that therefore rhetoric, being "synonymous" with persuasion, "needs to have a more central location in making sense of marketing management" (p. 806). Tonks' main concern in his paper, then, is to outline how the marketing manager can be seen as a Sophist, someone who is concerned with *phronesis*, or practical wisdom. The particular realm of the marketing manager's *phronesis* is the employment of rhetoric to manufacture consent. Standing against the anti-persuasion arguments of Duncan and Moriarty (1998), Tonks places persuasion at the heart of all marketing exchanges and relationships. He states that it is "in large measure" rhetoric which *energises* these exchanges. This is a remarkably important observation and the key to Tonks' vision of marketing rhetoric. Rhetoric suffuses all aspects of marketing work, in a way that it does not for other aspects of management and business—this is what makes marketing unique, and this is the true 'value added' that marketing brings to the firm, the energising of exchanges. The marketing manager seeks to "accumulate market power through initiating and controlling exchanges" (p. 812). Marketing is an attempt to control, "to beguile, to entice, to seduce and to entrap" (p. 813)—all wordings which echo not only critics of marketing and marketing communication but also the many criticisms of rhetoric through the centuries. Yet, Tonks seems to enjoy the contrarian position of affirming the aspect of marketing which so many marketing scholars have in various ways (via *manqué* scientism or dialogue-oriented 'relationship' positionings) tried to downplay or distance themselves from. Yes, Tonks is saying, marketing relationships *are* asymmetric, its practice does seek to "curtail consumer sovereignty" (p. 813), and it is concerned with seduction and entrapment via the energising of exchanges—but that's what we do, so let's not pretend anymore. While the linguistic and rhetorical turns in the social sciences can bring to marketing scholarship 'additional framing devices' for "contemplating marketing management and the range of marketing in its wider sense", the truly "radical claim" that Tonks finishes with is that "marketing *is* a reincarnation of rhetoric" (p. 816, emphasis retained). This is something that, once realised, not only can "enhance marketing practice" (p. 813) but potentially can re-orient the spirit of the discipline as a continuation of the "ancient song" of Corax.

Of course, Tonks' piece ends with the "radical claim", rather than starts with it as a proposition that is then argued for. It stands, therefore, as an inspiring, indeed, energising, piece of epideictic. It remains ambiguous regarding the relationship between understandings of marketing rhetoric as instruments of governmentality and practice-oriented attempts to use rhetoric to enhance marketing techniques. It also remains unclear whether all that is required is a simple adjusting of perspective, so that we may see marketing for what it always has been, or if a more substantial re-interpretation is necessary for marketing to be successfully understood as rhetoric.

Nilsson (2006) takes up the call of Laufer and Paradeise ([1990] 2016) and Tonks (2002) and seeks to explain in more detail "how the domain of marketing is closely associated with classical rhetoric" (p. 1) by describing how a variety of traditional rhetorical approaches and techniques (the figures, Aristotle's three artistic proofs, Quintilian's three duties, and the five canons) can be mapped onto the types of scenarios and practices encountered in everyday marketing. Furthermore, Nilsson (2006) argues that most mainstream marketing understandings of relationships are mired in simplistic dyadic (buyer<—>seller) understandings of how people act within markets imported from economic theory. He notes that Nordic service marketing, as exemplified for example in Gummesson (2002, 2004) and Håkansson et al. (2004), calls for an alternative conception, based upon a 'many-to-many' theory of marketing interactivity where all members of an organization are constantly involved in interactive communication with each other and other stakeholders. This "interactive marketing process" is the dominant arena of marketing communication, not the clearly bounded, comparatively small realm of promotional communication. This means, Nilsson argues, that a "many-to-many communication challenge emerges which calls for vast and sophisticated knowledge in the science and art of persuasion". This is why the study of rhetoric by marketing managers is essential—while there is "no specific rhetoric model that entirely matches the many-to-many communication challenge" (p. 8), nevertheless, an understanding of the rhetorical tradition will enable the construction of a "listening-rhetoric" (after Booth), which is "not another cunning persuasion strategy" but a commitment to "understand and acknowledge the deep interest of [each participant] in a communication situation" (ibid.). Nilsson (2006) is therefore proposing a rather different course than Tonks (2002), who dismisses the possibility of a non-persuasive marketing interaction. For Nilsson (2006), an education in the traditions of rhetoric can enable all actors in the marketing interaction process to communicate their "deep interest" in a sophisticated collaboration "that goes further than negotiating and bargaining". This echoes the types of calls for a dialogue-based marketing communication that we have seen come out of relationship marketing and service marketing research

(Duncan and Moriarty, 1998; Vargo and Lusch, 2004; Varey, 2000; Ballantyne, 2004).

I have also (Miles, 2010) advanced a rhetorical model of marketing communication (based upon Foss and Green's invitational rhetoric) designed to answer the calls in the relationship and services marketing literature for symmetrical, dialogue-based interactions between stakeholders. However, I have also been generally critical of that literature (2010, 2013) in terms of its unwillingness to engage with what a non-manipulative, symmetrical marketing communication would really be like and how it would work. My suspicion that much of this literature is based on unexplored but prejudicial attitudes towards persuasion has grown over the intervening years, bolstered by my analyses of other areas of marketing discourse which use (of course) rhetorical appeals around techniques of co-creation, transparency, and empowerment in order to position particular theories and practices as inclusive, egalitarian, and non-manipulative while remaining fully engaged in control orientations (Miles, 2014a, 2014b, 2016, 2017).

Conclusion

There has been, then, a not insignificant amount of marketing scholarship that has to some degree engaged with the link between marketing and some aspects of the Western rhetorical tradition. The vast majority of this scholarship, however, has either been narrowly focused on particular aspects of marketing communication practice (i.e. the use of tropes and schemas in advertising executions) or has tended to adopt rhetoric as a function of power relations within a broadly Foucauldian framework (analysing rhetorical strategies that serve to legitimize dominant professional hierarchies). That work which has positioned marketing as fundamentally rhetorical (Tonks' "radical claim") has done so in an effort to explain marketing's power as a legitimizing tool for the Bureaucratic Prince, or attempted to re-cast marketing rhetoric as a tool to answer the communication needs of the anti-persuasion service marketing theory platform. Only Tonks (2002) appears to be comfortable with the nitty-gritty of Sophistic persuasion as the basis for the marketing paradigm—and even then his position is somewhat ambiguous and not helped by the uniqueness of his pronouncement (the 'Marketing as Cooking' article remains the only engagement with rhetoric in Tonks' *ouevre*).

The marketing literature that engages with rhetoric exemplifies one of the main issues besetting the discipline (and profession)—a discomfort with persuasion. Persuasion is either something that the 'mainstream' does (and is therefore something that needs to be exposed and resisted) or it is something that marketing has foolishly engaged in and which it should now make every effort to move away from (a typical trope in the relationship and service marketing literature). In other words, the 'bad reputation' that has dogged rhetoric for centuries continues in marketing's own relationship with the pursuit of persuasion. The time is ripe, it would seem, for a fully articulated Sophistic theory of marketing which instead of demonising persuasion (or hiding it underneath layers of deliberately obfuscatory *scientism*) places it at the centre of the marketing enterprise. However, before we can confidently construct this Theory of Sophistic Marketing, there are a few steps left. We must first consider the nature of marketing itself. An exploration of the assumptions upon which the practice and discipline of marketing are based, and the various tensions around and between these assumptions, is essential in order to be able to distinguish the ways in which understandings of persuasion and rhetoric inform, influence, and haunt the fundamental nature of marketing. This will allow us to return to the beginnings of both Sophism and marketing in order to trace their similarities and symbioses. Once this is accomplished, we will turn to the relationship between persuasion, control, and magic. Without a full understanding of how humanity has tended to conflate these elements, we will not be in a position to place persuasion anywhere other than on the Outside of marketing, as so much modern marketing theory has tried to do.

Note

1. There's a lot of rhetoric going on in this small passage, but one notes the pun on "sleight", apparently reflecting a devalorising of the rhetorical.

References

Alvesson, M. (1993). Organizations as Rhetoric—Knowledge-Intensive Firms and the Struggle With Ambiguity. *Journal of Management Studies*, 30(6), 997–1015.

Aristotle (trans. H. C. Lawson-Tancred). (1991). *The Art of Rhetoric*. London: Penguin Books.

Ballantyne, D. (2004). Dialogue and Its Role in the Development of Relationship Specific Knowledge. *Journal of Business & Industrial Marketing*, 19(2), 114–123.

Billig, M. (1985). Prejudice, Categorisation and Particularisation: From a Perceptual to a Rhetoric Account. *European Journal of Social Psychology*, 15(June), 79–103.

Billig, M. (1996). *Arguing and Thinking: A Rhetorical Approach to Social Psychology*. Cambridge: Cambridge University Press.

Billig, M. (1998). Rhetoric and the Unconscious. *Argumentation*, 4(6), 199–216.

Bonet, E., and Sauquet, A. (2010). Rhetoric in Management and in Management Research. *Journal of Organizational Change Management*, 23(2), 120–133.

Boyd, J., and Waymer, D. (2011). Organizational Rhetoric: A Subject of Interest(s). *Management Communication Quarterly*, 25(3), 474–493.

Brown, S. (1995). The Eunuch's Tale: Reviewing Reviewed. *Journal of Marketing Management*, 11(7), 681–706.

Brown, S. (1999). Marketing and Literature: The Anxiety of Academic Influence. *The Journal of Marketing*, 63(1), 1–15.

Brown, S. (2002). The Spectre of Kotlerism: A Literary Appreciation. *European Management Journal*, 20(2), 129–146.

Brown, S. (2004). Writing Marketing: The Clause that Refreshes. *Journal of Marketing Management*, 20(3–4), 321–342.

Brown, S. (2005). *Writing Marketing: Literary Lessons From Academic Authorities*. London: Sage.

Brown, S. (2007). Are We Nearly There Yet? On the Retro-Dominant Logic of Marketing. *Marketing Theory*, 7(3), 291–300.

Brown, S. (2010). Where the Wild Brands Are: Some Thoughts on Anthropomorphic Marketing. *The Marketing Review*, 10(3), 209–224.

Brownlie, D., and Saren, M. (1992). The Four Ps of the Marketing Concept: Prescriptive, Polemical, Permanent and Problematical. *European Journal of Marketing*, 26(4), 34–47.

Brownlie, D., and Saren, M. (1995). On the Commodification of Marketing Knowledge: Opening Themes. *Journal of Marketing Management*, 11(7), 619–627.

Brownlie, D., and Saren, M. (1997). Beyond the One-dimensional Marketing Manager: The Discourse of Theory, Practice and Relevance. *International Journal of Research in Marketing*, 14(2), 147–161.

Capelli, S., and Jolibert, A. (2009). Metaphor's Validity in Marketing Research. *Psychology and Marketing*, 26(12), 1079–1090.

Cheney, G. (1983). The Rhetoric of Identification and the Study of Organizational Communication. *Quarterly Journal of Speech*, 69(2), 143–158.

Cheney, G., Christensen, L. T., Conrad, C., and Lair, D. J. (2004). Corporate Rhetoric as Organizational Discourse. In D. Grant, C. Hardy, C. Oswick, and L. Putnam (Eds.), *The SAGE Handbook of Organizational Discourse*. London: Sage, 79–103.

Cornelissen, J. P. (2003). Metaphor as a Method in the Domain of Marketing. *Psychology and Marketing*, 20(3), 209–225.

Cornelissen, J. P. (2006). Metaphor and the Dynamics of Knowledge in Organization Theory: A Case Study of the Organizational Identity Metaphor. *Journal of Management Studies*, 43(June), 683–709.

Cornelissen, J. P., and Kafouros, M. (2008). Metaphors and Theory Building in Organization Theory: What Determines the Impact of a Metaphor on Theory? *British Journal of Management*, 19(4), 365–379.

Duncan, T., and Moriarty, S. E. (1998). A Communication-Based Marketing Model for Managing Relationships. *Journal of Marketing*, 62(2), 1–13.

Durand, J. (1987). Rhetorical Figures in the Advertising Image. In J. Umiker-Sebeok (Ed.), *Marketing and Semiotics: New Directions in the Study of Signs for Sale*. Berlin: Mouton de Gruyter, 295–318.

Ellis, N., and Hopkinson, G. (2010). The Construction of Managerial Knowledge in Business Networks: Managers' Theories About Communication. *Industrial Marketing Management*, 39(3), 413–424.

Fairclough, N. (2013). Critical Discourse Analysis: The Critical Study of Language. London: Sage.

Foss, S., and Griffin, C. (1995). Beyond Persuasion: A Proposal for an Invitational Rhetoric. *Communication Monographs*, 62, 2–18.

Fox, G. L., Rinaldo, S. B., and Amant, K. St. (2015). The Effects of Rhetorical Figures and Cognitive Load in Word-of-Mouth Communications. *Psychology & Marketing*, 32(10), 1017–1030.

Gummesson, E. (2002). *Total Relationship Marketing*. Oxford: Butterworth-Heinemann.

Gummesson, E. (2004). *Many-to-Many Marketing*. Malmö, Sweden: Liber.

Hackley, C. (2001). *Marketing and Social Construction: Exploring the Rhetorics of Managed Consumption*. London: Routledge.

Hackley, C. (2003). 'We Are All Customers Now . . .' Rhetorical Strategy and Ideological Control in Marketing Management Texts. *Journal of Management Studies*, 40(5), 1325–1352.

Håkansson, H., Harrison, D., and Waluszewski, A. (2004). *Rethinking Marketing: Developing a New Understanding of Markets*. Chichester: John Wiley & Sons.

Hartelius, E. J., and Browning, L. D. (2008). The Application of Rhetorical Theory in Managerial Research: A Literature Review. *Management Communication Quarterly*, 22(1), 13–39.

Heath, R. L. (2011). External Organizational Rhetoric: Bridging Management and Sociopolitical Discourse. *Management Communication Quarterly*, 25(3), 415–435.

Hirschman, E. C. (2007). Metaphor in the Marketplace. *Marketing Theory*, 7(3), 227–248.

Kronrod, A., and Danziger, S. (2013). 'Wii Will Rock You!' The Use and Effect of Figurative Language in Consumer Reviews of Hedonic and Utilitarian Consumption. *Journal of Consumer Research*, 40(4), 726–739.

Lakoff, G. (1987). *Women, Fire, and Dangerous Things: What Categories Reveal About the Mind*. Chicago: University of Chicago Press.

Lakoff, G. (1993). The Contemporary Theory of Metaphor. In A. Ortony (Ed.), *Metaphor and Thought*. Cambridge: Cambridge University Press, 202–251.

Lakoff, G., and Johnson, M. (1980). Conceptual Metaphor in Everyday Language. *The Journal of Philosophy*, 77(8), 453–486.

Lakoff, G., and Johnson, M. (2003). *Metaphors We Live By*. London: University of Chicago Press.

Laufer, R. (2016). Marketing, Sophism, and Mystification. *Marketing Theory*, 16(3), 401–406.

Laufer, R., and Paradeise, C. ([1990] 2016). *Marketing Democracy: Public Opinion and Media Formation in Democratic Societies*. New Brunswick, NJ: Transaction Publishers.

Lowe, S., Ellis, N., and Purchase, S. (2008). Rethinking Language in IMP Research: Networking Processes in Other Words. *Scandinavian Journal of Management*, 24(4), 295–307.

McGuire, W. J. (2000). Standing on the Shoulders of Ancients: Figurative Language. *Journal of Consumer Research*, 27(1), 109–114.

McQuarrie, E. F. (1989). Advertising Resonance: A Semiological Perspective. In E. C. Hirschman (Ed.), *Interpretive Consumer Research*. Provo, UT: Association for Consumer Research, 97–114.

McQuarrie, E. F., and Mick, D. G. (1992). On Resonance: A Critical Pluralistic Inquiry Into Advertising Rhetoric. *Journal of Consumer Research*, 19(2), 180–197.

McQuarrie, E. F., and Mick, D. G. (1996). Figures of Rhetoric in Advertising Language. *Journal of Consumer Research*, 22(4), 424–438.

McQuarrie, E. F., and Mick, D. G. (1999). Visual Rhetoric in Advertising: Text-interpretive, Experimental, and Reader-response Analyses. *Journal of Consumer Research*, 26(1), 37–54.

McQuarrie, E. F., and Mick, D. G. (2003). Re-Inquiries: Visual and Verbal Rhetorical Figures Under Directed Processing Versus Incidental Exposure to Advertising. *Journal of Consumer Research*, 29(4), 579–587.

McQuarrie, E. F., and Mick, D. G. (2009). A Laboratory Study of the Effect of Verbal Rhetoric Versus Repetition When Consumers Are Not Directed to Process Advertising. *International Journal of Advertising*, 28(2), 287–312.

McQuarrie, E. F., and Phillips, B. J. (Eds.). (2007). *Go Figure! New Directions in Advertising Rhetoric*. London: Routledge.

Meisenbach, R., and McMillan, J. J. (2006). Blurring the Boundries: Historical Developments and Future Directions in Organizational Rhetoric. *Annals of the International Communication Association*, 30(1), 99–141.

Mick, D. G. (1986). Consumer Research and Semiotics: Exploring the Morphology of Signs, Symbols, and Significance. *Journal of Consumer Research*, 13(2), 196–213.

Mick, D. G. (1987). Towards a Semiotics of Advertising Story Grammars. In J. Umiker-Sebeok (Ed.), *Marketing and Semiotics: New Directions in the Study of Signs for Sale*. Berlin: Mouton de Gruyter, 249–278.

Mick, D. G. (1988). Schema-theoretics and Semiotics: Toward More Holistic, Programmatic Research on Marketing Communication. *Semiotica*, 70(1/2), 1–26.

Miles, C. (2010). *Interactive Marketing: Revolution or Rhetoric?* London: Routledge.

Miles, C. (2013). Persuasion, Marketing Communication, and the Metaphor of Magic. *European Journal of Marketing*, 47(11/12), 2002–2019.

Miles, C. (2014a). Rhetoric and the Foundation of the Service-Dominant Logic. *Journal of Organizational Change Management*, 27(5), 744–755.

Miles, C. (2014b). The Rhetoric of Managed Contagion: Metaphor and Agency in the Discourse of Viral Marketing. *Marketing Theory*, 14(1), 3–18.

Miles, C. (2016). Control and the Rhetoric of Interactivity in Contemporary Advertising Theory and Practice. In J. Hamilton, R. Bodle, and E. Korin (Eds.), *Explorations in Critical Studies of Advertising*. London: Routledge, 110–123.

Miles, C. (2017). The Rhetoric of Marketing Co-Creation. In G. Siegert and B. von Rimscha (Eds.), *Commercial Communication in the Digital Age—Information or Disinformation?* Berlin: De Gruyter.

Morgan, G. (1992). Marketing Discourse and Practice: Towards a Critical Analysis. In M. Alvesson and H. Wilmott (Eds.), *Critical Management Studies*. London: Sage, 136–158.

Morgan, S. E., and Reichert, T. (1999). The Message is in the Metaphor: Assessing the Comprehension of Metaphors in Advertisements. *Journal of Advertising*, 28(4), 1–12.

Nilsson, T. (2006). Marketing and Classical Rhetoric. In S. Lagrosen and G. Svensson (Eds.), *Marketing: Broadening the Horizons*. Lund: Studentlitteratur.

Nilsson, T. (2010). The Reluctant Rhetorician: Senior Managers as Rhetoricians in a Strategic Change Context. *Journal of Organizational Change Management*, 23(2), 137–144.

Nilsson, T. (2015). *Rhetorical Business: A Study of Marketing Work in the Spirit of Contradiction*. Lund: Lund University.

O'Malley, L., Patterson, M., and Kelly-Holmes, H. (2008). Death of a Metaphor: Reviewing the 'Marketing as Relationships' Frame. *Marketing Theory*, 8(2), 167–187.

O'Shaughnessy, J., and O'Shaughnessy, N. J. (2004). *Persuasion in Advertising*. New York: Routledge.

O'Shaughnessy, N. (2004). *Politics and Propaganda: Weapons of Mass Seduction*. Manchester: Manchester University Press.

Phillips, B. J., and McQuarrie, E. F. (2002). The Development, Change, and Transformation of Rhetorical Style in Magazine Advertisements 1954–1999. *Journal of Advertising*, 31(4), 1–13.

Phillips, B. J., and McQuarrie, E. F. (2004). Beyond Visual Metaphor: A New Typology of Visual Rhetoric in Advertising. *Marketing Theory*, 4(1), 113–136.

Phillips, B. J., and McQuarrie, E. F. (2009). Impact of Advertising Metaphor on Consumer Belief: Delineating the Contribution of Comparison Versus Deviation Factors. *Journal of Advertising*, 38(1), 49–62.

Phillips, B. J., and McQuarrie, E. F. (2010). Narrative and Persuasion in Fashion Advertising. *Journal of Consumer Research*, 37(3), 368–392.

Potter, J. (2005). *Representing Reality: Discourse, Rhetoric and Social Construction.* London: Sage.

Reddy, M. (1979). The Conduit Metaphor: A Case of Frame Conflict in Our Language About Language. In A. Ortony (Ed.), *Metaphor and Thought.* Cambridge: Cambridge University Press, 284–324.

Scott, L. M. (1990). Understanding Jingles and Needledrop: A Rhetorical Approach to Music in Advertising. *Journal of Consumer Research*, 17(2), 223–236.

Scott, L. M. (1994). Images in Advertising: The Need for a Theory of Visual Rhetoric. *Journal of Consumer Research*, 21(2), 252–273.

Shankar, A., Cherrier, H., and Canniford, R. (2006). Consumer Empowerment: A Foucauldian Interpretation. *European Journal of Marketing*, 40(9/10), 1013–1030.

Sillince, J. A. A., and Suddaby, R. (2008). Bridging Management and Communication Scholarship. *Management Communication Quarterly*, 22(1), 5–12.

Skålén, P., Fellesson, M., and Fougère, M. (2006). The Governmentality of Marketing Discourse. *Scandinavian Journal of Management*, 22(4), 275–291.

Skålén, P., Fougère, M., and Fellesson, M. (2008). *Marketing Discourse: A Critical Perspective.* London: Routledge.

Stathakopoulos, V., Theodorakis, I. G., and Mastoridou, E. (2008). Visual and Verbal Rhetoric in Advertising: The Case of 'Resonance'. *International Journal of Advertising*, 27(4), 629–658.

Stern, B. (1988). Medieval Allegory: Roots of Advertising Strategy for the Mass Market. *Journal of Marketing*, 52(3), 84–94.

Stern, B. (1990). Other-speak: Classical Allegory and Contemporary Advertising. *Journal of Advertising*, 19(3), 14–26.

Svensson, P. (2007). Producing Marketing: Towards a Social-phenomenology of Marketing Work. *Marketing Theory*, 7(3), 271–290.

Tadajewski, M. (2006). The Ordering of Marketing Theory: The Influence of McCarthyism and the Cold War. *Marketing Theory*, 6(2), 163–199.

Tadajewski, M. (2010a). Critical Marketing Studies: Logical Empiricism, 'Critical Performativity' and Marketing Practice. *Marketing Theory*, 10(2), 210–222.

Tadajewski, M. (2010b). Towards a History of Critical Marketing Studies. *Journal of Marketing Management*, 26(9–10), 773–824.

Theodorakis, I. G., Koritos, C., and Stathakopoulos, V. (2015). Rhetorical Maneuvers in a Controversial Tide: Assessing the Boundaries of Advertising Rhetoric. *Journal of Advertising*, 44(1), 14–24.

Tom, G., and Eves, A. (1999). The Use of Rhetorical Devices in Advertising. *Journal of Advertising Research*, 39(4), 39–43.

Tonks, D. (2002). Marketing as Cooking: The Return of the Sophists. *Journal of Marketing Management*, 18(7–8), 803–822.

Umiker-Sebeok, J. (Ed.). (1987). *Marketing and Semiotics: New Directions in the Study of Signs for Sale.* Berlin: Mouton de Gruyter.

van Dijk, T. A. (1993). Principles of Critical Discourse Analysis. *Discourse & Society*, 4(2), 249–283.

Varey, R. J. (2000). A Critical Review of Conceptions of Communication Evident in Contemporary Business and Management Literature. *Journal of Communication Management*, 4(4), 328–340.

Varey, R. J. (2002). *Marketing Communication: Principles and Practice*. London: Routledge.

Varey, R. J. (2008). Marketing as an Interaction System. *Australasian Marketing Journal*, 27(1), 79–94.

Vargo, S. L., and Lusch, R. F. (2004). Evolving to a New Dominant Logic for Marketing. *Journal of Marketing*, 68(1), 1–17.

von Koskull, C., and Fougère, M. (2011). Service Development as Practice: A Rhetorical Analysis of Customer-related Arguments in a Service Development Project. *Scandinavian Journal of Management*, 27(2), 205–220.

Watson, T. J. (1995). Rhetoric, Discourse and Argument in Organizational Sense Making: A Reflexive Tale. *Organisation Studies*, 16(5), 805–821.

Zaltman, G., and Coulter, R. H. (1995). Seeing the Voice of the Customer: Metaphor-Based Advertising Research. *Journal of Advertising Research*, 35(4), 35–51.

Zanoni, P., and Janssens, M. (2004). Deconstructing Difference: The Rhetoric of Human Resource Managers' Diversity Discourses. *Organization Studies*, 25(1), 55–74.

Zbaracki, M. (1998). The Rhetoric and Reality of Total Quality Management. *Administrative Science Quarterly*, 43(3), 602–636.

Zwick, D., Bonsu, S. K., and Darmody, A. (2008). Putting Consumers to Work: 'Co-creation' and New Marketing Governmentality. *Journal of Consumer Culture*, 8(2), 163–196.

3   Control and the Discourse of Marketing Science

In order to investigate how marketing may be seen as a form of rhetoric it is first necessary to establish how exactly marketing sees itself. Of course, like any academic discipline, marketing has evolved over time—but marketing is also a very young discipline with recognisable marketing courses at US universities becoming established only around 1915 (Hagerty, 1936) and the discourse regarding its identity can be summarised in a few core narrative streams. The first of these is the discipline's status as science or practice (or even art) and this has been a point of debate almost since the establishment of marketing as a discrete subject of scholarship. The second narrative concerns the relationship between advertising and distribution and this, too, has been a clear issue since the early days of marketing writing, with some authors treating the two as distinct but equal components of marketing and others attempting to subsume advertising into marketing-as-distribution as a small (and often rather inconsequential) element. The final narrative stream connects to both of these and concerns the *scope* of marketing—should it, for example, be expanded out (Borg-like) to include the work of government and administration or should it remain within the tight boundaries of commercial enterprise? I will argue that all three of these areas are primarily concerned with issues of control—in the sense of debating what business and social areas marketing should have control over (as a profession) but also in the sense of both how the debates function as arenas of discourse control and how they imply marketing's central function as one of control. In the next pages, I will explore the ramifications of each of these narratives, indicating how they reflect these different perspectives on control. This will then lead me to a deeper examination of what exactly *control* has meant for marketing and how marketing's relationship with the concept of control reflects its relationship with persuasion. From this foundation, I will then be able to construct an argument for understanding marketing as a discipline concerned exclusively with the management of attention (or regard) and thus as the contemporary manifestation of the rhetorical profession.

Marketing as Science

It has become usual to portray marketing as evolving initially from economics. Vargo and Lusch's (2004) presentation of the evolution of marketing thought, for example, starts by stating that "the formal study of marketing focused at first on the distribution and exchange of commodities [. . .] and featured a foundation in economics" (p. 1). The value of this foundation narrative seems to lie in the way that it serves to strengthen (by inheritance) the claims of marketing to be a science. As Vargo and Lusch (2004) go on to explain, at the time of the formal birth of marketing, economics had already become "the first social science to reach the quantitative sophistication of the natural sciences" (p. 3). So, although marketing thought might be concerned with far more immediate and tangible problems than most economic theory, the fact that it is framed as born from a rigorously quantitative discipline affords it outstanding rational and empirical credentials. Wilkie and Moore (2003) bring some more detail to this foundational narrative by describing how the "first era of formal marketing thought" (p. 117) arose because a particular aspect of the "business system", namely the challenges of distribution, began to be given more attention than it had previously garnered. As they point out, economists had traditionally "not been handling the topic" as their focus was instead on production. By the start of the twentieth century, however, the business environment had changed radically with a whole host of societal, technological, and infrastructure changes, meaning that market distribution had become a far more complex and critical component in a firm's success. Wilkie and Moore (2003) argue that there was a "genuine need for some economists to step forward" (p. 118) and provide an explanation of this new aspect of the business system. These economists ("professors at a number of universities across the [US]") are the founding fathers of the marketing discipline. An early analogue of this account can be found in Cassels' (1936) article for the second issue of the fledgling *Journal of Marketing*, where he notes that "in recent years . . . certain significant changes both in economic theory and in the methods of distribution which have aroused among economists in general a new interest in marketing problems and created an attitude towards them more likely to lead to practically useful results" (p. 133). This intellectual engagement with the issue of distribution uses "methods of theoretical analysis combined with empirical research" but is clearly positioned as stemming from a need to provide practical advice to current and future business leaders.

At the same time, the extent of the contribution of economic theory to this analysis of distribution is perhaps rather questionable. We can see from a rather exasperated article published in the late 1940s in the *Journal of Marketing* that it was clearly not the case that early US university marketing departments laid much emphasis on economic knowledge. Seelye (1947) notes that "some teachers of marketing apparently believe that economic theory has little or no place in marketing courses" (p. 223) and this is primarily because of the "assumption that economic theory is unrealistic and, therefore, has little or no application to the modern marketing structure" (p. 224). As a consequence, the "contribution of economic theory to the study of marketing is held to be negligible" (p. 223). Seelye contends that such an attitude places marketing in a "vacuum" (p. 226), blinding it to the relationships its functions have with "fundamental economic phenomena". Only through an appreciation of such relationships can marketing understand its "true position . . . as an applied branch of economics" (ibid.). The pure and applied dichotomy echoes the more established pattern in the scientific disciplines—it is also an attempt to *positively* frame the accusations of 'unrealism' that seem to have been commonly applied to economics by incumbent marketing faculty. If marketing is to be a 'science', then it must have its 'pure' theory as well as its practical implementation.

Whether most of its participants regarded themselves as performing 'applied economics' or not, it is fair to say that most marketing teaching and scholarship in the early years of the discipline was heavily descriptive rather than concerned with theory building or analysis. Certainly, the reports sponsored by the Carnegie and Ford Foundations (Gordon and Howell, 1959; Pierson, 1959) in the late 1950s, which investigated the state of US business education, found that the "core courses (such as marketing) were mostly descriptive, rather than analytical" (Hunt, 2012, p. 408). Given that these foundations (along with the Rockefeller Foundation) were important sources of funding for US business schools, it is not surprising that their judgements had significant effects upon the way in which marketing scholarship developed (Hubbard, 2005; Tadajewski, 2006a, 2006b, 2016). However, while the embarrassing reports of these foundations can certainly be considered to have had an impact upon the 'scientification' of business education in general and marketing in particular, there had already been strong internal evidence of a move towards considering the young discipline as a scientific endeavour. Jones and Monieson (1990), for example, have persuasively described the influence of the German Historical school (which emphasised an inductive scientific approach) on the marketing economists of Wisconsin University and the Harvard Business School in the early decades of the twentieth century. Furthermore, Edmund McGarry (1936) had stressed the need for "scientific method" in advertising work right back in the first edition of the *Journal of Marketing* and by the time of Converse's (1945) article on the "development of the science of marketing" the use of the descriptor appeared to warrant little editorial defence. Indeed, as Stephen Brown has noted, Converse's article assumes that "marketing was indubitably a nascent science" (1996, p. 244). At the time, Hutchinson (1952) noted the "ferment which had been started in the minds of students of marketing" (p. 287) in regard to this issue. Yet, while scholars such as Brown (1948), Alderson and Cox (1948), and then Bartels (1951) argued that marketing could (and even should) be considered a form of science, there were certainly voices raised in opposition. Hutchinson (1952), for example, wrote a coruscating critique of those scholars seeking to admit marketing "into the category of a science" (p. 286), arguing that such an "ill-advised" (p. 287) project has so far either involved "distorting the meaning of words" (p. 288) or vaguely criticising the weak foundations of economic theory (which does nothing to develop a viable theory of marketing). Hutchinson points out that the one real reason why marketing scholarship had so far been unable to make much headway in the construction off a "unique body of theory" was simply because "marketing is not a science" (p. 289). It is, instead, a *practice* (like architecture or medicine) which applies "the findings of many sciences to the solution of problems" (p. 290).

Hutchinson's message, however, was largely lost upon the audience of young marketing scholars coming into their voice in the late 1950s and 1960s, many of whose studies were being funded by the Ford Foundation (Tadajewski, 2006a). This shift towards thinking of marketing as a science was also echoed in the *Journal of Marketing*'s formation of an official editorial policy that sought to support rigorous, scientific advancements in marketing as well as the establishment in 1961 of the Marketing Science Institute (Kerin, 1996). While Buzzell's (1963) article in the *Harvard Business Review* made it clear that there were serious problems with marketing's performance as a science (mostly due to the fact that it needed to examine events that were "tightly coupled, nonlinear, and dynamic", p. 166), it was equally adamant that, slowly, the scientific project in marketing would be realised.

Hunt's (1976) article sought to settle the debate once and for all via an examination of the various competing claims concerning marketing's scope. It received the Harold H. Maynard Award in recognition of its "significant contribution to marketing theory and thought" (Anderson, 1994, p. 9) and became the most succinct and cogently argued expression of the pro-science viewpoint in marketing scholarship. Its argument was largely based upon the observation that the reason there continued to be a degree of reluctance to think of marketing as a science was that previous understandings of what science actually was were mistaken. In particular, Hunt describes Buzzell's (1963, p. 37) highly cited stricture that a science must be "organized around one or two central theories" as "overly restrictive" (Hunt, 1976, p. 25) and points out that it "confuses the *successful culmination* of scientific efforts with *science itself*". Buzzells' terms have constructed too high a bar for marketing to reach in its young life and the absence of "one or two central theories" does not mean that marketing is not engaged in scientific endeavour. Hunt argues that, for a discipline to be a science, it must have a "distinct subject matter"; it must also presuppose "the existence of underlying uniformities or regularities among the phenomena that comprise its subject matter", the discovery of which can lead to "empirical regularities, law-like generalizations (propositions), and laws"; and, finally, it must employ the "scientific method" based upon "the bedrock of empirical testability" (ibid.) in the discovery of its knowledge. Hunt stated clearly that he believed that marketing scholarship fulfilled all three of these criteria. Marketing's distinct subject matter is the transaction. While marketing's progress has been slow in identifying "underlying uniformities" across transactions, it is, opines Hunt, impossible to deny that there has been "some progress" in identifying "some uniformities". The final criterion regarding the use of scientific method is rather embarrassingly handled by Hunt, who acknowledges that there have been forthright criticisms of the scientific rigour of marketing scholarship but excuses the discipline with an argument that veers dangerously close to a *tu quoque* fallacy, namely that "researchers in marketing are at least as committed to the method of science as are researchers in other disciplines" (p. 28). Consequently, the final sentence of the paper proudly announces that "the study off the positive dimension of marketing can be appropriately referred to as marketing science".

One aspect of Hunt's (1976) paper that deserves some additional comment is the way in which he addresses the problem of marketing's definition. While acknowledging that the lack of agreement upon the nature and scope of marketing has so far made the provision of an unproblematic definition of the discipline impossible, Hunt writes that this should not be seen as a point of weakness. He notes that philosophy had also been beset with definitional questions some decades earlier, particularly focused around issues of scope and he approvingly quotes Karl Popper's commentary at the time, in which he stated that "there is no such thing as an essence of philosophy, to be distilled and condensed into a definition" because any definition can "only have the character of a convention, of an agreement" (Popper, quoted in Hunt, 1976, p. 23).

While Hunt's (1976) article employed the confident tone of settling the matter once and for all, in many ways it ironically acted as a rallying target for all those who had become disillusioned "with the dominant hypothetico-deductive perspective" (Brown, 1996, p. 255). Those young marketing scholars who had been exposed to the rising tide of relativism in the social sciences saw Hunt's article as the epitome of an arrogant, traditional mainstream approach to the marketing enterprise that was largely out of touch with what was happening elsewhere in the academy. The expression of dissatisfaction with the position that Hunt (1976) represented culminated in a series of articles by Paul Anderson (1983, 1986, 1988) in which he took issue with Hunt's logical positivist interpretation of science and argued that the bulk of recent writing in philosophy, social sciences, and the history of science pointed to the bankruptcy of such an interpretation. Instead, Anderson outlined a "critical relativist" approach to science, which constructed it as a "process of consensus formation" and "ultimately a social activity" (1983, p. 25). Central to the emotional power of Anderson's argument was the cutting observation that "despite its prevalence in marketing, positivism has been abandoned by these disciplines over the last two decades in the face of the overwhelming historical and logical arguments that have been raised against it" (ibid.). In other words, the "strong *honorific* overtones in labelling a discipline a science" (Hunt, 1976, p. 25), were beginning to be eroded by a general realisation that such labelling did not reflect access to unassailable, objective truth. For Anderson (1983), "a relativistic stance appears to be the only viable solution to the problem of scientific method"

(p. 25). Such a stance, which Anderson dubs "science$_2$", is founded upon "societal consensus", which determines that "science is whatever society chooses to call a science" (p. 26). Anderson intimates that, for marketing to be seen as scientific by society, it must move away from building marketing knowledge from the perspective of the marketer and instead move towards that of "the consumer or the larger society" (p. 27) and pursuit of knowledge for the sake of knowledge. A discipline that predominantly favours the hidden persuader, it seems, will not be valued enough by society to achieve the consensus that it deserves to be understood as a science.

Anderson's writing on these issues and the relativistic marketing scholarship that it to some extent precipitated resulted in a series of articles and dense monographs by Hunt (1984, 1990, 1994, 2002, 2003) in which he argued that relativism had, in fact, already been abandoned by philosophers of science, who had instead "adopted some version of scientific realism" (2002, p. 77). The influence of constructivist theories from scholars whom Anderson had relied upon in his arguments, people like Kuhn and Feyerabend, was dismissed as "exaggerated" (ibid.). Both Brown (1996) and Kavanagh (1994) contain overviews of the Hunt/Anderson positivism versus relativism debate. Even in 1994, Kavanagh was declaring the clash largely over, describing the debate as "repetitive" as well as "confusing and virtually impenetrable to the majority of marketing academics" (p. 28). Kavanagh (1994) argues that the "inexorable sparring match" between realism/relativism in marketing scholarship has become irrelevant, as both perspectives are ill-equipped to engage with what has become "postmodern marketing" (p. 36). Brown (1996) similarly declares the debate moribund, though his reasoning is a little more partisan. Like Kavanagh (1994), he notes that the legacy of the period of "internecine warfare" between scientific realism and relativism was a "widespread sense of perplexity and bemusement" (Brown, 1996, p. 250). However, Brown argues that the debate should be considered terminated because science has so clearly lost. Extending the postmodern to a consideration of academic discourse (rather than simply marketing practice, as Kavanagh did), Brown contends that the era of "Antiscience" has been ushered in by "the continental European versions of the postmodern" (p. 251). For thinkers aligned with this latest intellectual evolution, "the appellation 'science' is no longer considered honorific" (p. 251); indeed, "postmodern consciousness . . . [. . .] . . . is premised upon the repudiation of the Western scientific paradigm" (p. 250). Postmodernism sees science as "morally bankrupt, spiritually bereft, and intellectually barren" (p. 251). Importantly, while Brown is quick to concede that the "vast majority of marketing academics" "continue to work within the broad realist/empiricist/instrumentalist/positivistic tradition" (p. 249) and so therefore cannot be considered postmodern, or even relativist, scholars by any stretch of the imagination, he claims that the "revolutionaries of relativism have triumphed" precisely because they have not been killed off. As Hunt's mission was to destroy the intellectual foundations of relativism, reasons Brown, the fact that many marketing journals do currently contain scholarship based in interpretivist or constructionist perspectives demonstrates that he has clearly failed. In addition (and echoing some of Anderson's original arguments), as all the other social sciences have imbibed the postmodern perspective and seen the pursuit of science for the illusion it is, the general "denial of scientific authority cannot fail to strike a chord with the observers of the contemporary marketing scene" (p. 251). This, combined with the fact that "marketing scholarship has actually achieved very little of practical, implementable worth in the post-war period" (p. 252) means that the marketing academy is ripe for the realisation that the pursuit of science is an embarrassing snipe hunt.

Of course, Kavanagh and Brown were both writing before the publication of Hunt's (2002, 2003) mammoth tomes on the foundations and controversies of marketing theory, the second of which was helpfully subtitled, "for reason, realism, truth, and objectivity". Certainly, while significant schools of critical marketing, consumer culture theory, and broadly interpretivist approaches to consumer behaviour have established themselves in marketing scholarship over the past few decades there appears to have been little sign of a general retreat from the pursuit of marketing *science*. Indeed, perhaps the most successful stream of research in marketing theory since the early 2000s has been Vargo and Lusch's Service-Dominant logic (Vargo and Lusch, 2004, 2008, 2011, 2015, 2016; Lusch and Vargo, 2006, 2011, 2012). Vargo and Lusch's (2004) foundational *JoM* article for their logic is full of language designed to anchor their perspective within the legacy of Western scientific empiricism and which works persuasively to attract their readership and convince them of the logic's rigour and scholarly desirability (Miles, 2014, 2018). Clearly, the trappings of the scientific (or at least, scientism) still have "strong honorific overtones" for the broad mass of *JoM* readers. Additionally, much of S-D logic's evolution over the past decade has been focused on the (re-)integration of systems theory in to the S-D framework and this is very much done from a scientism perspective, where the scientific status of the systems approach is clearly a valuable marker of its rigour and scholarly desirability (e.g. Vargo and Lusch, 2011, 2016). While it is true that Vargo and Lusch have occasionally argued that S-D logic should not be understood as operating within the same context as the "sciences of the natural or social" (Lusch and Vargo, 2012, p. 195), this is because they wish to place it within the "science of the artificial" as conceived of by Herbert Simon (1996) in his study of artificial intelligence, complexity and dynamic systems—an even more modern and shiny type of science, in other words. Recently, however, Vargo and Lusch are content to use the descriptor of 'science' in order to situate their own evolution of "service science" within the broader 'economic sciences' and 'political sciences' (2011, 2015). Mainstream marketing scholarship's valorisation of science over any alternatives continues just as strongly as it did before, it appears.

Much of the dynamic across the realism versus relativism debate (and even across the science versus practice discourse) can be conceived of in rhetorical terms. As we have seen, Hunt (1976) admits the "honorific" power of the label of science, although he refrains from turning his observation back upon marketing's own obsession with the sobriquet. Yet the rancorous energy that is displayed in his vituperations of relativism speaks of great emotional investment in the issue of whether the discipline he has dedicated his life to can be thought of as uncovering objective truths in the way that chemistry or physics does. It might mean, of course, a great deal to both scholars and practitioners of marketing whether the rules and conclusions that the discipline expounds to the world are based upon 'facts' and 'analyses' which have the persuasive power of science behind them. In addition, much of academia is concerned with status, or *ethos*, at the personal, departmental, institutional, and disciplinary level. Despite Brown's (1996) protestations, science maintains a position of authority in much of the modern world (Cialdini, 2001). A 2015 Pew Research Center Report found that "science holds an esteemed place among citizens and professionals" in the US, despite some strongly diverging opinions between citizens and scientists on issues such as the safety of GM food (Funk and Rainie, 2015, para 2). Since the Ford and Carnegie reports, the intellectual status of business and marketing scholarship has seemed to depend (at least from *within* the discipline) upon projecting the impression that it is founded upon rigorous, positivist scholarship that can serve as a reliable source of decision making for management and enterprise. The promotion of 'marketing science' through the establishment of such institutions as the Marketing Science Institute and the Academy of Marketing Science (and its related journal) as well as through the tireless advocacy of scholars such as Shelby Hunt has meant that the concept of marketing science has become normalised and valorised. At the same time the efforts to promote relativistic, interpretive and aesthetic foundations for the marketing discipline are also closely tied to efforts to amplify the *ethos* of the work of those scholars and 'schools' who choose to work within such frameworks. Such amplification work is necessary in order to defend and build academic status, particularly as manifest in terms of promotion prospects and employability. If scholars are to engage in qualitative, interpretive research or concept building that relies upon critical, relativistic foundations, then it pays to promote and argue for these perspectives within the marketing academy using rhetoric which positions the positivistic approach as out-of-touch, old-fashioned, as well as fundamentally flawed. Allied to this, perhaps, is the fact that some scholars working within marketing might be more cognisant of how other scholars working within the social sciences might regard their discipline's approach—there is definitely a sense of embarrassment evident in much marketing writing from the relativistic or postmodern perspectives. How can a sensitive marketing academic familiar with much of the intellectual legacy of the twentieth century hold their head high in the company of communication scholars, media scholars, sociology scholars, and literature and history scholars, when the discipline is so clearly still in thrall to a 1950s scientism which these other disciplines have long since abandoned or heavily modified? In this sense, the relativism expounded by Anderson and others in opposition to Hunt's defence of scientific realism is an equally rhetorical reaction to the rhetoric of 'marketing science'. It attempts to increase the *cachet* of marketing scholarship within the social sciences and humanities, where relativism has become largely mainstream.

Looked at this way, the relativism/realism division collapses—both are rhetorical framings designed for the academy, wider university and government audiences, (very) occasionally the 'end users' of marketing knowledge, and perhaps most often the marketing academics engaged in these debates themselves (engaged in self-persuasion). Marketing is a both a manqué hard (realist) science and a manqué (relativist) social science. It convinces as neither because, ironically, its rhetoric of self-definition is always concerned with turning away from what it actually *is*, namely, rhetoric. Rhetoric does not fit the mould of twentieth-century scientism or 'humanities discipline'. As we have seen in Chapter 1, issues around its status, nature, and scope as a discipline have continually beset Western rhetoric. Furthermore, academic rhetorical studies in the twentieth century have tended to move towards rhetorical analysis rather than practice. Rhetoric in the modern academy does not look like many earlier manifestations of rhetoric because it has become (rhetorically) framed as a critical tool within a (North American liberal) construction of civic discourse. Similarly, marketing scholarship doesn't look like marketing practice, and this is largely because it has been (rhetorically) framed within a scientism/social scientism that obscures its nature in practice.

However, in addition to the rhetorical expediencies that have resulted in framings of marketing as a positivist/relativist (social) science, there exists one additional factor that unites marketing and the scientific enterprise—control.

Control and the Scope of Marketing

Marketing seems fundamentally concerned with control—control of resources, control of decision-making within the enterprise, control of moods, attitudes and behaviours, control of flow and distribution. No matter what era a definition of marketing originates in, its concern with control is always present. As Durkheim ([1959] 2009) noted (after Saint Simon), the "most vital trait" of the "spontaneous organization" of industrial order is "that its goal, and its exclusive goal, is to increase the control of man over things" (p. 107). Beniger (1986), in his study of the control orientation of modern information societies, argues that the industrial revolution, particularly the way it fuelled a rampant increase in the rate at which materials could be transported and processed, precipitated a "crisis of control" in America by the mid-nineteenth century in which "the social processing of material flows threatened to exceed in both volume and speed the system's capacity to contain them" (p. 219). Myriad problems arose as a result of this crisis. Railroads became increasingly unsafe and unmanageable, with companies deliberately delaying the introduction of larger systems "because they lacked the means to control them" (ibid.). Distributers and wholesalers began to find it increasingly difficult to keep track of raw material shipments, finished goods, and cash across the rapidly mushrooming manufacturing and retailing networks. Producers themselves were stretched to breaking point trying to respond to the increased speed of their own new production methods as well as the jump in upstream supply rates. All the rapid improvements in continuous processing technology had to be integrated into systems that had evolved for much lower rates of production and distribution. As a consequence, by the 1880s, production in many sectors was outstripping consumption and producers needed to create additional markets in order to "stimulate and control consumption" (ibid.). It is this requirement that Beniger identifies as generating the birth of modern marketing. He quotes Harry Tipper, Texas Company's (the precursor to Texaco) advertising manager in 1915, as saying that it was necessary for producers to educate consumers "to use more than they formerly had used, and to discriminate between different sellers or sections of the market in order to control the market" (quoted in Beniger, 1986, p. 264).

As an example of the way in which continuous processing technologies were integrated into a business sector and then caused a crisis of consumption control which needed to be addressed through early marketing, Beniger relates the story of Henry P. Crowell's adoption of automatic flour mill technology to his proto-assembly line production of packaged oatmeal in 1882. The production innovations he implemented allowed him, under one roof, to take raw oats as input and then output packaged oatmeal. However, there was little market for the vast amount of product his factory was generating—outside of the small constituency of Scottish immigrants, oats were not generally considered a fit food for human consumption. The result was that he was soon producing "twice as much oatmeal as the market could absorb" (p. 265). His answer was national advertising targeted directly at the mass consumer market using a number of innovative promotion techniques which have since become canonical. He created an easily identifiable brand label based around the figure of the Quaker, he re-packaged his product in smaller, friendlier 24-oz sizes, used testimonials, apparent scientific 'proof', free samples delivered door-to-door, and publicity stunts (hiring a train promoting his brand which ferried across states an actor dressed as a Quaker). As a result, Crowell "managed to dispose of surpluses created by the control revolutions in production and distribution by inventing not only the modern breakfast food industry but breakfast cereal itself—a product then almost entirely new to American tastes" (p. 266). Crowell's story, of course, is just one of the earliest in the history of advertising and marketing communication. However, its substance, and the way that Beniger frames it, raises a number of important questions regarding the nature and scope of marketing.

The definition of marketing as the 'control of consumption' certainly seems convincing within the context that Beniger provides for it. It includes advertising, branding, packaging (designed to sell itself), preprocessing (i.e. reducing the informational variety facing consumers so that their responses could be more predictable), as well as processing of the consumer via automated, self-service (nowadays we would say 'curated') retail experiences (as championed in Clarence Saunders' Piggly Wiggly stores). In other words, all the activities that a company might make use of to affect attitudes and behaviours of consumers towards their products, services, or brands—to "control the market", as Tipper had it. Most of the techniques that Beniger covers broadly fall into the category of advertising or promotion. However, if we look at the early years of academic marketing we find that our founding disciplinary fathers were rather divided on the significance of promotion for marketing work. Indeed, it is difficult to not note a division in the early decades of the *Journal of Marketing* between those scholars who are concerned with advertising (and salespersonship) and those who are concerned more broadly with *distribution* (i.e. the activities of bringing a product to market). Some of the origins for this division might well come from the fact that the functional approach to marketing which emphasised the study of the "functions of middlemen" (Jones and Monieson, 1990, p. 109) tended to be promulgated by economists who took a dim view of advertising. Those writers concentrating on advertising often already had a quite large choice of outputs for their musings on advertising and sales techniques including trade newspapers such as *Printer's Ink*, the publications of the various advertising associations, as well as the printing of books designed to aid the small business person (see Thompson and Adams, 1996, p. 270, n3 for a long list of representative texts). The study of the economic significance of middlemen, however, was not so well served and was not so popularly followed, but it did have a more respectable mien particularly for scholars trained in economics and economic history. Thomson and Adams (1996) note that the early American advertising industry was generally associated with "exuberant boosterism or imported 'grotesque' decorative forms" (p. 253). They quote Alfred Lasker's recollections of being an ad man at the start of the twentieth century where he recalls how "bankers refused to lend businessmen money if they revealed it would be used for advertising" and that the profession of advertising was "socially barred with very few exceptions" (ibid.). While the importance of advertising to successful business could not be denied, this didn't mean that society was particularly fond of what they did. Consequently, those engaged in developing the discipline of marketing chose to focus on another figure rather than the advertiser.

Control and the 'Middleman'

The term 'middleman' has not stood the test of time particularly well. Notwithstanding the obvious defects related to its sexist construction, the term carries with it the inevitable connotation of the activity being "of lesser consequence than that of manufacturing or retailing" (Steiner, 1976, p. 6) even of being in some sense "parasitic" (Brown, 2002, p. 30). It places the marketer in an inferior position and that is a hard place to remain content. Nevertheless, the term was common in the early days of marketing practice and scholarship and was used to indicate all those agents who had sprung up to help navigate and facilitate the increasingly long and irksome journey of goods from producer to user that the industrial revolution had brought about. This was, indeed, the descriptor term for marketers used by Arch Shaw (1912) in his article that formally heralded the birth of the functional approach to the discipline (Converse, 1945; Jones and Monieson, 1990). Cassels' (1936) paper on the place of economics in early marketing thought spends some time discussing the interesting dichotomy between the quite negative way that much of the general public regarded 'middlemen' and the far more "optimistic" view that classical and neo-classical economists had of such agents. He argues that Adam Smith's enthusiastic support for "agencies developed for commodity distribution" (p. 133) 'infected' the majority of economists, who consequently found it difficult to look critically at the place of the 'middleman' until problems of distribution (the types of problems outlined by Beniger, one presumes) forced them to look more carefully at the functions of agents and describe them in more sophisticated and nuanced terms—and so was born the academic study of marketing.

Cassels' paper is also interesting for the way in which it looks far, far back in history in order to provide a rounded foundation myth for the 'marketer as middleman' perspective. Indeed, the first persuasive gambit that Cassels uses is an *argumentum ad antiquitatem* to position marketing as an area of human endeavour which enjoyed the early attentions of great intellectuals, thereby proving that it is, contrary to popular perception, "one of the oldest" branches of economics (p. 129). He points out that it was one of the first areas of economics "to receive attention from the Greek philosophers and others who laid the foundations of the science" (ibid.) and that the central marketing question that concerned Plato and the greats remains at the core of twentieth-century understandings of the profession. This question, Cassels argues, is the problem of how to carry "through efficiently from the social point of view this final stage in the production process". He goes on to note how Plato, after recounting in *the Republic* the way in which increasing sophistication of exchange markets inevitably leads to specializations of roles, describes the way in which a special class of men will arise to meet the need of all those specialized professions. There will be times that a specialist artisan will have goods to sell when there are no customers available and therefore risks having to "sit idle in the marketplace" (quoted in Cassels, 1936, p. 129). This is the value of the middleman for Plato—someone who can "remain on the spot in the marketplace and give money for goods to those who want to sell, and goods for money to those who want to buy" (p. 130). Interestingly, Cassels has to defend Plato's curious stricture that

such middlemen will be made up of "persons of excessive physical weakness" (ibid.), explaining that this is a consequence of Plato's views on the
social division of labour. The Platonic marketer is someone who literally
is well-suited to sitting still in the middle of the marketplace and who can
therefore take advantage of that position to facilitate the exchange of goods.
At this early stage of market development, it is clear that the middleman is
basically a conduit of convenience—there is no hint of the persuasive 'control of consumption' that begins to typify the middleman's role after the
control revolution. Furthermore, in basing his exposition of Platonic marketing on *the Republic* he ignores the harsher treatment that philosopher
affords middlemen in the *Laws*, something that Kelley (1956) picks up in a
later JoM piece covering similar ground. The job of middleman should be
given to *metics* (immigrants or 'strangers') as there was far too much risk of
the retail trade infecting Athenians with a love of profit. As Kelley puts it,
"corruption of the moral fabric of the stranger would do less harm to the
state!" (p. 63). The *Laws* also forbid the 'flattering of goods' and the provision of guarantees as any form of persuasion with regard to the retailing
is considered to be dishonest. Cassels' (1936) attempt to provide middlemen with a sympathetic version of Platonic support is, perhaps, a misguided
attempt at the *argumentum ad antiquitatem*, implying that, if the oldest
and grandest of the Greek philosophers was convinced of the middleman's
necessity, then the profession should be assured a respected place in the
modern academy. From this perspective, this whitewashing of Plato's view
on middlemen is made all the more necessary, as the bulk of ancient opinion
that comes after Plato is set squarely against the morality of the merchant.
Indeed, he has to jump all the way up to Thomas Aquinas in the fourteenth
century to find even a grudging acceptance that, under certain very clear
circumstances, it was morally acceptable to charge more for a good than
was paid for it. As Kelley (1956) points out, this general lack of sympathy
for the middleman prevails "right through the medieval period of history",
when the idea of a "mutuality of benefit from a mere exchange of goods"
was simply inconceivable (p. 63).

There is, then, a dilemma for those who wish to amplify the antiquity and
importance of marketing's early roots. Being able to point out how central the
mercantile or middleman function has been throughout history amplifies the
ethos of the discipline. At the same time, any consideration of the evidence for
public perception of this function tends to indicate that societies in general did
not trust those performing the function and held them in low regard. Trade
was a corrupting influence on those performing it and those coming into
contact with it. If you want to link the names of the great philosophers and
thinkers with the practice of marketing, then you will mostly be dealing with
invective and mistrust, it seems. Of course, one option given this dilemma is
to ignore the historical *perception* of marketing and simply construct a history of how trade has grown over time. This is Fisk's (1967) approach, for
example, in his book on marketing systems; the opening sections provide a

bloodless narrative of the development of international trade development since the Mesopotamian merchants completely devoid of any sense of how these various traders and agents were perceived by society at large. Here we get the strategic narrative point that marketing is at the heart of growth and civilization without any consideration of its intellectual significance. We retain the *cachet* of ancient lineage without any of the awkward questions regarding the social status of that lineage.

Bartels (1976), in his *The History of Marketing Thought*, sidestepped the whole issue by largely dismissing the pre-nineteenth century importance of the middleman. In broad alignment with Beniger's (1986) argument, Bartels (1976) saw the middleman as of "incidental significance" (p. 17) until the explosion of production capacity in the years following the American Civil War. Previously, Bartels explains, middlemen individually "were necessary, but collectively they did not constitute what might be regarded as a distributive 'system'" (ibid.). However, as the widespread introduction of new industrial methods meant that production was "no longer carried on for an immediately available market but in advance of known markets and for unknown markets at great distances" (p. 16–7), so the intermediary position of market agents became increasingly vital. The responsibilities of such middlemen also grew, encompassing the creation of value through "time, place, and possession utilities" (p. 17). Price itself became "a managed phenomenon" rather than a "market or natural one" (ibid.). This significant increase in scope and impact of the middleman or market agent led directly to the birth of marketing thought. Middlemen became a distinct and substantial class of business managers dealing with issues that classical economics had not been designed for. As Bartels argues, this class of managers "required a type of scientific or academic thought that no prevailing theories provided, and [. . .] it became the objective of marketing thought and marketing literature to supply" it. (p. 18).

So, we can see that while the ancient origins of the middleman can occasionally (and awkwardly) be used to argue for the marketing profession's credibility, the transformation of middleman into marketer seems, according to general scholarly consensus, to occur in line with Beniger's (1986) identification of the control crisis in American industry in the mid to late 1900s. This is not to say that consideration of what ancient thinkers had to say about the profession of middleman is useful only for an *ad antiquitatem* amplification of the discipline's *ethos*. Indeed, we will return to consider more closely the significance of Platonic and Aristotelian censuring of middlemen for what it can tell us about the relationship between marketing and some of the other professions that these thinkers find untrustworthy. However, the narrative of the middleman's transformation under the pressure of the crisis of control does allow us to consider the way in which marketing's blurred disciplinary boundaries have come about and continue to exist.

Bartels' point that the transformation of the significance of the middleman was accompanied by a widening in the responsibilities and scope of the profession is an important one. Much of marketing's definitional chaos is a direct consequence of being a practice borne from the shifting sands of necessity. Bartels' (1976) study of the development of marketing thought makes this quite clear in its own structure. Initial chapters deal with separate areas of practice and research such as advertising, credit, sales, retail, and wholesale—as Bartels reviews the early literature across these topics it is clear they see little connection with each other. The writers and practitioners in these areas do not see themselves as part of a larger discipline of 'marketing'. Instead, 'marketing' begins to slowly be positioned by a small number of forward thinkers (Shaw, Butler, Weld and Cherington, in Bartels' narrative) as a concept that can serve to integrate the disparate functions, processes, and institutions that had been gradually growing in importance over the second half of the nineteenth century. Yet, despite the work by early pioneers of the integrative marketing outlook, the constituent areas continued to develop and publish and organise within themselves, with little regard to their place in this new umbrella discipline (which remained predominantly conceptual rather than functional in the sense that companies were not integrating these separate areas into marketing departments). It is not surprising, indeed, that the early marketing writing of the 1920s consisted of descriptive "commodity studies" (Bartels, 1976, p. 147). Those promulgating an integrative 'marketing' initially needed to position the necessity for such integration by persuasively describing the ways in which all of the distributive, sales, and advertising functions can be seen to lock together into one meta-function (as seen in work by Duncan, Hibbard, and Macklin). Only from such a base could the *principles* of the meta-function be identified and promoted.

One of the consequences of the integrative nature of marketing is that it subsumed some quite wildly different areas of activity. The middlemen that evolved to handle the crises of control in production, distribution, and consumption were necessarily highly specialised, and much of the thinking that developed around their various professions relied upon quite different knowledge sets and proficiencies. This continues to be an issue in modern marketing practice and scholarship—most advertising scholars will be quite unfamiliar with resource-advantage theory or theories of market entry, and supply chain specialists are ill-equipped to navigate the literature on consumer culture or social media marketing. Specialisms, and the silos they can inspire, are not just an issue for marketing, of course, but it is rare for an academic discipline (and a profession) to have emerged through the integration of so many disparate areas. The fact that advertising is taught in some universities around the world under the aegis of schools of Journalism or Media Studies rather than in Departments of Marketing in Business schools is an indication of just how unnatural and contentious some of this integration remains. In the professional environment, logistics is now rarely integrated with the marketing function in the organisational structure of most firms.

However, though there might be problems in integration at the practical level, the scholarly discipline of marketing is more integrative in approach than ever. For example, the debate that has occurred around social marketing (Kotler and Levy, 1969a, 1969b; Kotler, 1972; Luck, 1969, 1974; Arndt, 1978, Andreasen, 1994) is indicative of the way in which the urge to integrate (perhaps even co-opt) further areas of responsibility under the marketing banner remains hard-wired into the DNA of marketing scholarship. Despite discomfort from some quarters Kotler and Levy's conception of social marketing has become a largely accepted part of marketing's scope. While Kotler's (1972) subsequent expansion into "generic marketing" has not met with quite as much overt enthusiasm its transformation into the "holistic marketing" that he promotes in his successful (ubiquitous) textbook on marketing management (Kotler and Keller, 2015) is a further indication of the influential nature of the integrative urge. Furthermore, the small amount of criticism in print regarding Vargo and Lusch's (2004) Service-Dominant logic, a perspective which has managed to galvanise a wide variety of marketing scholars internationally and already resulted in a vast citation nexus, is often focused on its ambitious attempts to seemingly integrate a wide variety of marketing research streams from the 1980s and 1990s (Achrol and Kotler, 2006; O'Shaughnessy and O'Shaughnessy, 2009, 2011). Vargo and Lusch's project to create a new dominant paradigm for marketing which subsumes disparate, sometimes independent, discourses into one behemoth of theory has tended to resonate with the marketing academy precisely because the marketing academy is built upon such *panphageous* beginnings. A final example of this avaricious appetite will suffice. The tremendous popularity of co-creation and co-production as a contemporary marketing technique, both with practitioners and scholars, is clearly indicative of marketing's urge to control product and service research and development, an area that it has historically been envious of yet remained relatively powerless to influence (Miles, 2016). The broader idea of the co-creation of value, which has been central to the premises of Vargo and Lusch's S-D logic, provides a powerful argument for marketing's purview over re-positioned R&D and production departments.

So, the argument that I am making is that the discipline (and, to a certain extent, the practice) of marketing comes out of a concern with conceptually unifying a broad variety of burgeoning middleman functions. While many of these functions could be said to have roots in the early growth of trade, they had all evolved significantly in the second half of the nineteenth century as a response to spiralling crises in control. Additionally, these functions had been working largely independently, but early marketing thinkers proposed that firms might benefit from managerial consolidation across them. In this sense, and adapting Beniger's (1986) terms, marketing is a discipline built upon the need for meta-control—it has sought to integrate under central control practices that are motivated by the desire to control production, distribution and consumption. This need for meta-control is reflected, fractal-like, in many smaller issues relating to marketing's search for increased scope and responsibility.

Before moving on to a discussion of the ramifications of this urge for control that I am arguing characterises the marketing discipline, I would like to address one particular alternative vision. The search for a common denominator behind all the functions and practices that marketing seeks to bundle together has been continuing for some time, if not very successfully. The changing definitions of the American Marketing Academy represent the ways in which the discipline has sought to explain its central concerns to itself and those it seeks to persuade of its status. The 1960 AMA definition states that marketing is "the performance of business activities that direct the flow of goods and services from producer to consumer or user" (quoted in Hunt, 1976, p. 17). This covers classic middleman territory in a manner that clearly situates the marketer in between the producer and consumer. In that the responsibility of marketing is the direction of the flow of goods and services the definition is consistent with marketing as a control function. Yet, the nature of that control is rather weakly framed—'direction' seems simply a matter of choosing the right trajectory, making sure flow doesn't get held up or caught in cross traffic. The emphasis seems to be on distribution and the terminology does not lend itself well to considerations regarding the control off consumption. As Sheth and Uslay (2007) point out in their study of the AMA definitions, the above definition was actually the original AMA formulation and reaches back all the way to 1935. It was changed only in 1985, a full fifty years into the discipline's evolutionary journey. The 1985 revision stated that marketing was to be understood as "the process of planning and executing the conception, pricing, promotion, and distribution of ideas, goods, and services to create exchanges that satisfy individual and organizational objectives" (quoted in Lusch, 2007, p. 264). The scope has clearly expanded here and marketing is now positioned at the "conception" of "ideas, goods, and services", right at the start of production, in other words. Marketers are also strongly framed as agents of "organizational objectives" (rather than just the self-interested objectives of the middleman). We can, also, see a clear reference to the marketing mix in the way in which the definition is structured. More importantly, however, the 1985 definition recognised what had been an increasingly concerted attempt by marketing scholars to conceptualise marketing around the concept of exchange (Sheth and Uslay, 2007).

Bagozzi's (1975) article on "Marketing as Exchange" remains the epitome of scholarship seeking to orient marketing as a whole in terms of the concept of exchange, or the "exchange paradigm" as the author put it. It comes out of assumptions explicit within Kotler's (1972) formulation of "generic marketing" that depicted the practice and discipline as concerned with answering the questions of "Why do people and organizations engage in exchange relationships?" and "How are exchanges created, resolved, or avoided?" (Bagozzi, 1975, p. 32). Kotler (1972) had argued that there

was a radical "consciousness" beginning to emerge amongst some marketers which extended the boundaries of the discipline beyond the customer
to include "all other publics" of an organization. (p. 48). He noted that
this understanding of marketing did not rely upon a structural perspective
(whereby marketing is defined as dealing with particular institutions to be
found in the business environment) but rather based itself upon a functional approach wherein marketing occurs wherever a marketing function
is performed. In considering what "core concept" can constitute the marketing function, Kotler identified the transaction, which he defined as "the
exchange of values between two parties" (ibid.). Bagozzi (1975) takes up
this position, stating that "there appears to be a growing consensus that
exchange forms the core phenomenon for study in marketing" (p. 32). He
then proceeds to explain what he identifies as the three different types of
exchange (restricted, generalized, and complex), which allows him to analyse how even the decision to watch a television programme can be thought
of as a "complex circular exchange" in which "different tangible or symbolic entities" (p. 34) are transferred between the viewer, the programme
makers, and their advertisers and advertising agencies. As Bagozzi analyses
in more depth the nature of exchange in society, he begins to frame it in
a manner that is fundamentally concerned with influence. He argues that
"social actors obtain satisfaction of their needs by complying with, or influencing, the behavior of other actors" and this is achieved through "communicating and controlling the media of exchange, which, in turn, comprise
the links between one individual and another, between one organization
and another" (p. 35). Bagozzi is careful to admit that not all of marketing is concerned with influence, in that it is also must deal with "meeting
existing needs and anticipating future needs" (ibid.). However, this is surely
short-sighted: according to the exchange paradigm that Bargozzi is outlining, those existing needs are certainly the product of previous exchanges and
any future needs are necessarily going to be the result of future influence.

The most far-reaching aspect of Bagozzi's (1975) analysis is his assertion that exchange should be divided into three different "classes of meaning": "utilitarian exchange", "symbolic exchange", and "mixed exchange".
The first of these, he explains, has been the focus of marketing for most of
its development; it describes "an interaction whereby goods are given in
return for money or other goods and the motivation be-hind the actions
lies in the anticipated use or tangible characteristics commonly associated
with the objects in the exchange". It is a conception of exchange that stems
from an understanding of humans as *economic* agents. Symbolic exchange,
however, is based upon what people understand the media of exchange
to *mean* rather than what they can *do* (to paraphrase Levy, 1959, whom
Bagozzi identifies as one of the first scholars to recognise this truth). It
describes the "mutual transfer of psychological, social, or other intangible
entities between two or more parties" (ibid.). Bagozzi asserts that marketing exchanges involve a mixture of the utilitarian and symbolic and the

recognition of this truth allows us to uncover how the discipline of marketing deals not with "economic man" but "marketing man" (p. 37). The clear implication here is that the practice of marketing has always been concerned with mixed exchanges but the academic discipline's early debt to economics blinded it of its true "core concept", something that was also perhaps exacerbated by the variegated distribution focus of early marketing practice. The exchange paradigm therefore promises to provide marketing with an unveiled understanding of its disciplinary and professional identity. It also supports marketing in its attempts to seek a wider base within the firm and society. Bagozzi paper finishes with the assertion that marketing is a "general function of universal applicability" and that it can be defined as "the discipline of exchange behavior" (p. 39). Keeping in mind Bagozzi's conception of "mixed exchange", it is not difficult to see how this perspective was widely applauded throughout the academy—it constitutes a strong defence of the discipline, based around an already popular "core concept" that can include older, economic conceptions of marketing as well as the more modern social and symbolic ones. It also neatly ties together the distributive and the communicative aspects of the field.

The intellectual confidence that the exchange paradigm began to afford many in the marketing academy is best represented by Kiel et al. (1992), an article which can be seen as the foundation for Vargo and Lusch's (2004) introduction of S-D logic (Miles, 2018). In this paper, Kiel et al. argue for marketing to be seen as part of a larger "universal system of exchange" (p. 62). By "universal", the authors mean situated within the universe, so that marketing can be understood as being embedded in larger physical (i.e. non-human) systems of exchange. Kiel et al. (1992) advance what they term a "natural science of exchange" (ibid.) as an antidote to the predominantly "anthropocentric microtheory building" of extant marketing approaches to exchange. Their conception of the "natural science of exchange" attempts to explain "the evolution of all exchange systems and properly positions marketing in this evolutionary exchange paradigm" (ibid.) and implements a General Systems Theory perspective that sees all systems in the universe as exhibiting the fundamental characteristics of exchange, attraction, dynamic equilibrium, and the evolution of complexity (via circular movement through the stages of emergence, convergence, proliferation, and divergence). Within this framework, marketing is seen as one of the most recent expressions of universal exchange within the human system and is a function of the increasing complexity of human social systems. Kiel et al.'s (1992) paper is a highly compressed but nevertheless tremendously ambitious argument in favour of placing exchange at the heart of not just marketing but the whole universe. In doing so, they not only attempt to explain the connection between marketing and all the other social and physical sciences but also situate marketing as a discipline that has a clear place in the universe through its consideration of the basic constructive forces of the universe. The dynamic of exchange stands as the central motif throughout the paper, and, as such, it is working within the tradition of Kotler (1972) and Bagozzi (1975), yet in its serious engagement with the terms of General Systems Theory it elevates the marketing conception of exchange into something fundamental to not just human life but the workings of the universe. To study marketing from this perspective is to study the universe.

The 1985 AMA (re)definition of marketing, therefore, can be seen as a natural (if tardy) reflection of the way in which the exchange paradigm had come to dominate academic marketing understandings of the discipline's "core concept". At the same time, the 1985 definition was accused by some of not recognizing "(implicitly or explicitly) marketing as a societal process" and did not easily lend itself to extensions of marketing beyond the traditional scenario of "organizations marketing to customers" (Lusch, 2007, p. 264). Dissatisfaction with the definition, as well as recognition that marketing theory appeared to be moving towards an obsession with value, led to another revision of the AMA definition in 2004. The wording of this version, however, completely dropped any reference to exchange as well as continuing with the move towards a more managerial and less societal understandings of the discipline and profession (Sheth and Uslay, 2007). The 2004 definition stated that marketing "is an organizational function and a set of processes for creating, communicating and delivering value to customers and for managing customer relationships in ways that benefit the organization and its stakeholders" (quoted in Wilkie and Moore, 2006, p. 227). It is difficult to know whether the absence of exchange here is a function of the more recent focus on value being seen to necessarily imply exchange or whether there was some more oppositional intent informing its absence. Lusch was involved in the definition's construction but is on record as preferring his own formulation which does explicitly contain reference to the exchange paradigm: "Marketing is the adaptive process, in society and organizations, of collaborating to communicate, create, provide, and sustain value for customers through exchange relationships while meeting the needs of diverse stakeholders" (Lusch, 2007, p. 265). Quite why the AMA committee decided to abandon exchange (while adopting an emphasis on value and stakeholders) is not clear. Certainly, the fact that it did was seen by some as a victory. Sheth and Uslay (2007) are positively delighted with the elision, as they see marketing as "amidst a paradigm shift from exchange (value in exchange) towards value cocreation (value for all stakeholders) with an intermediate iteration at value creation (value in use and relationship marketing" (p. 305). They equate exchange with what Vargo and Lusch (2004) have identified as Goods-Dominant logic, and they even use some re-heated terminology from Vargo and Lusch (2004) when they state that "exchange masks the value creation capabilities" of goods and services (Sheth and Uslay, 2007, p. 305). For Sheth and Uslay (2007), it is value co-creation which is fundamental to marketing and which generates exchange. However, given the extent to which Vargo and Lusch's writing on S-D logic is used by Sheth and Uslay (2007), it is curious that they ignore the central place that exchange has within it. For Vargo and Lusch (2004), the emerging service paradigm does not do away with (or de-emphasise) exchange at all. Instead, it keeps it at the heart of marketing. The goods-dominant logic is characterised as being concerned with "commodities exchange", whereas the new service paradigm starts from the assumption that "people exchange to acquire the benefits of specialized competencies (knowledge and skills)" (p. 7). S-D logic still sees marketing as based upon exchange; it is just that the paradigm's view of what is being exchanged has transformed from the tangible to the intangible. Indeed, their phrasing through the foundational 2004 paper makes it clear that they are promulgating a "service-centered mode of exchange" (p. 14). Exchange has remained at the centre of the S-D logic even as many other aspects of its formulation have evolved and transformed. Lusch and Vargo's (2014) book-length presentation of the logic, for example, still frames it as a way of "viewing human exchange systems" (p. 5).

The 2004 AMA abandonment of exchange as a defining characteristic of marketing was short-lived. Indeed, Sheth and Uslay's 2007 paper included an epilogue which notes that the journal's special sections editor has informed them that "a revised definition of marketing has already been proposed by the 2007 AMA task force" (p. 306). This revised definition, which they include in this final paragraph to the article, has re-included exchange in its wording, though the manner in which it is done clearly limits exchange by now distinguishing it from other equally important marketing processes. The 2007 revision remains the ratified AMA definition at the time of writing and conceives of marketing as "the activity, set of institutions, and processes for creating, communicating, delivering, and exchanging offerings that have value for customers, clients, partners, and society at large" (AMA, 2017). If exchanging is separate from communicating, creating, and delivering, then it is unclear what exactly it is but it is certainly not what Kotler, Bagozzi, Kiel et al., and Vargo and Lusch mean by the term. There is clearly a degree of confusion here, and much of this is located in the way in which value (co)creation and exchange have become seen by some marketing thinkers as originating in mutually incompatible paradigms, or at least in deserving of dramatically different emphasis. While Vargo and Lusch have been quite clear concerning the continuing exchange basis of S-D logic, other proponents of value co-creation have been more vague. Prahalad and Ramaswamy (2004) are perhaps the most prestigious voices in the co-creation of value movement. They are writing as scholars of enterprise and business strategy, rather than from inside the marketing academy and so therefore their view of exchange is not marketing-focused. Nevertheless, they do characterise the "traditional concept of a market" as being one where products and services are the subject of an "exchange of value" (p. 120), whereas the new "emerging concept of a market" is based upon co-creation converting "the market into a *forum* where dialogue among the consumer, the firm, consumer communities, and networks of firms can take place" (p. 122, emphasis in original). Prahalad and Ramaswamy do not actually deny that the emerging market is not based upon exchange—instead they use the word "interaction" to describe the "locus of co-creation of value and economic value extraction by the consumer and the firm" (ibid.). Although clearly this locus of interaction, along with the depiction of the market as a "forum", is perfectly amenable to the idea of the market as a place of exchange, the adoption of new terminology rhetorically underlines the emphasis on a particular form of exchange that the authors are favouring.

In the next chapter, I advance an understanding of marketing as exchange which seeks to include the creation and co-creation of value, looks back on marketing's intermediary past, and looks forward to its future in what is increasingly being understood as a global society based upon an 'attention economy'. In doing so, my motivation is to construct a conception of marketing as exchange which is rigorous enough to inform the broadest as well as narrowest definition of marketing while enabling the discipline to be clearly identified as an extension of the rhetorical tradition. It is important that this understanding of marketing as an extension of rhetoric does not just refer to marketing communication. As we have seen above, most scholarly consideration of marketing's nature and scope has not focused overtly upon its communicative aspects. On the other hand, most scholarly work linking the rhetorical tradition to marketing has indeed narrowly understood marketing through its communicative function, with the consequence that the majority of marketing scholars and practitioners assume that a rhetorical perspective has little to offer the other practice areas of marketing and, therefore, marketing in general.

References

Achrol, R., and Kotler, P. (2006). The Service-Dominant Logic for Marketing: A Critique. In R. Lusch and S. Vargo (Eds.), *The Service-Dominant Logic of Marketing: Dialog, Debate, and Directions*. Armonk, NY: M. E. Sharpe, 320–333.

Alderson, W., and Cox, R. (1948). Towards a Theory of Marketing. *Journal of Marketing*, 13(October), 137–152.

AMA. (2017). *Definition of Marketing*. www.ama.org/AboutAMA/Pages/Definition-of-Marketing.aspx [Accessed March 6, 2017].

Anderson, L.M.T. (1994). Marketing Science: Where's the Beef? *Business Horizons*, 37(1), 8–16.

Anderson, P. F. (1983). Marketing, Scientific Progress, and Scientific Method. *Journal of Marketing*, 47(4), 18.

Anderson, P. F. (1986). On Method in Consumer Research: A Critical Relativist Perspective. *Journal of Consumer Research*, 13(2), 155–173.

Anderson, P. F. (1988). Relativism Revidivus: In Defense of Critical Relativism. *Journal of Consumer Research*, 15(3), 403–406.

Andreasen, A. (1994). Social Marketing: Its Definition and Domain. *Journal of Public Policy & Marketing*, 13(1), 108–114.

Arndt, J. (1978). How Broad Should the Marketing Concept Be? *Journal of Marketing*, 42(1), 101.

Bagozzi, R. P. (1975). Marketing as Exchange. *Journal of Marketing*, 39(4), 32–39.

Bartels, R. (1951). Can Marketing Be a Science? *Journal of Marketing*, 15(3), 319.

Bartels, R. (1976). *The History of Marketing Thought*. Columbus, OH: Grid.

Beniger, J. (1986). *The Control Revolution: Technological and Economic Origins of the Information Society*. London: Harvard University Press.

Brown, L. O. (1948). Toward a Profession of Marketing. *Journal of Marketing*, 13(1), 27–31.

Brown, S. (1996). Art or Science? Fifty Years of Marketing Debate. *Journal of Marketing Management*, 12, 243–267.

Brown, S. (2002). The Spectre of Kotlerism: A Literary Appreciation. *European Management Journal*, 20(2), 129–146.

Buzzell, R. D. (1963). Is Marketing a Science? *Harvard Business Review*, 40(1), 32–40, 166–170.

Cassels, J. M. (1936). The Significance of Early Economic Thought on Marketing. *Journal of Marketing*, 1(2), 129–133.

Cialdini, R. (2001). *Influence: Science and Practice*. London: Allyn and Bacon.

Converse, P. D. (1945). The Development of the Science of Marketing—An Exploratory Survey. *Journal of Marketing*, 10(July), 14–23.

Durkheim, E. ([1959] 2009). *Socialism and Saint Simon* (trans. C. Sattler). London: Routledge.

Fisk, G. (1967). *Marketing Systems: An Introductory Analysis*. London: Harper & Row.

Funk, C., and Rainie, L. (2015). *Public and Scientists' Views on Science and Society*. Pew Research Center. www.pewinternet.org/2015/01/29/public-and-scientists-views-on-science-and-society/ [Accessed February 15, 2017].

Gordon, R. A., and Howell, J. E. (1959). *Higher Education for Business*. New York: Columbia University Press.

Hagerty, J. E. (1936). Experiences of an Early Marketing Teacher. *Journal of Marketing*, 1(1), 20.

Hubbard, R. (2005). Examining the Influence of Articles Involving Marketing History, Thought, and Theory: A Journal of Marketing Citation Analysis, 1950s–1990s. *Marketing Theory*, 5(3), 323–336.

Hunt, S. D. (1976). The Nature and Scope of Marketing. *The Journal of Marketing*, 40(July), 17–28.

Hunt, S. D. (1984). Should Marketing Adopt Relativism. In P. F. Anderson and M. J. Ryan (Eds.), *Scientific Method in Marketing*. Chicago: American Marketing Association.

Hunt, S. D. (1990). Truth in Marketing Theory and Research. *Journal of Marketing*, 54(July), 1–15.

Hunt, S. D. (1994). On Rethinking Marketing: Our Discipline, Our Practice, Our Methods. *European Journal of Marketing*, 28(3), 13–25.

Hunt, S. D. (2002). *Foundations in Marketing Theory: Toward a General Theory of Marketing*. Armonk, NY: M. E. Sharpe.

Hunt, S. D. (2003). *Controversy in Marketing Theory: For Reason, Realism, Truth, and Objectivity*. Armonk, NY: M. E. Sharpe.

Hunt, S. D. (2012). Toward the Institutionalization of Macromarketing: Sustainable Enterprise, Sustainable Marketing, Sustainable Development, and the Sustainable Society. *Journal of Macromarketing*, 32(4), 404–411.

Hunt, S. D., and Edison, S. (1995). On the Marketing of Marketing Knowledge. *Journal of Marketing Management*, 11(December), 635–640.

Hutchinson, K. D. (1952). Marketing As a Science: An Appraisal. *Journal of Marketing*, 16(4), 286–293.

Jones, D. G. B., and Monieson, D. D. (1990). Early Development of the Philosophy of Marketing Thought. *Journal of Marketing*, 54(January), 102–113.

Kavanagh, D. (1994). Hunt Versus Anderson: Round 16. *European Journal of Marketing*, 28(3), 26–41.

Kelley, W. T. (1956). The Development of Early Thought in Marketing and Promotion. *The Journal of Marketing*, II, 62–67.

Kerin, R. (1996). In Pursuit of an Ideal: The Editorial and Literary History of the Journal of Marketing. *Journal of Marketing*, 60(1), 1–13.

Kiel, D. L., Lusch, R. F., and Schumacher, B. G. (1992). Toward a New Paradigm for Marketing: The Evolutionary Exchange Paradigm. *Behavioral Science*, 37(1), 59–76.

Kotler, P. (1972). A Generic Concept of Marketing. *Journal of Marketing*, 36(April), 46–54.

Kotler, P., and Keller, K. L. (2015). *Marketing Management*. Boston: Pearson.

Kotler, P., and Levy, S. J. (1969a). Broadening the Concept of Marketing. *Journal of Marketing*, 33(1), 10–15.

Kotler, P., and Levy, S. J. (1969b). A New Form of Marketing Myopia: Rejoinder to Professor Luck. *Journal of Marketing*, (July), 55–57.

Levy, S. J. (1959). Symbols for Sale. *Harvard Business Review*, 37(4), 117–124.

Luck, D. (1969). Broadening the Concept of Marketing—Too Far. *Journal of Marketing*, 33(July), 53–63.

Luck, D. (1974). Social Marketing: Confusion Compounded. *Journal of Marketing*, 35(July), 70–72.

Lusch, R. F. (2007). Marketing's Evolving Identity: Defining Our Future. *Journal of Public Policy & Marketing*, 26(2), 261–268.

Lusch, R. F., and Vargo, S. L. (2006). Service-dominant Logic: Reactions, Reflections and Refinements. *Marketing Theory*, 6(3), 281–288.

Lusch, R. F., and Vargo, S. L. (2011). Service-dominant Logic: A Necessary Step. *European Journal of Marketing*, 45(7/8), 1298–1309.

Lusch, R. F., and Vargo, S. L. (2012). The Forum on Markets and Marketing (FMM): Advancing Service-dominant Logic. *Marketing Theory*, 12(2), 193–199.

Lusch, R. F., and Vargo, S. L. (2014). *Service-Dominant Logic: Premises, Perspectives, Possibilities*. Cambridge: Cambridge University Press.

Mcgarry, E. D. (1936). The Importance of Scientific Method in Advertising. *Journal of Marketing*, 1, 82–86.

Miles, C. (2014). Rhetoric and the Foundation of the Service-Dominant Logic. *Journal of Organizational Change Management*, 27(5), 744–755.

Miles, C. (2016). Control and the Rhetoric of Interactivity in Contemporary Advertising Theory and Practice. In J. Hamilton, R. Bodle, and E. Korin (Eds.), *Explorations in Critical Studies of Advertising*. London: Routledge, 110–123.

Miles, C. (2018). Service-Dominant Logic—The Evolution of a Universal Marketing Rhetoric. In M. Tadajewski, M. Higgins, J. Denegri-Knott, and R. Varman (Eds.), *The Routledge Companion to Critical Marketing*. London: Routledge.

O'Shaughnessy, J., and O'Shaughnessy, N. J. (2009). The Service-dominant Perspective: A Backward Step? *European Journal of Marketing*, 43(5/6), 784–793.

O'Shaughnessy, J., and O'Shaughnessy, N. J. (2011). Service-dominant Logic: A Rejoinder to Lusch and Vargo's Reply. *European Journal of Marketing*, 45(7/8), 1310–1318.

Pierson, G. W. (1959). *The Education of American Businessmen*. New York: McGraw-Hill.

Prahalad, C., and Ramaswamy, V. (2004). *The Future of Competition: Co-Creating Unique Value With Consumers*. Boston: Harvard Business School Press.

Seelye, A. L. (1947). The Importance of Economic Theory in Marketing Courses. *Journal of Marketing*, 11(2), 223–227.

Shaw, A. W. (1912). Some Problems in Market Distribution. *Quarterly Journal of Economics*, 26, 703–765.

Sheth, J. N., and Uslay, C. (2007). Implications of the Revised Definition of Marketing: From Exchange to Value Creation. *Journal of Public Policy & Marketing*, 26(2), 302–307.

Simon, H. (1996). *The Sciences of the Artificial*. Cambridge, MA: The MIT Press.

Steiner, R. L. (1976). The Prejudice Against Marketing. *Journal of Marketing*, 40(3), 2–9.

Tadajewski, M. (2006a). The Ordering of Marketing Theory: The Influence of McCarthyism and the Cold War. *Marketing Theory*, 6(2), 163–199.

Tadajewski, M. (2006b). Remembering Motivation Research: Toward an Alternative Genealogy of Interpretive Consumer Research. *Marketing Theory*, 6(4), 429–466.

Tadajewski, M. (2016). Academic Labour, Journal Ranking Lists and the Politics of Knowledge Production in Marketing. *Journal of Marketing Management*, 32(1–2), 1–18.

Thomson, E. M., and Adams, H. F. (1996). 'The Science of Publicity' an American Advertising Theory, 1900–1920. *Journal of Design History*, 9(4), 253–272.

Vargo, S. L., and Lusch, R. F. (2004). Evolving to a New Dominant Logic for Marketing. *Journal of Marketing*, 68(1), 1–17.

Vargo, S. L., and Lusch, R. F. (2008). Service-dominant Logic: Continuing the Evolution. *Journal of the Academy of Marketing Science*, 36(1), 1–10.

Vargo, S. L., and Lusch, R. F. (2011). It's All B2B . . . and Beyond: Toward a Systems Perspective of the Market. *Industrial Marketing Management*, 40(February), 181–187.

Vargo, S. L., and Lusch, R. F. (2015). Institutions and Axioms: An Extension and Update of Service-Dominant Logic. *Journal of the Academy of Marketing Science*, 1–19.

Vargo, S. L., and Lusch, R. F. (2016). Service-dominant Logic 2025. *International Journal of Research in Marketing* (In Press, Accepted Manuscript). http://doi.org/10.1016/j.ijresmar.2016.11.001

Wilkie, W. L., and Moore, E. S. (2003). Scholarly Research in Marketing: Exploring the '4 Eras' of Thought Development. *Journal of Public Policy & Marketing*, 22(2), 116–146.

Wilkie, W. L., and Moore, E. S. (2006). Macromarketing as a Pillar of Marketing Thought. *Journal of Macromarketing*, 26(1), 224–232.

4 A Rhetorical Approach to Marketing as Exchange

Marketing is the art of intermediation. The marketer stands in the middle in order to profit from facilitating exchange. This facilitation can take a large number of forms that work together in the forum of exchange. Some of these forms concern the physical design and movement of products (or service vehicles depending on your perspective), other concern pricing and packaging, still others concern the areas of wholesaling, retailing, and consumer financing, while others are concentrated upon the creation and manipulation of consumer markets and stakeholder attitudes and behaviour. The one thing that all these practices have in common is their intermediary nature in the facilitation of exchange. The facilitation of exchange is where marketing adds value. This is not to say, of course, that it is only marketing that adds value—the consumer (indeed, all stakeholders) also adds value, sometimes through exchanges facilitated or taken advantage of by marketers. However, the *core function* of the marketer is to add value through facilitating exchange.

Facilitation is a form of control. More particularly it is a control of flow. What marketing ultimately seeks to control is the flow of value, but this is achieved through the control of the flow of a large number of other variables. Some of these can be grouped under the larger headings of attention (mental presence), physical presence (locations of goods and services and locations of consumers and other stakeholders) and virtual presence (location of representations of goods, services, brands online and the online presence of consumers and other stakeholders).

Control of the Flow of Value

A marketer profits by adding value via the control of flow. So, Plato's middleman creates value by buying goods from a producer and then staying in the market permanently in order to take advantage of the consumer's need for the good when that need arose. The producer does not have to stay in the market and is therefore free to spend their time more productively (or enjoyably). Similarly, the consumer does not have to spend their time hunting down the producer. The intermediary position of the marketer produces value in the form of convenience for both producer (who pays for that value via a sacrifice in price asked) and consumer (who pays via an increased price tendered). We might regard this, then, as the model of *urmarketing*. In this consideration of the role of the intermediary, there needs to be no control of flow other than the act of buying to hold and then sell at a later date, but it is this control of flow which defines the value of the practice.

It is important at this point to note the difference between the nature of the relationship produced when the producer and consumer exchange face-to-face and the relationship produced by mediated exchange. As Plato[1] describes it in the *Republic*, the direct exchange of goods between producer and consumer is characterised by barter, the swapping of one good for another. It is the form of relationship, "giving and taking" (369c), which initially leads to the establishment of Plato's thought-experiment city as people come together in order to share what they produce. However, this simple form of exchange, by which a cobbler might share a pair of shoes in return for clothing or food, will, in Plato's theorising, rapidly evolve beyond practical means. Although imagining a city starting with only five professions (farmer, builder, weaver, cobbler, and doctor) the logic of the division of labour begins to necessitate a far more complex society, with metalworkers to make tools, carpenters to help the builder, tanners to provide leather and so on. It is at this stage, and as a direct result of the division of labour that is a cornerstone of Plato's thinking about society, that the issue of the middleman arises. If a farmer is to be a farmer and therefore spend his time efficiently in the production of crops, then it makes no sense for him to waste his time sitting in the marketplace waiting for customers to come along. As Adeimantus (Socrates' interlocutor) notes, "there'll be people who'll notice this and provide the requisite service" (371c). More specifically, the "service" that they will provide is described as "buying and selling" (371b). This is important because it makes a clear distinction between the barter exchange characterised as "giving and taking" and the market exchange founded on "buying and selling". Consequently, for Plato, the market is based upon mediation. The exchange of "buying and selling" is defined by the separation of producer and consumer by those services associated with the market (retailing, merchandising, transporting, etc.).

Shaw (1995) admirably uses Plato's arguments in the *Republic* to (re-) construct a "first dialogue on macromarketing" which is designed to both celebrate Plato's prescience and intellectual acuity and demonstrate the logical flaws in Kotler's attempt to establish a "generic exchange concept". He notes that Plato's arguments clearly describe how "market exchange is the bridge connecting parties arising out of considerations of efficiency in production resulting from the division of labour and comparative advantage" (p. 9). He underlines that what drove Plato's vision of how society comes together in cities was not just any form of exchange but, specifically, the market exchange of buying and selling. While he admits that there might be "superficial similarities in all forms of exchange" (p. 12), he appeals to

Polyani's tripartite distinction to demonstrate that market exchanges are based upon "voluntary agreements and specified terms" (p. 11).

Weinstein (2009) goes further than Shaw (1995) in contrasting Plato's conception of barter and market exchange. For him, the change from one to the other that takes the Athenian barely ten lines of text represents a "veritable revolution" (p. 439). The system of sharing that the city is initially founded upon is "organized communally, much as a single household might be" (ibid.) but this is then "overturned" by the far more complex market exchange which "integrates a variety of needs into a single framework that is capable of satisfying them, while avoiding the pitfalls of less sophisticated approaches" (p. 440). Complexity inevitably emerges from a realistic consideration of the needs that must be met as people come together in a city with the single goal of *autarky* (self-sufficiency). As Weinstein notes, "satisfying each need leads to new needs, which must in turn be satisfied if self-sufficiency is to be achieved" and so the "city arises tier by tier through cyclical applications of the logic of autarky" (p. 443). This iterative nesting of needs means that the city cannot logically be expected to remain entirely self-sufficient—it must look to trade with other cities and other regions to supply it with the raw materials that its various artisans require for their professions. At this point, Plato's interlocutors rather matter-of-factly agree that of course this will mean the city will have to be organised around "buying and selling" rather than the simple sharing of the family-like commune. Weinstein (2009) notes that this "fundamental shift itself seems unexplained" (p. 444) and is unsure of the reasons for this elision. However, his reconstruction of the logic of this revolution from the "signs, [. . .], suggestions, and indications" (p. 445) that are to be found in the text is sufficiently important to a marketing understanding of exchange that it is worthwhile rehearsing here. What, he asks, "does the market provide that is missing from the communal city and denies it its self-sufficiency once there are merchants in the picture?" (ibid.). The answer, he argues, is "some nexus, some way of interconnecting and harmonizing imports with exports" (p. 446). The exact nature of this nexus Weinstein (2009) thinks can be found in the distinction that the *Republic* makes between artisans/producers (*demiourgoi*) and service-providers (*diakonoi*). Indeed, if we quickly return to our *urmarketing* scenario, we can recognise that the middleman between consumer and producer is the epitome of the service-provider—they do not make anything but rather take advantage of an opportunity to serve both the producer and the consumer. Plato keeps producers and service-providers "clearly distinct from one another" (Weinstein, 2009, p. 447) and it is the service-providers who embody the transformation to a "buying and selling" market exchange economy. The way in which Weinstein (2009) describes the nature of service in the market is particularly interesting. He points out that *diakonos* can be used by Plato in a number of ways, sometimes pejoratively to refer to a slave, sometimes more positively to refer to something which is subordinate but still useful (in the way that cooking is a *diakonos* to medicine), and sometimes in a far more noble manner to describe the way that a functionary or politician is in service (and so still subordinate) to the public. The final use that Plato makes of the term is to be found exclusively in the discussion of the market that we have been considering in the *Republic*. Weinstein (2009) argues that here the term is used to emphasise usefulness but significantly de-emphasise any sense of subordination. Plato does not accompany the term with the usual irony or sarcasm with which he treats the figure of the trader in other dialogues. Instead, the *diakonos* is portrayed as someone vital to the success of the city in that they "make up for the weakness of the various crafts, and brings the city closer to self-sufficiency" (p. 449). Finally, Weinstein is able to arrive at a formulation of the innate specialism of the service-providing market intermediary. Starting from an understanding that all types of service mean "doing what other ask of one, without knowing in advance precisely what their needs and demands will turn out to be" (p. 449), he focuses in on the necessity for a service-provider to find out what it is that is required of him, to fill the gap of "missing knowledge" (p. 450). It is this ability, to be able to reckon what is needed and provide it when required under "conditions of uncertainty" that characterises the successful service-provider. In the city systems based upon market exchange that Plato envisions uncertainty regarding the time and quantity of needs is endemic. No artisan/producer will be able to forecast the amount they must produce and therefore the amount of raw materials they will need. Instead, it is the job of the service-providers to act as the nexus for the resolution of this uncertainty. As Weinstein (2009) describes it, "the market is the single locus where all this disparate knowledge is integrated, converted into useful concretes, distributed, and made effective for the city as a whole" (p. 453).

Weinstein's (2009) deep analysis of Plato's vision of the market is important for its portrayal of the marketing intermediary as a service-provider whose value lies in a *kairotic* response to the uncertainties of human need. It situates the profession of marketing clearly within a frame of "buying and selling" exchange but anchors it to that exchange with the ties of knowledge and reckoning. This reading supports Shaw's (1995) understanding of Platonic marketing as a system which by definition excludes any sort of extension of the profession out to the broad realms of social exchange typified by Kotler's (1972) generic exchange concept. Even the "giving and taking" of barter is seen to be fundamentally different to the "buying and selling" of market exchange.

If we were to construct a definition of marketing based upon a Weinsteinian interpretation of Platonic thought, we might arrive at something resembling the following:

Marketing is the provision of intermediary services which facilitate buying and selling under conditions of uncertain demand.

Such a formulation adequately reflects the central logic underlying Plato's exposition of the market. The definition gives a clear scope for the marketing discipline but also contains a worrying ambiguity. So, one reading might infer that the marketing intermediary only *reacts to* the ebb and flow of demand. Yet, marketers have also been proactive. Indeed, while the early passages in the *Republic* that we have been examining here are remarkably positive about the position of market intermediaries in society, in later sections of that work, along with passages in the *Laws*, and in many other dialogues, traders are generally treated with suspicion and disdain. The reason for this is that they indulge in manipulation—of product, opportunity, and demand. So, a trader might adulterate their wares to receive a greater profit, they might set up shop at a place or time which gives them an unfair advantage over the appetites of their prospective customers (Plato gives the example of selling provisions at remote, deserted crossroads!), or they rise or lower their prices in a day, "push" their wares, or "take an oath on its quality" (*Laws*, XI, 917c). Aside from the first, each of these practices has come to be standard and accepted elements of the marketing intermediary's profession. Of course, the fact that Plato is declaiming the need for tight regulation of market intermediaries in the hypothetical Cretan colony of *Laws* is a certain indication that such practices were common in the 'real' world. These practices can, in fact, be understood under the terms of the definition above if we concede that facilitating buying and selling under conditions of uncertain demand would naturally include efforts to make the demand more certain. In other words, the market intermediary should not be conceived of as someone who simply attempts to forecast the vicissitudes of demand and react accordingly, but rather should be understood as someone who considers the variables of the environment and tries to maximize them to their advantage. This leads directly to the manipulation of demand. For Plato, of course, the market intermediary is there to help the city perform as efficiently as possible in its goal of self-sufficiency. If a market intermediary attempts to maximize their own profit through the manipulation of demand, then they are succumbing to the greed that Plato sees as leading to "a city with a fever" (*Republic*, II, 372e), a city obsessed with luxury and the amassing of wealth. This is why the manipulation of demand is to be forbidden. And this is why the merchant and the trader are portrayed so regularly with suspicion and distaste. Like so many areas of life in Plato's idealised societies, harmony and balance must be carefully regulated—while the market exchange of "buying and selling" is vital to the life of the city, its normal functioning always threatens to tip over into avarice. Indeed, in *Laws*, Plato attempts to protect the citizens of the new colony of Magnetes from any such corruption by ensuring that they are barred from taking market intermediary positions, such professions being reserved for "a resident alien or a temporary visitor" (*Laws*, XI, 920)—in other words, those who are naturally in liminal, intermediary positions (and are clearly Other).

The manipulation of demand by market intermediaries who seek to profit from it is something, then, that Plato would not countenance in his understanding of the market and its relationship to society. It is striking that the sort of condemnation that Plato reserves for the techniques of what we would today call marketing strategy and advertising is also regularly to be found in modern discourses that concern themselves with the health of society. Marketing is commonly held to be the driving force behind the increase in obesity (Critser, 2003; Moss, 2013; Schlosser, 2002), the widespread use of cancer-causing products (Malkan, 2007), and the general obsession with consumption above all else (Klein, 2009; Ewen, 2001). Yet there are many things that Plato would not want to encourage in the ideal society. The sort of highly censorious approach he has towards poetry and entertainment, for example, is indicative of the way in which he feels human social relations are injured by those who manipulate sentiment and emotion. Such practices threaten to upset the good sense of citizens who should be guided by rationality and temperance in all things.

However, we are not interested here in the markets of ideal societies. Rather, we are trying to find our way towards an understanding of the basic characteristics of the marketing profession—its true scope. Plato's early analysis allows us to strip away many of the distracting superstructures that have been built upon the practices of marketing and return to basics. Yet, at the same time, we can also recognise some of the bias inherent in his discussion and acknowledge that what he specifically is at pains to outlaw might be a natural part of the market's functioning. In particular, Weinstein's (2009) reading of the *Republic* provides us with a vision of the marketer as someone who rides the ebb and flow of uncertainties, who is able to react appropriately to the latest knowledge of market demands and it is clear from what Plato forbids that an active manipulation of those demands is part of those "very powerful inducements to vice" (*Laws*, XI, 920b) that the practice of the market intermediary offers.

The reduction of uncertainty is a basic, powerful human need. Indeed, Maslow (1943) discusses what he calls "safety needs" (p. 376) as part of his description of the most basic level in his hierarchy of needs. Once we have our physiological hungers satisfied, we begin to focus on the need to minimise danger in our lives. We search for "some kind of undisturbed routine of rhythm" (p. 377) in our lives, trying to make the world predictable and orderly. So, too, in social organisations. As Beer (1993, 1994, 1995) and Bateson (2000) have amply demonstrated using Ashby's (1957) work as a foundation, complex dynamic systems seek stability through "continual nonprogressive change" (Bateson, 2000, p. 125). In order to deal with a market of uncertain demand, marketers are inevitably going to attempt to control that demand to their own advantage. Whether this means changing prices, seeking out new markets, offering guarantees, or stimulating enthusiasm for the goods they offer these are all natural tools employed by the intermediary to control the instability the uncertainty of the market brings.

Contained within our understanding of marketing distilled in the definition provided above, then, is the recognition that the facilitation of buying and selling in an uncertain market will involve the manipulation of demand. The marketer's intermediary role is one founded upon the attempt to control buying and selling exchange in a way that benefits all parties (including the intermediary).

Let us now move on to consider the stricture, arising both from Weinstein's (2009) and Shaw's (1995) readings of Plato, that marketing concerns itself with only "buying and selling". For Shaw (1995), Plato's model of how the market should support the city through the service of buying and selling serves to demonstrate how Kotler's concept of generic exchange is misconceived. Yet this does lead him into some rather tortured logic. So, while he concedes that there are many forms of exchange in society which use "marketing-like activities" (such as "advertising, transfer of moneys, persuasive communication", p. 11), these exchanges are not actually marketing because they are not being used to facilitate "buying and selling". Adhering tightly to Plato's vision of the ideal city and the place that marketing plays in it allows Shaw (1995) to maintain a tightly curtailed sense of marketing's scope. Yet, as we have seen, Plato's own boundary setting is intensely idealistic, in fact outlawing just those activities that Shaw concedes are signs of "marketing-like" activity. Surely, the point of returning to Plato's considerations of the ideal market is that they allow us to examine the way in which the practices of marketing where conceived of in earlier, less developed, less complex eras? But we cannot forget that Plato is talking of the market in terms of thought-experiments (of the Republic of the philosopher-kings and of the Magnetes colony) and we cannot ignore the ramifications of Plato's wider system of thought. As such, Plato's marketing theory should be seen as an initial stepping stone in the discipline. The focus on "buying and selling" makes sense for Plato when he can arbitrarily militate against the greed such exchanges can foster with draconian punishments and strictures. It is also the case that there is little consideration of the *representative* nature of money by Plato. The fact that currency, which is essential for the service of market intermediaries, *stands for* something else is an important detail that is avoided by the philosopher despite (or, perhaps, because of) its inconvenience within Plato's larger censuring of representation (see Weinstein, 2009, footnote on p. 454; see also Moore, 2014, for a discussion of the problematic status of representation in Plato).

Plato's strictures regarding marketing reveal an intense effort to bound it and, most particularly, to keep persuasion away from it. Yet, in also seeking to quarantine the valued citizens of a city from taking part in its practice, Plato makes it clear that, by its very nature, it is a corrupting force. The promise of gain will mean that persuasion will always work its way into marketing practice. Plato does not say that marketing should be practiced only by those who have received a strong education in the pursuit of truth and have the wisdom to control their appetites. No, marketing will infect even those citizens who have had the most advantage and the most instruction. Indeed, the *Laws* go so far as to state that those citizens who re-offend by returning to marketing activities after having being punished before will have their imprisonment doubled. Imprisonment, clearly, does not dim the allure of the market.

The market infects. In the *Republic*, the market intermediary is portrayed as a service provider in language akin to that used for public servants (Weinstein, 2009), but this has the effect of framing them as selflessly motivated. As soon as the issue of personal gain, of profit, is brought into the equation, the service-provider becomes an *infected, liminal stranger* who must be kept quarantined from the rest of civil society and who must be heavily bound by laws in order to prevent their use of persuasive strategies. Consequently, we can imagine the *urmarketer* as a biphasic practitioner—acting in service to producers and consumers in one phase of operations and acting *in their own* service (i.e. via a profit maximising motivation) in the other. It is, of course, the latter phase, which spirals around the manipulation of demand, which is of most danger to society in Plato's view—and in the view of many social commentators after him. However, if the history of marketing practice shows anything, it is that the dangerous, persuasive edges of the profit-maximising phase of marketing operations have moved towards the core of marketing practice. Modern Western societies have tended towards an increasingly laissez-faire policing of the manipulation of demand, often acting as if it were not even an issue. Guarantees are expected rather than outlawed, and testimonials and persuasive statements regarding a product's worth are part of the everyday, normalised media landscape in such societies. Advertising is celebrated in international awards and exhibitions in major art and design galleries and is even allowed to mostly regulate itself. Yet, at the same time, the old Platonic mistrust remains, and marketing is used as a reliable scapegoat for all manner of human failings and social problems. I will examine what I consider to be some of the major causes of this oscillating regard below. At this stage, however, let us return to the construction of our definition of marketing.

If we are to explicitly include the manipulation of demand in our definition of marketing as well as reflect some of the substance of the above discussion, we might construct something along the following lines:

> *Marketing is the provision of intermediary services which facilitate buying and selling under conditions of uncertain demand. Facilitation can include activities which seek to reduce this uncertainty through the manipulation of the flow of demand as well as practices which aim to control the flow of resources and finished products.*

By glossing 'facilitation' we make it clear that market intermediaries can display a range of activities that include the manipulation of logistical flows as well as demand flows. The motivation for providing the service remains unstated, and the exchange system that marketing operates within remains that of "buying and selling". However, we must now once and for all address the recurrent question regarding this latter characteristic. Is "buying and selling" something that can be taken metaphorically? Or, perhaps more succinctly, how symbolic can market exchange be? So, if we speak of political and social marketing campaigns and discuss the "selling" of a party, or the "selling" of a religion, or a set of values, are we necessarily making a category mistake? Certainly, Shaw (1995) uses Plato's vision of the market to argue just this. Kotler and Zaltman (1971) and Kotler (1972) argue the opposite, for the applicability of the "logic of marketing to social goals" (Kotler and Zaltman, 1971, p. 3). This perspective is founded upon the idea that the "core idea of marketing lies in the exchange process" (p. 4) and, while most marketing might be performed around the buying and selling of goods and services, this does not mean that *all* marketing must. Once Kotler has defined marketing management as a practice based upon the awareness "of an opportunity to gain from a more careful planning of their exchange relationships" (ibid.), then it becomes clear that a marketer might just as well perform their marketing service for a client who wishes to create social change as for a brand wishing to increase demand for a product. This does, of course, assume that all exchange relationships are of the same type and would benefit in the same way from the intermediary services of marketing. Kotler and Zaltman's (1971) logic relies upon the assertion that marketing has changed from having a selling focus (changing perceptions of a product or service to increase demand) towards having a response focus (researching nascent demand in order to respond to it via the creation of appropriate products or services). The truth is, of course, that both of these perspectives continue to be used within business. Indeed, as Mitchell (1999) argues, product-orientation has remained hugely powerful throughout the rise of the brand management paradigm, and firms that truly implement a customer-oriented marketing tend to remain the exception rather than the rule. This is, after all, the complaint that successive 'revolutionary' systems try to address; *vide*, amongst many others, Ries and Trout's (2001) positioning, Levine et al.'s (2000) cluetrain manifesto, Lanning and Michael's (1988) business as a value delivery system, Prahalad and Ramaswamy's (2004) DART model, and even Vargo and Lusch's (2004) Service-Dominant logic. Might it perhaps be more useful to look at a full customer-orientation as a goal to which all marketing exchange systems might be moving towards? Any understanding of marketing, however, must be able to contain (and account for) the marketing done from a product-orientation as well as that more 'evolved' form grounded in initial research of consumer needs and wants.

Perhaps the adoption of 'value' as the key term in contemporary marketing theorisation is a reaction to this constant tension between the product and customer orientations? It certainly might provide us with a way of thinking about marketing as a facilitation of exchange which can include both market exchange (i.e. exchange dependent upon currency) as well as the types of broader exchange described by Kotler and Zaltman (1971). Indeed, Kotler (1972) himself based his "generic concept of marketing" upon the core concept of the transaction defined as "the exchange of values between two parties" (p. 48). The changes in the AMA definition of marketing recounted above have also brought the discipline to a position where the exchange of "offerings that have value" is seen as the final goal of the profession. While not explicitly stated in the definition, value here is clearly meant to be interpreted in its Bagozzian mixed modality as both utilitarian and symbolic. Following this long trend in marketing theorisation of the nature of exchange, then, it makes sense for us to address the question of whether 'buying and selling can be taken metaphorically' by determining if we can usefully frame it within the broader terms of value exchange without sacrificing the clarity of scope that our Platonic/Weinsteinian formulation promises to provide.

It will be remembered that what made the Platonic evolution to market exchange significant was the introduction of a currency as a means to allow the facilitation of the flows of the market. Without currency, the city must remain at the simple level of barter and will not be able to grow and thrive into the complex organisation that Plato (and we) are familiar with. The currency is a token of value, one that can facilitate exchange through its universal acceptance within the market. Marketing is dependent upon this token of value. When we talk of the buying and selling of market exchange, what fundamentally distinguishes it from barter is the mediating action of currency as a token of value. Of course, other things can have value for the inhabitants of a market system. As Kotler (1972) points out, "time, energy, and feelings" are also "things-of-value" (p. 48) which can be exchanged. So, to think through a typical social marketing campaign—a government department needs to reduce a particular behaviour that is considered to be deleterious to the citizens of the country. They hire a marketing agency who put together a campaign to persuade those citizens to eliminate or reduce that behaviour. The currency-mediated buying and selling here occurs in terms of the marketing service offered by the agency—the government pays them and they in turn pay suppliers, employees, media companies, etc. But, in terms of our definition above, is the marketing agency providing "*intermediary services which facilitate buying and selling under conditions of uncertain demand*"? No. Surely, the target audience of the resulting campaign are not being persuaded to use currency to 'buy' something'? The sticking point is the issue of currency, the medium that allows market exchange. Perhaps our understanding of currency needs a little revision?

Certainly, this is Richard Lanham's (2006) point in *The Economics of Attention*. He argues that contemporary society, in moving from being based on tangible "stuff" to intangible "fluff", has transformed into a "market attention economy" (p. 20). This is becoming an increasingly familiar argument as scholars adapt to the weaknesses in existing understandings of contemporary markets (Wu, 2016; Davenport and Beck, 2001; McCloskey, 1995). It is attention which firms, governments, causes, and individuals truly vie for, not capital and currency. Indeed, attention has become the prime currency—not in a metaphorical sense but in a literal sense. While money is still used, of course, to buy attention, we are moving towards a recognition that attention itself is a medium of exchange. A very simple example of this can be found in current online gaming platforms. In a mobile game such as *Modern Combat 5*, I have the option to acquire more in-game (virtual currency) in two ways—I can either use my own 'real world' pounds sterling to buy more in-game credit units or I can buy those credits *with my attention*, by electing to watch an advertisement. Digital marketing has become reliant upon attention- and sentiment-based metrics such as views, likes, follows, visits, dwell time, etc., not only because they are easier to measure in online environments but also because the consumer attention that they appear to index is the currency that brands, governments, causes, and individuals seek to acquire (and, even, hoard). To 'pay' attention is, of course, a fine metaphorical expression of just how much we value something, but it also reflects the more fundamental truth that the relationships that human society is built upon are dependent upon a currency of *regard*. In the generic social marketing example outlined above, the client (the government) is paying the agency to facilitate the exchange of attention. Attention is not the campaign objective (that would be some form of attitude and/or behaviour change)—rather, attention is the currency via which these can be effected. In our generic example, the government requires the attention of the target audience in order to successfully build a relationship with them that could lead to attitude or behaviour change. In the same way, the target audience, too, needs to feel that they are the object of attention or regard. An electoral demographic will desert a party if it feels that they are no longer being paid attention to, no longer held in sufficient regard. This works in exactly the same way in the context of brand relationships; a brand wants its target audience to pay attention to it, and its target audience wants to feel that the brand pays attention to them. Humans are used to equating value with attention. The apparent ease of online attention measurement is now simply allowing this equation to act openly as the foundation for economic, social and political structures and processes. From Lanham's (2006) perspective, this naturally makes those professionals of the art of persuasion, such as advertisers, public relations agents, lobbyists, etc., central to the new 'economy of attention'.

If we look at commercial marketing and social marketing from the perspective of Lanham's (2006) 'attention economy', we would see no difference—they are clearly both facilitating the exchange of attention. As such, it is not surprising that they use the same set of strategies and tactics, for there is no question that they are performing the same professional function. Interestingly, if we momentarily turn our minds back to Plato's original description of the place that the marketer has in society, we might also notice that it is attention which is at the root of the move from barter to market exchange in the ideal city state. The motivation for the establishment of the retailer is so that a craftsmen does not "sit idly in the marketplace, away from his own work" (*Republic*, II, 371c), in other words, the marketer frees the producer to pay attention to the things that are important to them. What is more, the function of retail marketer comes into existence because of attention—"there'll be people who notice this and provide the requisite service" (ibid.)—the marketer pays attention to the agora and recognises, in that *kairotic* spirit which typifies his function, the opportunity. Attention, in the end, is what makes Plato's republic function—attention to one's reason, attention to one's function, attention to one's place within the city, attention to the laws, attention to the Guardians.

However, if an appreciation of the currency value of attention can collapse any distinction between social and commercial marketing, surely it also brings us back to the other dichotomy we have been struggling with, namely, the difference between the marketing elements of communication/persuasion and the elements of production, logistics, and distribution (the more traditional 'middleman' functions)? While Lanham (2006), like many others before him, is happy to point to the waning of the world of "stuff", it is an inescapable fact that the global production of "stuff" continues to increase. The areas of marketing that are not directly concerned with persuasion but are instead focused on the creation, moving, storing, and shelving of "stuff" have not lost their significance. Is there a sense in which their management is also founded upon attention? Might the hints of attention in Plato's telling of marketing's *paramyth* provide us with a way of understanding how it could suffuse all aspects of marketing?

When we 'bring something to market' we are bringing it to the attention of the market. The various marketing processes that might be engaged in by a firm (product design, supply chain management, distribution, warehousing, retailing, branding, communication) are all part of efficiently achieving the goal of bringing the attention of the market to the firm's offerings. Traditional marketing middlemen provided services that facilitated this 'bringing to attention' in the same way that Plato's traders and merchants acted in order to bring goods to the attention of those likely to buy them. Goods have to be made physically available before a prospect will exchange currency for them, and it is this aspect of the attention economy that marketing middlemen mostly focused upon. If we return to Beniger's (1986) description of the birth of modern market control, and his example of Henry Crowell's oat surplus, we can understand that the principle problem besetting Crowell was one of how to facilitate the flow of attention towards his oat surplus. This facilitation was carried out through a combination of physical extensions and communication extensions designed to bring a previously unattended to commodity (in terms of human consumption) to the regard of a national household audience. The packaging choices, distribution choices, and communication choices all combined to construct a strategy designed to bring oats to the attention of the US market as a breakfast option. Once they could see the value in the product, they also found that it was physically available to them in a form and supply which made sense to their household practices. It can make sense, then, to think of the marketing job as one that involves the coordination and management of the facilitation of attention with a view to the exchange of currency for offerings that have or can be made to have value for stakeholders. Value and attention here are strangely contiguous in meaning, flip-flopping between distinction and identity. Value is impossible without attention: we value those things that our attention is drawn to, so the value you assign things is a token of how much they draw our attention. At the same time, attention is a measure of value, a token of it (we might judge that something is worthy of our attention only to the degree that we value it). While some of this haziness might simply be due to the usual semantic drift, ambiguities, and lazy usages that are part and parcel of language use, there is a real sense in which the ideas of value and attention are tightly entwined in human society. Perhaps, in English, the crux of this relationship is to be found in the concept of *regard*. This word synthesises both value and attention in a way that connects nicely back to Aristotle's rhetorical proof of *ethos*—the way we look at, consider, judge, the character of the speaker before us.

Thinking a little more about the origins of the market place itself, we can recognise in the trading practices surrounding the Athenian Agora the fundamental importance of attention in market exchange. As Dixon (1995) recounts, the Agora was the central site for social gathering in Athens from the sixth century BCE onwards, co-locating administration offices, religious shrines, artisan workshops, and the retail marketplace. He cites an address made by Lysias to the Athenian Council in the fourth century BCE, who speaks of the fact that citizens are more likely to visit those "tradesmen who have their establishments nearest the Agora" (Dixon, 1995, p. 80). Being able to command the attention of consumers through apt location is clearly of prime importance even at this early stage of marketing strategy. The market of the Agora was also arranged in a circular manner in order to facilitate the play of the consumer's attention (and their memory). As much shopping was done by slaves under instructions from their owners, this meant also that once a retailer had secured the attention (and regard) of a consumer, having a position in the Agora meant that they could be easily navigated to again by a simple series of directions (ibid.). The display of goods across the stalls of the Agora played with the attention, and thus the appetites, of the browsers. As one fourth-century BCE denizen of the marketplace recounts, the sight of so many wares was "a great joy for anyone who has money; a great torture for those who have not" (ibid., p. 81). Developments in retailing over the subsequent centuries have tended to focus around more and more sophisticated means to direct the attention (and regard) of prospects and consumers. The Agora itself underwent a famous period of what might nowadays be called 'gentrification' in the second century BCE, when an area on its east side was converted into a gated, two-storey retail mall that would be familiar in layout and atmosphere to any modern shopper (ibid.).

Attention is also directed by price. Low prices can help to initially capture consumer attention, but they more importantly then contribute to the overall 'value proposition' (in Lanning and Michaels, 1988, formulation) in combination with the perceived benefit, itself expressed through imagery and copy designed to capture and hold attention. High prices, as well attested to throughout years of marketing research, can also be used to capture and maintain *regard*. Or they can be a means whereby consumers come to lose attention in a brand, as the high price paid makes it no longer seem worthy of continued regard.

Furthermore, the way that marketing engages with a firm's distribution system is closely connected to the engineering of attention that we can see beneath strategies of pricing, retailing, and design. The motivation behind just-in-time or lean manufacturing, for example, is the ability to respond as quickly as possible to changes in the attention focus of consumers so that products which have attracted attention are able to be placed on retail shelves as quickly as possible without the losses of producing and maintaining stock which no longer attracts attention.

It is, in other words, not difficult to shift our traditional marketing perspective (inherited mostly from the early economists and economic historians who largely established the academic identity of marketing in the US) on 'demand', the production, allocation, and distribution of resources, and product/brand lifecycles towards a rather different approach whereby the practice of every aspect of marketing is centred around efforts to control the attention (understood as *regard*) of stakeholders. The marketing goal is therefore to capture, direct, and maintain attention in order to assure as high a valorisation of the firm's offerings as possible (with value understood in both utilitarian and symbolic senses). Offerings might be physical, service-based, or entirely conceptual. In most cases, marketing is designed to facilitate the transmutation of regard into monetary exchange. But, to shamelessly adapt Vargo and Lusch's (2004) formulation, such exchanges mask the fundamental unit of exchange: attention. So, if offerings are largely conceptual (as they can be in political or social marketing), then an exchange of attention is the primary exchange that is designed to occur. And it is truly an *exchange* of attention. Marketing *focuses upon* the consumer—it *pays attention* to particular target audiences with a view to having those audiences pay attention to the offerings around which it is operating. So, a brand uses marketing to pay attention to particular audiences so that they will pay attention to the brand. And, again, this exchange is not just a matter of marketing communication; it motivates all aspects of marketing. A firm manages resources in order to bring a product to market in a way, manner, and price that it hopes will attract the regard of a particular group of consumers. All firms have an idea of the market that they wish to exchange attention with—it might be a very vague, uninformed, unrealistic idea, but there will still be an idea of who 'our customers' are. Marketing's value for a firm lies precisely in researching to whom the firm should pay attention and then being able to facilitate that exchange through influencing production, distribution, company organisation and culture, and, of course, communication with those prospects and consumers.

So, let me try to finalise a definition of marketing that takes into account the intermediary nature of the marketer, the principle of exchange, and the control of attention in a way that maintains a unique scope for the profession while also being able to include the wide variety of scenarios that marketing professionals and agencies find themselves practicing in.

Marketing is the provision of intermediary services which facilitate the continuing exchange of attention between firm and stakeholders

The definition no longer needs to speak of conditions of uncertain demand because human attention is, almost by definition, something that is constantly being redirected. The definition sacrifices the simplicity of 'buying and selling' because this simplicity cannot help describe areas in which marketing is clearly practiced without immediately having to be interpreted metaphorically. It seems clear that the sorts of gymnastics of metaphorical interpretation that one has to go through in order to see political or social marketing (and even some areas of contemporary branding and social media marketing) as facilitating 'buying and selling' are not signs of clear and useful terminology. By going back to the earliest marketing model we have, however, been able to investigate what elements of 'buying and selling' are essential to the marketing process. Plato allows us to see that currency exchange enables the engineering of attention in the market place. It allows those who produce to attend to production and those who wish to consume to attend to consumption when and where they wish. And the marketer facilitates this by existing in the middle, seeking to control attention via the flow of goods, display, price, and address.

Although the definition sacrifices the (always utopian) simplicity of 'buying and selling', it instead underlines that attention is exchanged in the marketing process. This is essential to an effective understanding of what value marketing brings to the firms, organisations, networks, and individuals who choose to use it. Marketing facilitates the direction of the firm's attention (its *regard*) to the right segments of the market so that it can then organise itself to most effectively attend to those segments so that it might earn in return the regard of those segments. The definition further makes it clear that such an exchange of attention must be continually worked at—attention is a scarce resource and can be redirected at any time. If a consumer feels that a firm's attention has wandered, if they feel that its regard has been placed elsewhere, and as a consequence their requirements and expectations are being ignored, then they will redirect their attention elsewhere, too. Marketing seeks to prevent this happening, or at least to make such shifts of attention conscious and strategic.

One important consequence of the terms of this definition of marketing is the reframing of the idea of the manipulation of demand. In particular, it collapses the traditional division within marketing between those aspects of practice that are concerned with persuasion and those which are concerned with production and distribution. If (marketing) choices around the latter elements are understood as being concerned with attempts to control the exchange of attention ('where do we put what in order to facilitate the regard of segment x?'), then their focus becomes identical to that of marketing communication. This is an important antidote to the rather nonsensical divisions within the academic discipline of marketing that have seen marketing communication and marketing often broken into separate departments and then housed in entirely different faculties and buildings on university campuses.

In the next chapter, I will explain in detail how marketing, seen as a profession that facilitates the continuing exchange of attention between firm and stakeholders, is essentially a rhetorical enterprise.

Note

1. All references to passages from *Republic* are to the 1997 edition of the complete works edited by John Cooper, published by Hackett Publishing, Indianapolis.

References

Ashby, W. R. (1957). *An Introduction to Cybernetics*. London: Chapman & Hall.

Bateson, G. (2000). *Steps to an Ecology of Mind*. Chicago: University of Chicago Press.

Beer, S. (1993). *Designing Freedom*. Toronto: House of Anansi Press.

Beer, S. (1994). *Decision and Control: The Meaning of Operational Research and Management Cybernetics*. Chichester: John Wiley & Sons.

Beer, S. (1995). *Brain of the Firm*. Chichester: John Wiley & Sons.

Beniger, J. (1986). *The Control Revolution: Technological and Economic Origins of the Information Society*. London: Harvard University Press.

Critser, G. (2003). *Fat Land: How Americans Became the Fattest People in the World*. London: Penguin.

Davenport, T., and Beck, J. (2001). *The Attention Economy: Understanding the New Currency of Business*. Boston: Harvard Business School Press.

Dixon, D. F. (1995). Retailing in Classical Athens: Gleanings From Contemporary Literature and Art. *Journal of Macromarketing*, 15(1), 74–85.

Ewen, S. (2001). *Captains of Consciousness: Advertising and the Social Roots of the Consumer Culture*. New York: Basic Books.

Klein, N. (2009). *No Logo*. New York: Picador.

Kotler, P. (1972). A Generic Concept of Marketing. *Journal of Marketing*, 36(April), 46–54.

Kotler, P., and Zaltman, G. (1971). Social Marketing: An Approach to Planned Social Change. *Journal of Marketing*, 35(3), 3–12.

Lanham, R. (2006). *The Economics of Attention: Style and Substance in the Age of Information*. Chicago: University of Chicago Press.

Lanning, M. J., and Michaels, E. G. (1988). A Business Is a Value Delivery System. *McKinsey Staff Paper* (No. 41, July), 1–16.

Levine, R., Locke, C., Searls, D., and Weinberger, D. (2000). *The Cluetrain Manifesto: The End of Business as Usual*. Harlow: Pearson Education.

Malkan, S. (2007). *Not Just a Pretty Face: The Ugly Side of the Beauty Industry*. Gabriola Island, Canada: New Society Publishers.

Maslow, A. H. (1943). A Theory of Human Motivation. *Psychological Review*, 50(4), 370–396.

McCloskey, D. (1995). Metaphors Economists Live By. *Social Research*, 62(2), 215–237.

Mitchell, A. (1999). Out of the Shadows. *Journal of Marketing Management*, 15(1–3), 25–42.

Moore, K. R. (2014). Plato's Puppets of the Gods: Representing the Magical, the Mystical and the Metaphysical. *Arion*, 22(2), 37–72.

Moss, M. (2013). *Salt, Sugar, Fat: How the Food Giants Hooked Us*. London: WH Allen.

Prahalad, C., and Ramaswamy, V. (2004). *The Future of Competition: Co-Creating Unique Value With Consumers*. Boston: Harvard Business School Press.

Ries, A., and Trout, J. (2001). *Positioning: The Battle for Your Mind*. London: McGraw-Hill.

Schlosser, E. (2002). *Fast Food Nation: What the All-American Meal Is Doing to the World*. London: Penguin.

Shaw, E. H. (1995). The First Dialogue on Macromarketing. *Journal of Macromarketing*, 15(1), 7–20.

Vargo, S. L., and Lusch, R. F. (2004). Evolving to a New Dominant Logic for Marketing. *Journal of Marketing*, 68(1), 1–17.

Weinstein, J. (2009). The Market in Plato's Republic. *Classical Philology*, 104(4), 439–458.

Wu, T. (2016). *The Attention Merchants*. London: Atlantic Books.

5   Marketing and Sophism—A Comparison

In taking the control of attention as the focus of marketing, I have obviously constructed an understanding of the profession that makes it more amenable to a rhetorical interpretation. However, it is my aim in this section to draw enough connections between the two practices to convince the reader that we really are dealing with two sides of the same coin or, at least, two aspects of the same rich intellectual tradition.

I will start by returning once more to Plato. Much of the way that we have come to think of the pre-Aristotelian nature of rhetoric, its earliest history, schools, and tensions comes directly from Plato. In particular, our understanding of the Sophists, those charismatic fifth-century BCE superstars of public argument and declamation, such as Protagoras, Gorgias, Hippias, Antiphon, and Critias, has been largely formed by Plato's depiction of them in such dialogues as *Gorgias*, *Phaedrus*, *Protagoras*, *Sophist*, *Theaetetus*, *Hippias Major*, and *Meno*. Sophism, or an understanding of it mediated via Plato, has been at the centre of two important pieces of marketing scholarship that have attempted to describe the rhetorical nature of marketing practice, namely Laufer and Paradeise (1990) and Tonks (2002). It seems sensible, then, to start this mapping of rhetoric onto marketing with a consideration of the figure of the Sophist. While, as I have said, much of how we think of Sophism comes from Plato, we cannot ignore the fact that in many respects Plato is a hostile witness. The Sophists were direct competitors of Socrates and the traditions and schools they founded remained as competitors for Plato. Much recent scholarship has attempted to disentangle 'real' Sophism from the strategic, oppositional construction found in Plato and Aristotle (Cole, 1991; Corey, 2015; Gagarin, 2002; Tell, 2011). While enticing and often persuasive, this is not the venue for a review of such research. Indeed, much of what I wish to point out regarding the link between Sophism and the practice of marketing simply requires the acknowledgement of Plato as an oppositional voice against Sophism. In a similar way to my previous use of Plato as a source of interesting perspectives on marketing to be considered and examined, so I will use some of his depiction of Sophistic practice to aid in the consideration of how persuasion relates to marketing.

The Middle Position of the Sophist and the Marketer

The most vital passage in the whole of Plato's works for any consideration of how the marketer and the Sophistic rhetor relate to each other is to be found in the *Gorgias*. Towards the beginning of the dialogue, Gorgias (who was, of course, a real and famous Sophist) recounts to Socrates an example of how his skill in oratory "encompasses and subordinates to itself just about everything that can be accomplished" (*Gorgias*, 456b). He recalls how:

> Many a time I've gone with my brother or with other doctors to call on some sick person who refuses to take his medicine or allow the doctor to perform surgery or cauterization on him. And when the doctor failed to persuade him, I succeeded, by means of no other craft than oratory.
>
> (ibid.)

Within this short passage there is much to unpack. Initially, we should again remember that Plato is putting these words into Gorgias' mouth in order to characterise to his audience the type of person the great Sophist rhetor was. Plato is trying to make the audience baulk at the absurdity of the situation. How can someone with no medical training be listened to by a patient when the wise and practiced doctors' words fall upon deaf ears? Plato increases the sense of iniquity even further when he has Gorgias cap this example with the following words:

> And I maintain too that if an orator and a doctor came to any city anywhere you like and had to compete in speaking in the assembly or some other gathering over which of them should be appointed a doctor, the doctor wouldn't make any showing at all, but the one who had the ability to speak would be appointed.
>
> (*Gorgias*, 546c)

So, not just addled, distracted patients would favour the orator over the doctor, but an educated, sober body of citizens would judge the rhetor to be the one worthy of being appointed the medical professional! Plato here seems to be using a hyperbolic example to demonstrate both the dangerous folly inculcated in audiences by the techniques of the Sophists and also Gorgias' own disturbing pride in being able to secure such injustice.

However, if we pause and consider the story from the perspective of the marketer, I think we might come to quite a different conclusion. This passage is so important because it places rhetorical practice in an environment outside the public assembly and the law courts. Aristotelian rhetoric, particularly through its systematisation of the genres of rhetoric (forensic for the law courts, deliberative for the political assembly, and epideictic for ceremonial occasions) has tended to pull the attention of rhetoric scholars away from the nitty gritty of everyday arenas of persuasion. Gorgias' example locates rhetoric right at the patient's bedside. It indicates that rhetoric is necessary in so many scenarios outside the formalised, privileged arenas of Athenian civic life. Garver (2009) makes the interesting argument that Aristotle distinguishes only three kinds of rhetoric even though it is obvious that rhetoric is used in a multitude of other areas of life because these are the only sites of rhetorical endeavour where his "claims that the best and most rational argument will carry the day will be anything more than a pious hope" (p. 10). Aristotle's distinction between them in Book 1 of his *On Rhetoric* thus serves to provide an idealised model of rational persuasion. Subsequent scholarship has somewhat, therefore, missed the point and often turned its back upon rhetoric outside of the strict Aristotelian genres. The rhetoric that allows Gorgias to achieve something that the doctors cannot is precisely the type of rhetoric that Aristotle has deliberately left out of formal consideration in his philosophical consideration of rhetoric. However, that does not mean that it is not rhetoric and that does not mean that it should be ignored.

So, what is the story really demonstrating to us? The doctors tell Gorgias of the *necessity* for treatment and what *kind* of treatment is needed and then Gorgias goes and persuades the patient of these points. They know this information better than Gorgias yet are unable to get the patient to listen to them. Gorgias is an intermediary agent, here, providing a service that facilitates the doctors' profession (the healing of the sick). Indeed, it does not require a significant leap of imagination to frame the story in social marketing terms. Gorgias listens to what the doctors want their patients to do and then creates a campaign designed to persuade them to do it. It's the type of thing that marketing agencies do for NGOs and governments all the time—a classic piece of marketing communication. The principal difference here is that Gorgias is working on a one-to-one basis rather than for a mass audience.

Gorgias' doctor friends cannot get their patients to listen to them, to attend to them. Gorgias has that ability—the *treatment* is the same, but Gorgias makes it valuable in the patients' eyes where the doctors could not. Of course, doctors in ancient Athens were rather similar to doctors nowadays, knowledgeable and skilled but often with little *regard* for the patient. It is the *exchange* of attention that is so often the root of complaints in the marketing of medical services. A patient does not feel that the doctor is listening to them, taking them into account, really understanding them, interested in them—and, as a consequence, they withdraw their own attention and seek to place it elsewhere (in a second opinion, an interested pharmacist, an empathetic alternative healer, or simply towards the internal dialogue of anxiety). Plato's outrage (echoed by Aristotle and probably many doctors down the centuries) is rooted in two truths of human nature—the apparent powerlessness of specialist knowledge and rational argument to sometimes capture the regard of an audience and the ability of rhetoric to succeed where knowledge and rationality cannot. Gorgias is comfortable with these truths. The Sophists, indeed, sought to take advantage of them, offering any who could pay their fees education in the construction of persuasive arguments so that they might no longer be caught powerless in life despite position, knowledge and experience. Fee-taking is something that Plato came back to again and again as evidence of the decadence of the Sophistic perspective. For Plato, knowledge should not be bought and sold like any other commodity. Yet, the Sophists are "knowledge merchants" (as he calls them in *Sophist*, 231d and e). They market their own knowledge, a knowledge that is designed to surpass and confound the knowledge of others, as we see in the *Gorgias*. The Sophists engaged in public demonstrations of their persuasive techniques that were designed to catch the attention of Athenian youth (and strategically minded parents, one presumes) so that they would clamour to learn at the feet of such masters. And clamour they did. The scene-setting opening of *Gorgias* is a great depiction of the type of charmed adulation that the visiting Sophists could muster from the young minds of Athens.

The type of situation that Gorgias' doctors find themselves in is, of course, not just limited to the medical profession. In modern marketing terminology, we might say that the doctors fail to understand and communicate the 'value proposition' of the treatment to their patients. As was made very clear in the original consultancy work by Lanning and Michaels (1988) that gave rise to the concept, many firms fail to regard their products or services from the perspective of the consumer and have therefore constructed a business with no value proposition. In such situations, it is no wonder that firms find their customers increasingly attending to their competitors. The value proposition is something that can be understood only by the firm when they attend to the customer and try to formulate the benefit their offering can bring to the consumer's life. This perspective can be arrived at only through a focusing of attention upon the prospect/customer.

The story of Gorgias and the doctors, then, provides us with a microcosmic illustration of the way in which marketing echoes Sophistic rhetoric. Before we move on from Plato's considerations of the Sophists, however, it is worth noting some further connections between his reactions to Sophistic practices and the figure of the marketer.

Of most importance, perhaps, is the relationship between of Sophism and relativism. Now, interestingly, the subject of relativism has been of much interest to certain marketing scholars. As we have seen when discussing the marketing as science debate above, there have been tense exchanges between scholars espousing a "critical relativist" stance (Anderson, 1983, 1986, 1988) and others defending a position of "scientific realism" (Hunt, 1990, 1994, 2002, 2003; Hunt and Edison, 1995). However, these debates and theorisings have all been focused upon the status of the academic marketing discipline rather than the fundamental nature of the practice of marketing itself. Looking at marketing through Sophist eyes, however, allows us to see the absolute centrality of relativism in how marketers go about what they do. So, first of all, let us consider the way in which relativism is manifest in Sophistic practice.

There are two main ways in which thinkers identified as Sophists can be considered to display a relativistic approach to truth. The first stems from the words of Protagoras in a famous fragment, "Of all things the measure is man" (Lavery, 2008, p. 31). This is generally taken to mean that the only form of truth available to a human is that available via the (perhaps flawed) human senses and mind—we can have no access to an absolute truth outside our own understanding of the universe. This is certainly the way in which Plato understands the dictum and he spends half of the *Theaetetus* demonstrating why Protagorean relativism is unsupportable and morally dangerous (Corey, 2015)—arguments which will be familiar to readers of Shelby Hunt. As Conley (1990) summarises, "the truth, for all practical purposes, was held by Protagoras to be inaccessible; and matters of prudence, virtue, and honor were all contestable" (p. 5). The second source of Sophistic relativism is found at the centre of their pedagogical method—the *dissoi logoi*, or opposite arguments. This phrase refers to an anonymous Sophist text from the late fifth century BCE consisting of a number of examples of how to "argue both sides of an issue" (Kennedy, 1994, p. 17). No one position was judged by the text to be the 'correct' one. Instead, the text provided models of how to construct effective arguments for whichever side one found oneself on. It was this type of training, combined with the relativism embodied in much of Protagoras' approach, that led to the later judgement that the Sophists sought to "make the weaker cause the stronger", as Aristotle put it (Aristotle, 1991, p. 211).

If one carefully considers the realities of marketing practice, Sophistic relativism can be seen as a highly appropriate guiding framework. A marketer must persuade a chosen audience of the superior value of the brand they are working for, no matter their personal belief nor any objective criteria that might be able to prove the precedence of any competition. A marketing agent must be able to find a strategy in order to cause that chosen audience to regard their offering as the right one at a particular time and within a particular context. There is no 'objective truth' for the marketer outside the 'measure of man', namely market research that can help them to understand the attention focus of a chosen market segment. The arguments that marketing scholars have had regarding how relativistic marketing 'science' is (or should be) completely miss the mark. Marketing practice is entirely relativistic—it is concerned with how to elevate regard for any brand, any client. Even in the realm of social and political marketing, the same marketing agent could, in principle, one year work for an HIV charity and the next year for a pharmaceutical company trying to recover from a reputation hit over the artificially high prices of its HIV drugs. A marketing manager might commonly move between competitors within the same industry and at all of them work to convince consumers of their superior value. Granted, we might spend time arguing whether the ways in which we measure and evaluate consumer regard are built upon assumptions of scientific realism or critical relativism, but such disagreements are largely immaterial to the fundamental relativism that is at the heart of marketing. Even when compared with the rhetorical practice of the advocate in the courtroom (another form of intermediary), we must judge the marketer as far closer to the Sophistic ideal, for the marketing system has no appeal to an idealised, external truth (such as justice or 'rightness')—instead the marketer must forever be mindful of the shifting, uncertain object of human regard.

It is just this relativistic Sophism that has made of the marketer such a slippery character. As we have seen already, the way Plato understands the marketer is as a figure who is central to the existence of the city and yet is also a dangerous, infecting, liminal stranger. This is also, of course, his view of the Sophists—"merchants of knowledge" who were strangers in Athens and threatened to infect the citizenry with a love of intellectual display and trickery at the expense of any attention to truth and virtue. Both marketer and Sophist appeal to the appetites. As Plato describes it, when having Socrates grill Gorgias on the nature of rhetoric, Sophistic rhetoric works primarily because it produces "a certain gratification and pleasure" (*Gorgias*, 462c) in the audience, employs a type of flattery which facilitates an audience's acceptance of the rhetors' position. It takes advantage of human weaknesses of character, of the imbalanced appetites that the majority of citizens will suffer from. In the same way, we will remember, Plato fears that any profession based upon the market will infect citizens with uncontrollable greed. And, of course, Sophists are very much connected to the market, being "merchants of knowledge".

One might reason, indeed, that the Sophists are *infected by* the market that the marketers bring to the city. For Plato, the market is, of course, necessary, but cannot be allowed to infect what should be the instruction of virtue. In other words, the Marketer and the Sophist are infected with the same virus—the greed that the market inevitably brings. Society's mistrust of marketers comes from the same place as Plato's use of fee-taking as evidence of Sophist degeneracy. The infection of market exchange inflames its victims with the urge to influence demand in order to turn an ever greater profit. Plato sees the Sophists succumbing to this infection as they tout their services around cities using demonstrations of their marvellous skills as persuasive gambits. Naturally, their skills also infect those who attend these demonstrations—they become fevered with the prospect of persuasive power. Sophistic displays function as value propositions to influence demand for their service. And, of course, those services include the inculcation of influence strategies in their clients as well as the construction of specific influence strategies for clients in the form of speeches for delivery in political assemblies or the law courts.

In Plato's thought, then, there are many points of similarity and relationship between the Sophist and the marketer. I think perhaps the most important point of similarity, however, must be the suspicion with which Plato regards both sets of figures. This suspicion, this distrust, has been reproduced century after century. It continues just as strongly today. Both marketing and rhetoric have become popular codes for either nefarious manipulations which attempt to make 'us' do things we shouldn't do or empty, wasteful blathering. We may look at the sorts of strictures against marketing that Plato enshrined in his *Laws* and conclude that our modern world has, by comparison, absolutely embraced the manipulation of the appetites. Yet, the idea that the market is a contagion, and that marketers are the carriers of that contagion (perhaps ironically) remains very strong in our societies. Suspicion of marketers is not just something that we can blame on occasional journalistic exposés such as Vance Packard's (1957) *Hidden Persuaders* and Wilson Bryan Key's (1973) alarmist diatribes on subliminal advertising. Instead it exists as a continual background radiation throughout modern society. Marketing is "an organised form of deceit" (Chomsky, 2012, p. 292). Public perception of marketers, advertisers, and public relations communicators inevitably focuses around suspicion—these professionals are trying to influence us, indeed, are successfully influencing us to pursue all sorts of unhealthy, damaging appetites. As Pollay (1986) notes regarding the public perception of advertising's "unintended consequences", it is "seen by many as a pollution of our psychological and social ecology" (p. 19). It should come as no surprise, then, that when we look at various indications of public trust we find the same sentiment. A 2015 Gallup poll on honesty in the professions sees advertising personnel, telemarketers, and lobbyists right down at the bottom along with members of congress and car salespeople—all professions that in the public eye are seen to rely upon a mastery of duplicitous language (Gallup, 2015). We can also see the recently published results of the Edelman (2017) trust barometer survey, in which respondents globally were found to be mired in a "trust crisis" as indicative of the way in which the public have reacted to commercial and political marketing use of social influencers.

The mistrust of marketing that can be found in both academic and non-academic audiences is fundamentally the same as the mistrust of the practice of rhetoric and, as I will investigate in the following chapter, the mistrust of those accused of (or espousing to practice) magic and witchcraft. Humans are extremely wary of those who seek to control them. Modern marketing is constantly accused of influencing, manipulating, forcing, or tricking us into doing things that are bad for us or that we at least don't really need to spend money purchasing or doing. Marketing scholarship has tended to have an oscillating relationship with these accusations. Most of the time it acts as if they simply do not exist. There are precious few marketing textbooks, for example, which devote any space to examining negative public perceptions of marketing, let alone to serious considerations of why such perceptions might exist. However, there is a small but significant body of literature in the journals that seeks to empirically investigate public attitudes towards marketing practice. Perhaps the first study to attempt to empirically measure attitudes towards marketing was Barksdale and Darden's (1972) investigation into consumer attitudes in the US. The researchers found that "many consumers register a high level of apprehension about certain business policies and considerable discontent about specific marketing activities [. . .] the most obvious example is the lack of confidence in advertising" (p. 34). A decade or so later, Gaski and Etzel's (1986) proposal for an "index of consumer sentiment toward marketing" (p. 71) kickstarted a small slew of studies seeking to either adopt or adapt their scale for measuring differences in sentiment towards marketing across nations and cultures (Wee and Chan, 1989; Varadarajan and Thirunarayana, 1990; Webster, 1991; Lawson et al., 2001; Lysonski et al., 2003; Chan and Cui, 2004; Ferdous and Towfique, 2008). Gaski and Etzel (2005) conducted a further, retroactive, study that analysed changes in sentiment over thirty years of measurement in the US. Although the literature finds differences between sentiment towards particular aspects of marketing (generally categorised according to the elements of the traditional marketing mix) amongst different populations in different stages of economic and marketing development, most of the studies tend to make predictable and depressing reading. One also cannot help but wonder if the urge to quantify hostility to marketing is not just a particularly 'marketing science' way of engaging with the issue, one that helps to transform it into just another subject for measurement and analysis. Certainly, this literature has done little to influence the broader conspiracy of silence in the discipline regarding the unfavourable light it is seen in. As Heath and Heath (2008) observe, "despite the importance of consumers to marketers, there is a surprising dearth of research into consumers' feelings about marketing itself (especially since the nineties)" (p. 1026). Even amongst those studies that have been done, as Lysonski et al. (2003), summarise, "the preponderance of the historical studies point to negative opinions about marketing and consumerism issues in developed and developing countries while some studies find that consumers do express satisfaction with certain elements of the marketing system" (p. 390–1). Occasionally, the titans of marketing academia do come together in order to try to deal somewhat directly with the issue of marketing's low reputation with the public and the perception of its ineffectiveness by business. Perhaps one of the largest collections of such self-examinations is Sheth and Sisodia's (2006a) edited collection, which includes contributions from such usual suspects as Kotler, Hunt, Belk, and Holbrook. In their introduction (Sheth and Sisodia, 2006b), the editors speak of the "mistrustful, adversarial" (p. 3) nature of the relationship between marketer and consumer. They note that "year after year" marketing does "less with more", only succeeding in delivering "flat or declining customer satisfaction level, shockingly low customer loyalty levels, and increasing numbers of alienated customers" (ibid.). Indeed, they conclude, "the more a customer is marketed to, the more frustrated or irritated he or she becomes, and the more manipulated and helpless he or she feels" (p. 4). While generally acknowledging this dire state of affairs, the authors of the collection generally come down to the conclusion that all this is because marketing is not being done correctly. If only marketing practitioners would listen to the assorted academics who offer their particular spins on how to perform marketing in a manner that puts consumers first then this whole problem would be solved. If we could just get rid of "wasteful marketing", "unethical marketing", and "dumb marketing", then we would be left with the sort of "exemplary marketing" (p. 5) which represents a "win-win" for producer and consumer. Fundamentally, Sheth and Sisodia (2006b) argue that "aggressive sentiments and mindsets have no place in marketing" and that we must re-orientate the profession around a set of "seemingly forgotten but timeless virtues" (p. 10) such as truth, integrity, authenticity, trust, respect, manners, etc. All the things, one presumes, which marketing is not associated with now.

Cluley (2016) has recently argued that the negative image of marketing held by the public is certainly reinforced by the way that it is depicted in the news media. He points to the way in which "mass media texts cultivate mainstream reputations concerning who does certain jobs, what those jobs involve and the status of those jobs in society" (p. 755). His survey of the UK news media indicates that when marketing is talked about it is often done in a negative manner, focusing on such practices as irritating cold-calling and aggressive tactics and "is routinely portrayed as a way businesses force goods and services onto people which they do not want or need" (p. 760). However, Cluley actually found in his research that there were more stories in his sample with a positive sentiment towards marketing than negative. In attempting to explain how this could be the case given the poor public sentiment towards marketing, Cluley suggests that these positive stories demonstrate to the public that "marketers are able to shape the news agenda" (p. 765) and so make them even more suspicious in the eyes of the public. In the end, then, it is the nature of marketing practice that remains fundamentally mistrustful to its audiences. It is not that the public misunderstand what marketing is or that they have been fed biased scare stories about what its intentions are, rather it is "that some of its most public-facing activities, which influence people's perceptions, are the kinds of things people are uncomfortable with and suspicious of" (ibid.). Some of the things that marketing is concerned with are just things that make people suspicious. They do not like other people (whether working on behalf of organisations or not) trying to manipulate what they think or feel. This is exactly the same problem that initially Sophism and then latterly the whole of the discipline of rhetoric has tended to suffer from.

Marketing and rhetoric, when they are done well, succeed in controlling what audiences value, what they hold in regard. That success, when it is attributable to either marketing or rhetoric then provides further reason to hold them in suspicion. So, we might ridicule poor rhetoric or marketing as clumsy attempts to influence us, but we will equally be outraged at the manipulation of good rhetoric and marketing (one we have realised that it is through them that we have been brought to regard an idea, a product, a brand, or a person as valuable). The suspicion and mistrust that accompany marketing and rhetoric are inevitable consequences of their practice.

The Gap

If, then, rhetoric and marketing are so closely connected, why is there so little investigation into marketing by rhetoric scholars and so little attention paid to rhetoric by marketing scholars and practitioners? Regarding the dearth of rhetorical scholarship engaging with advertising, I am not the first person to wonder why this state of affairs has come about. McKenna (1999), at a conference celebrating the thirtieth anniversary of the Rhetoric Society of America, notes that "the largest, most pervasive, and most successful rhetorical enterprise on the planet is advertising . . . [yet] . . . it is perplexing to note that scholars of rhetoric give advertising scant attention" (p. 103). He goes on to observe that "the best place to read scholarly studies of advertising rhetoric" is in the journals of consumer researchers, namechecking marketing scholars such as McQuarrie and Mick, Scott, and Stern. Similarly, almost a decade later, Marsh (2007) states that "advertising may be the most pervasive form of modern rhetoric, yet the discipline is virtually absent in rhetorical studies" (p. 168). Both McKenna and Marsh provide a number of reasons for why scholars of rhetoric ignore the largest, most powerful instantiation of rhetoric in modern society—it is vulgar and so unworthy of the attention of communication intellectuals, it is mostly performed in very short texts and so it's better off left to linguists, it is predominantly visual and so is best left to semioticians and semiologists, or even that rhetorical analysis of advertising would be too easily co-opted by the malicious forces of capitalist industry. While there are some noteworthy exceptions (I might point to Longaker and Walker's (2011) handbook, *Rhetorical Analysis: A Brief Guide for Writers*, which puts advertising examples firmly at the centre of their exposition) to judge them by the journals, textbooks, and monographs, we would be forgiven for assuming that scholars and students of rhetoric find nothing of relevance in the world of marketing communications. Of course, ironically, this lack of research engagement with "the largest, most pervasive, and most successful rhetorical enterprise on the planet is advertising" might well be connected to the suspicion and mistrust of marketing I have just been discussing. Rhetoric scholars are just as much a part of the general public as anyone else—their perception of marketing undoubtedly reflects the broadly negative sentiments identified by the researchers above. However, in the case of rhetoric scholars we might also posit that an extra level of embarrassment and discomfort will be present when they consider marketing as rhetoric, having to align their own discipline with one so commonly associated with suspicion and mistrust. Certainly, the turn towards rhetorical *analysis* as the proper *métier* of the rhetorical scholar that we have seen since the twentieth century has tended to find rhetorical scholarship framing the study of rhetoric (i.e. being a rhetorician) as something which contributes to rational, honest debate in the public sphere, a civilizing discipline which can help reduce conflict, mistrust, and suspicion. Marketing has no such motivation (discounting some of the wilder claims made for social marketing or the service perspective for the moment)—its practice is intent on creating regard, amplifying the valorisation of brands, manipulating demand. When marketing 'scientists' analyse marketing practice, they are, in the vast majority of cases, trying to identify heuristics for best practice rather than uncover the way in which attention is being controlled so that misunderstandings can be avoided, assumptions can be examined, and harmony between competitors can be achieved. Marketing is agonistic—even if we were able, by some great miracle, to eliminate the aggressive way in which marketers think (and talk) about markets and consumers, we would still be left with the simple truth that the marketplace is unavoidably a competition *between firms*. For rhetorical scholars it is, perhaps, more comforting to deal with the realms of political debate and judicial argumentation for these are places where, at least ostensibly, rational civilised argument *should* prevail. Rhetorical scholarship dedicated to uncovering how political discourse around certain issues is constructed to have particular persuasive effects on particular audiences can expect that such investigations might contribute in some way to a more reasoned, less agonistic, public dialogue around those issues. What expectation might rhetorical scholars expect from an engagement with marketing practice?

Marsh (2001, 2013), perhaps, gives us an idea of what might happen if rhetorical scholars were to engage more strongly with marketing. Marsh has not just complained of rhetorical scholarship's lack of involvement with marketing; he has actually done a lot to demonstrate what such involvement should look like. His work on how public relations can be re-configured through a rhetorical lens is a convincing example of how the understanding of rhetoric as an 'improving' or humanising discipline can be made to square with marketing ideals. Rather than using the twentieth-century arguments of such figures as I. A. Richards or Kenneth Burke, Marsh looks to Isocrates' fourth-century BCE rhetorical tradition as a model that can provide a "moral, symmetrical rhetoric" ideally suited to implementing a non-adversarial, modern public relations. Of course, Marsh's conception of public relations is here driven by recent research that has pointed out both the ineffectiveness and the ethical dubiousness of agonistic, asymmetrical public relations, research that has instead called for practitioners to adopt a position of "responsibility to the societies in which they operate and from which they profit" (Baker, 1999, quoted in Marsh, 2001, p. 82). In Marsh (2013), we find a detailed exposition of exactly how a rhetorical perspective steeped in the tradition of Isocrates can be used a guiding framework all aspects of modern PR practice, from an ethical approach to persuasion to media planning decisions. It is, however, indicative of the engagement of rhetorical scholarship with marketing in general that the one fully worked-through, committed study of how the rhetorical tradition can be fruitfully adopted as the principal theoretical foundation for a branch of marketing understands that branch (i.e. public relations) in a way that runs counter to the evidence of the sort of overwhelmingly negative public sentiment that we have been discussing above. Marsh sees public relations as a way for firms to engage responsibly, civically, with society. For him, effective public relations should be built upon "Isocrates' core values of moderation and justice" (Marsh, 2013, p. 117). So, in order to engage with this aspect of marketing is has to be made into *un*marketing. Indeed, it is noticeable that Marsh, throughout the whole of his wildly erudite and enjoyable monograph, does not once address public relations as a part of marketing. The only time he even mentions the word is to list it as a "newer discipline" alongside public relations and advertising. He is unwilling, then, to understand public relations and advertising as parts of marketing. One wonders how much of this is motivated by a lingering Platonic sense of marketing as infecting sickness. What it certainly does allow Marsh to do is to turn public relations away from the marketplace, making it instead a discursive tool for the (political) public sphere. In other words, he can remain within the general trajectory of twentieth-century rhetorical scholarship that seeks to understand the tradition in order to help humanise and harmonise civic discourse.

What of the Sophistic view of rhetoric, though? What of a relativistic, agonistic, asymmetrical approach to persuasive communication? As described above, Sophism has many similarities with the actual practice of marketing. Marketing is about competition, the changing of minds and behaviours, the manipulation of public understandings of value, the constant dynamic of the exchange of regard. Sophism is perfectly suited to explain such practices without the need to first construct an ideal vision of marketing which bears little to no resemblance to how it is actually practiced. We do not need to make marketing into an instrument of social responsibility in order to see how it is Sophistic through and through.

Of course, a Sophistic approach to rhetoric does not mean that we have to ignore Aristotelian or Isocratean perspectives (or the fruits of any other rhetorical traditions). Indeed, the relativistic foundations of Sophism surely encourage an investigation into alternative understandings and toolsets. However, there are certain characteristics of Sophism which do align it more strongly with marketing as it has come to be practiced and which also account for the generally problematic relationship marketing has with other disciplines and with society at large. The various manifestations of distrust of marketing that we have discussed have at their root a suspicion of, unease with, efforts to control us, to persuade us, to make us do things we probably shouldn't do. We see the same sorts of unease and suspicion in Plato and Aristotle's reactions to Sophist figures like Gorgias. Marketers and Sophists are often framed by their critics (or rivals) as exercising unnatural, unhealthy, magical influence over audiences. In the next chapters, I will examine the reasons for the links between magic, persuasion, rhetoric and marketing. My intention here is to try to open up some of the hidden assumptions that influence the ways that consumers, journalists, and scholars within and without marketing end up understanding what marketing does. Deep-seated suspicion of the links between rhetoric/persuasion and magic (and, therefore, marketing) has a large part to play in the way that these stakeholders think. At the same time, the allure of magic has a significant impact on the form and content of much marketing communication. So, the next three chapters explore the ambiguous, nuanced connections between magic, persuasion, the tradition of Sophistic rhetoric, and the practice of marketing.

References

Anderson, P. F. (1983). Marketing, Scientific Progress, and Scientific Method. *Journal of Marketing*, 47(4), 18.

Anderson, P. F. (1986). On Method in Consumer Research: A Critical Relativist Perspective. *Journal of Consumer Research*, 13(2), 155–173.

Anderson, P. F. (1988). Relativism Revidivus: In Defense of Critical Relativism. *Journal of Consumer Research*, 15(3), 403–406.

Aristotle (trans. H. C. Lawson-Tancred) (1991). *The Art of Rhetoric*. London: Penguin Books.

Baker, S. (1999). Five Baselines for Justification in Persuasion. *Journal of Mass Media Ethics*, 14, 69–81.

Barksdale, H. C., and Darden, W. R. (1972). Consumer Attitudes Toward Marketing and Consumerism. *Journal of Marketing*, 36(4), 28–35.

Chan, T.-S., and Cui, G. (2004). Consumer Attitudes Toward Marketing in a Transitional Economy. A Replication and Extension. *Journal of Consumer Marketing*, 21(1), 10–26.

Chomsky, N. (2012). *How the World Works*. London: Hamish Hamilton.

Cluley, R. (2016). The Depiction of Marketing and Marketers in the News Media. *European Journal of Marketing*, 50(4), 752–769.

Cole, T. (1991). *The Origins of Rhetoric in Ancient Greece*. Baltimore: John Hopkins University Press.

Conley, T. (1990). *Rhetoric in the European Tradition*. White Plains, NY: Longman.

Corey, D. (2015). *The Sophists in Plato's Dialogues*. Albany, NY: State University of New York Press.

Edelman. (2017). *Edelman Trust Barometer 2017—UK Findings*. www.edelman.co.uk/magazine/posts/edelman-trust-barometer-2017-uk-findings/ [Accessed July 25, 2017].

Ferdous, A. S., and Towfique, B. (2008). Consumer Sentiment Towards Marketing in Bangladesh: The Relationship Between Attitudes to Marketing, Satisfaction and Regulation. *Marketing Intelligence & Planning*, 26(5), 481–495.

Gagarin, M. (2002). *Antiphon the Athenian: Oratory, Law, and Justice in the Age If the Sophists*. Austin: University of Texas Press.

Gallup. (2015). *Honesty/Ethics in Professions*. www.gallup.com/poll/1654/honesty-ethics-professions.aspx [Accessed July 25, 2017].

Garver, E. (2009). Aristotle on the Kinds of Rhetoric. *Rhetorica: A Journal of the History of Rhetoric*, 27(1), 1–18.

Gaski, J., and Etzel, M. (1986). The Index of Consumer Sentiment Toward Marketing. *Journal of Marketing*, 50(3), 71–81.

Gaski, J., and Etzel, M. (2005). National Aggregate Consumer Sentiment Toward Marketing: A Thirty-year Retrospective and Analysis. *Journal of Consumer Research*, 31(4), 859–868.

Heath, T. P. M., and Heath, M. (2008). (Mis)trust in Marketing: A Reflection on Consumers' Attitudes and Perceptions. *Journal of Marketing Management*, 24(9–10), 1025–1039.

Hunt, S. D. (1990). Truth in Marketing Theory and Research. *Journal of Marketing*, 54(July), 1–15.

Hunt, S. D. (1994). On Rethinking Marketing: Our Discipline, Our Practice, Our Methods. *European Journal of Marketing*, 28(3), 13–25.

Hunt, S. D. (2002). *Foundations in Marketing Theory: Toward a General Theory of Marketing*. Armonk, NY: M. E. Sharpe.

Hunt, S. D. (2003). *Controversy in Marketing Theory: For Reason, Realism, Truth, and Objectivity*. Armonk, NY: M. E. Sharpe.

Hunt, S. D., and Edison, S. (1995). On the Marketing of Marketing Knowledge. *Journal of Marketing Management*, 11(December), 635–640.

Kennedy, G. (1994). *A New History of Classical Rhetoric*. Princeton, NJ: Princeton University Press.

Keys, W. B. (1973). *Subliminal Seduction*. Englewood Cliffs, NJ: Prentice-Hall.

Lanning, M. J., and Michaels, E. G. (1988). A Business Is a Value Delivery System. *McKinsey Staff Paper* (No. 41, July), 1–16.

Lavery, J. (2008). Protagoras. In P. O'Grady (Ed.), *The Sophists: An Introduction*. London: Duckworth, 30–44.

Laufer, R., and Paradeise, C. ([1990] 2016). *Marketing Democracy: Public Opinion and Media Formation in Democratic Societies*. New Brunswick, NJ: Transaction Publishers.

Lawson, R., Todd, S., and Boshoff, C. (2001). Relationships Between Consumer Sentiment Towards Marketing and Consumer Lifestyles. *Australasian Marketing Journal*, 9(2), 7–22.

Longaker, M., and Walker, J. (2011). *Rhetorical Analysis: A Brief Guide for Writers*. Boston: Longman.

Lysonski, S., Durvasula, S., and Watson, J. (2003). Should Marketing Managers Be Concerned About Attitudes Towards Marketing and Consumerism in New Zealand? A Longitudinal View. *European Journal of Marketing*, 37(3/4), 385–406.

Marsh, C. (2001). Public Relations Ethics: Contrasting Models From the Rhetorics of Plato, Aristotle, and Isocrates. *Journal of Mass Media Ethics*, 16(2), 78–98.

Marsh, C. (2007). Aristotelian Causal Analysis and Creativity in Copywriting: Toward a Rapprochement Between Rhetoric and Advertising. *Written Communication*, 24(2), 168–187.

Marsh, C. (2013). *Classical Rhetoric and Modern Public Relations*. London: Routledge.

McKenna, S. (1999). Advertising as Epideictic Rhetoric. In C. Jan Swearingen and D. S. Kaufer (Eds.), *Rhetoric, the Polis, and the Global Village: Selected Papers From the 1998 Thirtieth Anniversary Rhetoric Society of America*. London: Lawrence Erlbaum Associates, 103–109.

Packard, V. (1957). *The Hidden Persuaders*. New York: McKay.

Pollay, R. W. (1986). The Distorted Mirror: Reflections on the Unintended Consequences of Advertising. *Journal of Marketing*, 50(2), 18–36.

Sheth, J. N., and Sisodia, R. S. (Eds.). (2006a). *Does Marketing Need Reform? Fresh Perspectives on the Future*. London: Routledge.

Sheth, J. N., and Sisodia, R. S. (2006b). Introduction. In J. N. Sheth and R. S. Sisodia (Eds.), *Does Marketing Need Reform? Fresh Perspectives on the Future*. London: Routledge, 3–11.

Tell, H. (2011). *Plato's Counterfeit Sophists*. Washington, DC: Center for Hellenic Studies.

Tonks, D. (2002). Marketing as Cooking: The Return of the Sophists. *Journal of Marketing Management*, 18(7–8), 803–822.

Varadarajan, P. R., and Thirunarayana, P. N. (1990). Consumers' Attitudes Towards Marketing Practices, Consumerism and Government Regulations: Cross-national Perspectives. *European Journal of Marketing*, 24(6), 6–23.

Webster, C. (1991). Attitudes Toward Marketing Practices: The Effects of Ethnic Identification. *Journal of Applied Business Research*, 7(2), 107–116.

Wee, C.-H., and Chan, M. (1989). Consumer Sentiment Towards Marketing in Hong Kong. *European Journal of Marketing*, 23(4), 25–39.

6 Magic, Sympathy, and Language

In the previous chapters, I have slowly been building an argument that marketing, in all its manifestations, can be seen to be a rhetorical discipline—one concerned with the persuasive control of the flow of people and resources, and most of all, attention.

Deep in the roots of rhetoric, however, there is a connection to something else that also seeks to control people, resources, and attention—magic. Magical practices use words and symbols in attempts to effect change in the world—the object of that change might be someone's mind (in the sense of a change of affections, a common goal of love spells, for example), a natural process (the healing of a disease or, indeed, the inculcation of sickness in someone), a supernatural process (the conjuring of spirits of the dead, perhaps, the invocation of an animal spirit in order to confer its power upon the magician, or even the materialisation of angels for purposes of discourse on heavenly matters). In all such cases, magic is used in order to circumvent the 'way things are', to provide "power capable of bypassing standard structures", as Chlup (2007, p. 154) says of the purview of Hermes, the god of Greek magicians. Magical words are used in attempts to attain those things that are, due to our position in society, the world, the universe, ordinarily denied us. The connection to rhetoric is clear to see and, if we squint our eyes just a little bit, so too the relationship with marketing.

Understanding the ways in which societies have dealt with the often unclear, perhaps even porous, boundaries between rhetoric and magic will afford us a stronger, more nuanced, appreciation of what we expect words and symbols to do, how they do it, and how we tend to feel about these expectations. This is important when we try to reflect upon what we think marketing is. Magic has often been ranged against 'science' and rationalism and, as we have already seen, the debate about how scientific marketing can be is a long and rancorous one in the discipline. There are many serious critiques of marketing and advertising that accuse it of being 'magic', where magic is understood as a pejorative description of something that casts a web of illusion over people. As we shall see, such accusations have a great deal to do with the way that magic, rhetoric, and persuasion are conflated in the minds of many intellectuals—and this tradition continues in critiques of marketing. In this chapter, then, I will explore the ways that magic and rhetoric (as the art of persuasion) have been, and remain, intimately connected.

Definitions

It is strangely gratifying when looking at the history of Western scholarly attempts to define magic to realise that marketing is not alone in the uncomfortable suffering of definitional purgatory. As Stark (2001) memorably puts it, "the term magic has been a conceptual mess" (p. 102). For example, there are longstanding disagreements over whether magic is to be differentiated from religion or seen as a part of it, or indeed if both categories have any meaning whatsoever outside of scholarly analysis (for interesting overviews, see Bremmer, 1999; Wax and Wax, 1963; Hammond, 1970; Geertz, 1975). Even the exact origins of the word 'magic' are clouded in some confusion and dispute (Bremmer, 1999). If we are going to talk about the relationship between rhetoric and magic, however, we certainly need to have some idea of what it is we are referring to when we use the term. Firstly, it is unavoidable that use of the word 'magic' (along with its close cognates such as 'sorcery', 'goetia', and 'witchcraft') has tended to have a rhetorical component. It often been used to indicate spiritual practices which are felt to involve trickery, foreign influence, or which are outside the established way of doing things in a particular location, social/cultural/ethnic grouping, or spiritual doctrine. So, the term 'magic' comes from Greek usage (*magos* and *mageia*) designating the practices of wandering Persian priests (perhaps more familiar to Western European audiences as 'Magi') or those who had adopted (and adapted) such practices. In this sense, *magos* and *mageia* usually had a derogatory connotation and were used to describe charlatans, beggars, quacks, or "people of an inferior theology and an inferior cosmology" (Bremmer, 1999, p. 4). At the same time, while the Greek culture that used these terms clearly did so in a pejorative manner, we should not forget that it also treated many aspects of Persian culture with fascination and intrigue and "in many spheres of life busily copied them" (ibid., p. 6). As Bremmer (1999) notes, "in tragedy, rhetorics and earlier philosophy, *magos* is a term of abuse, whereas historians and Aristotelian philosophers tend to take the Magi seriously" (ibid.). So, our word 'magic' already comes to us with a complex of rhetorical associations even before it finds itself transferred into a Judeo-Christian context and the languages of Western Europe. It refers to something decidedly Other, at times deceitful and vulgar, at times mysterious and powerful. The associations of alluring exoticism, however, seem to have won out at the end of the day—the reputation of the Persian Magi as possessors of powerful spiritual knowledge in Roman and then European Medieval cultures meant that, while there might be equivalent words in their indigenous languages (as well as in Greek), "later magicians called themselves [. . .] *magos/magus*" (Bremmer, 1999, p. 9).

So much for the origins of the word that I will be using here. But to what exactly does it refer? How can we think of magical practice in fifth-century Athens as equivalent in some way to magical practice in seventeenth-century England, let alone the Trobrian Islanders studied by Malinowski (1935)? And how does that magical practice relate to persuasion and rhetoric? In the same way that a fifth-century Athenian would be using the term to refer to a quite constructed sense of what Others might have been doing, so are all descriptions of 'magic' necessarily constructed. Malinowski's (1935) understanding of what the Trobrianders did when they did magic is necessarily influenced by his own intellectual paradigm, as Wax and Wax (1963) argue. Malinowski was concerned to establish the "Trobrian—and the savage in general—as a practical man, pragmatic and utilitarian if unreflective" (p. 498). The way Malinowski defines magic is therefore intimately bound up with seeing it as part of an attempt to control nature for practical benefit. Similarly, James Frazer's (1894) influential view of magic as a form of early pseudoscience inspired by a clumsy appreciation of the order that exists in the universe is a reflection of Frazer's own intellectual paradigm that sought to categorize religion and magic as fundamentally different and marking separate developmental stages of humanity. For Frazer, sympathetic magic, "which plays a large part in most systems of superstition" (p. 9), represents a "germ of the modern notion of natural law or the view of nature as a series of events occurring in an invariable order without the intervention of personal agency" (p. 9). Magic seeks to "bend nature" to human wishes (p. 12). Instead of seeking to change the course of nature by religious supplication to a god (praying for that god to intervene in a drought, for example), the magician seeks to use an understanding of sympathetic correspondences that they have discerned in the natural order in order to cause a change in that order. So, sympathetic magic assumes that "any effect may be produced by imitating it" (p. 9)—a hunter can take on the slipperiness of a frog by using a charm and ritual which imitate aspects of the frog. Frazer argued that, although it was "misapplied", such practices displayed "the modern conception of physical causation" (p. 12). In this, of course, he betrays a very Victorian, mechanistic understanding of the natural sciences, a rather paternalistic view of "primitive man", as well as a determination to neatly (bluntly) compartmentalise the spiritual practices and traditions of humanity into simple categories and dichotomies. As Tambiah (1968) points out, spiritual rituals usually display a rich mixture of forms and registers, some of which might be described as 'magical' and others as 'religious', in Frazer's terms. To keep arguing that "magic was thoroughly opposed to religion" (p. 176) was a position that made increasingly little sense especially when faced with the realities of ritual around the world. However, it did make sense for someone like Frazer who was generally sceptical of what religion had brought to the world and who wished to see science as the force that progressed humanity. By framing magic as a mistaken but conceptually sophisticated attempt to engage with the order of nature, he could cast it as an early evolutionary stage that later blossomed into science itself. The assertive, masculine derring-do of magic and science is ranged against Frazer's framing of religion as "feminine and sycophantic" (Wax and Wax, 1963, p. 496) in ways that are perhaps all too familiar to readers of 'marketing science'.

Even when historians of religion and anthropologists have been more reflective regarding the pitfalls of categorisation, the exact nature of magic remains quite unclear. As Smith (2004) notes, in "academic discourse 'magic' has almost always been treated as a *contrast* term, a shadow reality known only by looking at the reflection of its opposite ('religion', 'science') in a distorting funhouse mirror" (p. 216). Additionally, magical practice is so variegated that defining it in opposition to something invariably leaves that definition open to being undermined by a few well-chosen counter-examples. Collins (2003), for example, points out how "public, state-sponsored curses [. . .] seem to defy a simple 'public/private' or 'social/antisocial' contrast for magic" as do "formularies that employ for their efficacy propitiation, slander, and compulsion of divine forces" which therefore "blur perhaps the most conventional and misleading contrast, that between religion as propitiatory and magic as coercive in their respective attitudes toward divinity" (p. 18). Arriving at a coherent, stable definition of what magic is seems highly problematic, then. What is defined as magic depends on who is talking, when they are talking, and to what audience they are talking. This, perhaps explains why "an amazing number of scholars have been content to write about magic at length while leaving it undefined" (Stark, 2001, p. 102). Certainly, a clear context is vital when discussing what magic might consist of or mean at any one time and trying to draw out fundamental similarities across different centuries (if not millennia) and cultures is fraught with traps and pratfalls. I will look in more detail at the ways in which magic has been used as a "contrast term" for marketing in the next chapter, but what I am at pains to determine at this point is the nature of the connection between magic and rhetoric. In order to achieve this, there must be some points of description that can be generally agreed upon. So, given that rhetoric is about language, I will focus on those aspects of magical practice that can be seen to deal with language and representation, while trying to avoid falling into *too* much reliance upon general theoretical pronouncements of what magic is.

A good point to start, perhaps, is with Lehrich's (2007) suggestion that "comparison is indeed typically magical", which he glosses as meaning "usually magical, typical of magic, of a type with magic" (p. 83). Two of the most characteristically magical approaches to the world, according to Frazer (1894), were based upon the principles of sympathy and contagion. Now, while we have seen that Frazer goes on to explain how the magical approach to causation that sympathy and contagion epitomise is fundamentally "misapplied", it is worthwhile detaching it from its Frazerian evolutionary framework and examining the way in which the operation of comparison underlies both sympathy and contagion. This will then go some way towards demonstrating the magical aspects of language and linguistic persuasion.

As Greenwood (2000) has argued, Frazer's concept of sympathetic magic can usefully "still be taken as a basic definition today" of magic and has been adopted into most of the major theorisations of magic and religion that have followed him, including those of Malinowski, Mauss, and Evans-Pritchard. Indeed, Greenwood also states that sympathetic magic is the "underlying theme behind communicating with the otherworld in the diversity of contemporary magical practices" (p. 38). What exactly does it mean, then? Frazer (1894) writes that "one of the principles of sympathetic magic is that any effect may be produced by imitating it" (p. 9). He illustrates this principle by recounting the use of what we would now popularly refer to as 'voodoo dolls', but which can be found in various forms across many cultures. So, "if it is wished to kill a person an image if him is made and then destroyed"—through "a certain physical sympathy between the person and his image" it is thought that when harm is done to the image so that harm will be inflicted upon the intended victim. This is a tremendously powerful and common way of thinking across time and cultures. Even if one is nervous of reproducing 'Frazerian categories', it is clear that "the basic notion that objects made to resemble certain people or things, or symbolically linked to them, might convey power to their possessor is evident in many widely separate contexts" (Bailey, 2006, p. 18). We all have probably caught ourselves indulging in such notions—it is, surely, the root of the whole 'signature series' marketing trope, and intimately informs the trade in celebrity and historical memorabilia, amongst many other things. As a guitarist, for example, I am all too aware of the almost irresistible draw of instruments and equipment which have been imbued with some form of "physical sympathy" with a revered artist, whether that be through a simple silk-screened signature on a headstock, the completely faithful replication of a well-worn guitar, or even an entirely new model designed by the artist specifically for the brand. While we (and the marketing communication department) can make half-hearted attempts to rationalise such purchases in terms of the 'search for authentic tone' (itself, of course, embedded in a broader sympathetic magic of imitation) such product lines are operating at a far deeper, simpler level—if I play something that has some connection to a favoured artist, then I will take on something of their ability, their spirit, their musicality.

In actuality, such magical thinking demonstrates a mixture of two magical perspectives—the imitative one we have already met and Frazer's other category (introduced in the second edition and formally named in the vastly expanded third edition of *The Golden Bough*), contagious magic. In a move that has led to a degree of confusion that still occasionally haunts discussion of the subject, Frazer finally decided to describe both the imitative and contagious branches of magic as being grounded in the overarching originating category of "sympathetic magic". So, the two subcategories are formally distinguished by observing that imitative magic (also referred to by Frazer as "homeopathic magic") revolves around the conviction that "like produces like, or that an effect resembles its cause", while contagious magic depends upon the idea that "things which have once been in contact with each other continue to act on each other at a distance after the physical contact has been severed" (Frazer, 1920, p. 52). The distinctions between the two are somewhat artificial, and even Frazer acknowledges that "in practice the two branches are often combined" (p. 54). We can, then, adopt Frazer's subsuming title of "sympathetic magic" to describe the patterns of thinking around the powers of imitation and contagion that tend to occur in magical practice but which we also see in many other walks of life.

We see similar patterns of sympathetic relationship working across sports, cuisine, and arts marketing. We even have a whole raft of fallacies to identify the irrational, illogical thinking involved (arguments of composition, division, association, *post hoc ergo propter hoc*, etc.). Yet it seems that it is difficult to break the hold such thinking has upon us no matter how much our cultures might ostensibly valorise rational and logical thought and decision making. Take, for example, an excellent study by Albas and Albas (1989) of the ways in which university students "participate in magic at exam time" (p. 603). Exams are, of course, events where students "no matter how well prepared, encounter a number of uncertainties" (ibid.) and might therefore wish to use any (legal) tool at their disposal to reduce those uncertainties and associated anxieties. The researchers found that many of the practices that students used to control their luck (and therefore their anxiety) operated on the simple associations of sympathetic magic. So, one respondent "always wore a three-piece suit that he had found particularly efficacious when he wore it on one occasion to a job interview" (p. 607)—a good example of the mixing of the contagious and imitative (the student wears the suit to imitate the same set of circumstances that had previously produced success and also sees the suit as imparting success to him through contact). A number of other students wore specific pieces of jewellery that belonged to their parents but "in all of these cases, the students mentioned that the parent was particularly bright and successful, thus implying a faith in magic by contagion" (ibid.). Examples of pure imitative magic used by respondents are practices that involve the creation of an artefact or pattern that mimics the desired examination result. So, on every exam day one student would cook a breakfast consisting of "one sausage placed vertically on the left of the plate and beside it two eggs sunny side up to make the configuration '100' (percent)". Another would stir his coffee exactly twenty times before his examinations, as "he was taking 5 courses and aspired to an A in each (which is the equivalent of 4 grade points), and 5 times 4 equals 20" (p. 608). While we may joke as much as we want about the febrile imaginations and illogic of undergraduate students, the simple reality is that Albas and Albas' (1989) respondents represented a broad sample of those engaged in higher education across a broad range of subjects (including the sciences) in a large, provincial university in the United States. Not somewhere where we would immediately expect to discover the rampant practice of sympathetic magic. Albas and Albas (1989) make the final point that the modern sympathetic magic of students is clearly expressed in ways that can differ from more traditional magical practices. The student magic that they uncovered was generally individually performed for individual purposes rather than related to public or community concerns, often quite "spontaneously generated" rather than culturally dictated, and "highly variable and even contradictory" (p. 612) in its rituals. Yet, despite these 'modern' or 'postmodern' variations, the basic assumptions of sympathetic magic are clearly present and link the actions (and the thinking) of these undergraduates with the magical practices of the Ancient Greeks, the Romans, the Trobriand Islanders, Cornelius Agrippa and the Renaissance occult philosophers, the practitioners of Santeria, etc. Indeed, let us not forget that we are not linking magic with anything laughingly called 'primitive' society. Their practices do not make Albas and Albas' (1989) students 'primitive' (whatever that might possibly mean). Rather, their spontaneous recourse to sympathetic magic illustrates the way that the law of similarity and the law of contact seem 'natural', 'right', 'correct' at some level to humans in need of control over their lives wherever and whenever they might be.

The basic assumptions of sympathetic magic can be used to build up truly impressive feats of intellectual creativity. In Renaissance Europe, for example, the assumptions of homeopathic and contagious magic were expanded into highly complex systems of correspondences that uncovered the hidden (occult) relationships within the variety of the natural world. "Natural magic", as it was called, sought to investigate, catalogue, and then exploit these "occult sympathies" (Yates, 2003, p. 53), aiming to control natural forces (and a person's place within them) to the magician's advantage. Cornelius Agrippa, indeed, in his treatise on natural magic first published in 1531, provides us with exactly the same division between magics of similarity and contact that Frazer was to propose some many centuries later. What Agrippa calls the "occult virtues" of things can be discovered through the magician's attention to the similarities between things and to the way that things come into contact with each other. While God has infused everything with these "occult virtues" nevertheless He has hidden them from the eyes of humanity. Yet we are also created by God and have been given the tools to uncover these properties, using our "experience and conjecture" to inquire into the nature of the world and discover its secrets (which is, of course, the root of the scientific method mainstream marketing prizes so highly). For Agrippa, when we inquire into the world, we should first consider that "everything moves and turns itself into its like"; "so fire moves to fire, water moves to water, and he that is bold moves to boldness" (Agrippa, [1651] 1898, p. 71). It therefore follows that if

> we would obtain any property or virtue let us seek for such animals, or such other things whatsoever, in which such a property is in a more

eminent manner than in any other thing, and in these let us take that part in which such a property or virtue is most vigorous.

(ibid.)

So, if we wish to "promote love" we should, seek out the animal that is "most loving" (for example a pigeon or a turtle), and then "take the members or parts" which display this property most vigorously (say, its heart or its breast) at the time when its love is the most intense (in Spring, perhaps). Agrippa then moves on to talk of ways in which the magician can also manipulate occult virtues by contact. He explains that "so great is the power of natural things that they not only work upon all things that are near them, by their virtue, but also besides this, they infuse into them a like power, through which, by the same virtue, they also work upon other things" (p. 74). He uses the commonplace example of the lodestone to demonstrate how true this is, for when iron rings are drawn near to the lodestone they also become infused with the same qualities as the lodestone and are themselves able to draw further iron pieces. From this material example of infection through contact, Agrippa then moves on to one based in human personality—"after this manner it is, as they say, that a wanton, grounded in boldness and impudence, is like to infect all that are near her, by this property, whereby they are made like herself". It is then but a very small step for Agrippa to argue that "if any one shall put on the inward garment of a wanton, or shall have about him that looking-glass which she daily looks into, he shall thereby become bold, confident, impudent and wanton" (ibid.). In this way, the principles of similarity and contact are seen to provide the explanatory mechanisms for all of Agrippa's natural magic.

These occult sympathies did not just exist on the natural (or elemental) level, however, but were also mirrored (in far more complex fashion) in the celestial and supercelestial realms—knowledge of which would enable the magician to communicate with angels, demons and, at the most rarefied level, God Himself. In an instance of spiritual bootstrapping, once magic has provided you with the means by which to converse with such spirits, then they will be able to provide you with the "knowledge of the whole universe, and of the secrets of Nature contained therein" (Arbatel, [1655] 1978, p. 211). All of this will make you someone who is aware of their place in the universe, who is able to interpret correctly what is happening to them in their life. As the pseudonymous Arbatel (author of the famous Renaissance treatise *Of Magick*) writes, the magician becomes someone who

understandeth when the minde doth meditate of himself; he delibereth, reasoneth, constituteth and determineth what is to be done; he observeth when his cogitations do proceed from a divine separate essence, and he proveth what order that divine separate essence is.

(p. 213)

All of this is neatly contrasted with the fate of the non-magician, who "is carried to and fro, as it were in war with his affections; he knoweth not when they issue out of his own minde, or are impressed by the assisting essence; and he knoweth not how to overthrow the counsels of his enemies by the word of God, or to keep himself from the snares and deceits of the tempter" (ibid.). In other words, even the highly elaborate magical systems of Renaissance scholarship are seen as routes to the confidence and mental strength that will allow the magician to be decisive and clear in their thinking about the universe, and avoid being blown about by the vicissitudes of a mysterious and complex world. For Hammond (1970), this is the "central concept" of magic—"the power that makes magic effective is a projection of man's capacity to act effectively by means of his knowledge and skill" (p. 1353). An understanding of the sympathetic relations in the universe reflects humanity's active stance towards nature and the environment—it is about taking control through knowledge and active comparison. The practice of magic, Hammond argues, expresses "the belief in human powers as effective forces" (p. 1355). And perhaps here it is worth remembering Gorgias' pride in the power of rhetoric. The way that it can effect ascendency in any realm of human endeavour provides a confidence to Gorgias that almost seems magical.

Which brings us to an important question. If sympathetic relations of similarity and contact are to be placed at the centre of a general description (if not a definition) of magic, where does that leave language? For language is most definitely something that seems to have an important part to play in magical practice. Words accompany the making of magical artefacts, they are inscribed upon such artefacts, they direct spirits, they banish them, and they even cajole and persuade them. For quite some time, mainstream anthropological approaches to magic "devalued the role of words in ritual which was seen as stereotyped behaviour consisting of a sequence of non-verbal acts and manipulation of objects" (Tambiah, 1968, p. 175). However, although the "ratio of words to actions may vary between rituals" (ibid.), Tambiah (1968) argues that "in most cases it would appear that ritual words are at least as important as other kinds of ritual act" (p. 176). Furthermore, he notes that even when words might seem to play a secondary role in a particular magical practice, if the performer is questioned as to what makes the ritual work it is often the case that "the reply takes the form of a formally expressed belief that the power is in the 'words' even though the words become effective only if uttered in a very special context of other action" (ibid.). Words become magically powerful when uttered in the right way in the right place at the right time, then—a perspective that is fundamentally rhetorical. Indeed, many words uttered in magical rituals can seem, when examined in isolation, to have almost no meaning—they seem to be jumbled syllables or babble. They might originate in a language unknown to the magician or the client, they might be amalgams of words from different languages, they might be almost unrecognisable mutations of snatches of older liturgies, they might be onomatopoeic creations, or entirely synthetic exoticisms. But they have a nascent power that is brought out within a particular ritual context. They are given a *perlocutionary* force, in the terminology of Austin's (1962) speech act theory. If a sentence's *locutionary* force is its function to describe something, its illocutionary force is the speaker's motivation in uttering it, its performative power. If I shout "Cthulhu's behind you!", my words have a descriptive function but they also are working as a warning (my motivation to scream these words is to warn you)—the illocutionary act is "performance of an act *in* saying something as opposed to performance of an act *of* saying something" (Austin, 1962, p. 99). The words' *perlocutionary* force, however, is the power they have to get you to do something (in this case, start running, gibbering, voiding your bowels, etc.). The perlocutionary force of words refers to the effects that those words can have, their consequences. Chlup (2007) makes the point that just because the words of magical ritual may not have any apparent locutionary force (or may have lost it over time and cultural/linguistic shifts) does not mean that they have no illocutionary or perlocutionary power. Speaking of the language of the *Hermetica* (the second century CE collection of Egyptian-Greek magical spells and invocations), Chlup (2007) argues that although it "stands beyond logic and seems incoherent", "that is not to say, though, that it becomes meaningless—only that locutionary meaning is replaced by a performative one" (p. 144). Of course, a vast amount of magical language does have locutionary as well as performative meaning and it is the play between the two that can itself produce what we might think of as the magical moment. Through the sorts of patterning, sequencing, and redundancy that Tambiah (1979) contends is typical of magical language, a "sense of heightened and intensified and fused communication" is produced (p. 140). This has a perlocutionary force, altering mental states, inducing euphoria or even "subordination to a collective representation" (p. 141). Tambiah (1979) further argues that the formal elements of magical language must be considered to work in tandem with the symbolic elements that it contains. An interesting consequence of this is that in his description of the spells of the Trobriand Islanders, Tambiah depicts a discourse which has striking similarities with rabble-rousing political rhetoric (or advertising copy, come to that):

> the formulaic pattern of the Trobriand spells insistently introduces a variety of metaphorical expressions or metonymical parts into a stereotyped stream of repeated words intoned with modulations of speed, loudness, and rhythm, thereby foregrounding them as well as telescoping or fusing them into an amalgam that is given motion and direction by compelling illocutionary words of command and persuasion or declaration.
>
> (p. 138)

I find this a remarkably powerful description not only of magical ritual but also of rhetorical force, the sort of force that Tonks (2002) claims allows marketing to *energize* exchange.

So, magic can broadly be seen as a way of trying to effect change in the world, change that is advantageous for the magician, his client, or his community. In order to effect this change magic tends to rely not upon simple appeals to divinity but instead on the performance of ritual that feature the logic of sympathy and the performative power of language. There are, of course, many other aspects to magical practice—the use of music, for example, or the construction of material artefacts. And, as Evans-Pritchard (1929) famously demonstrated, what one community's magic looks like can be quite different from another's just a few hundred miles away. Furthermore, the things that we point to and call magic change significantly over time. Smith (2004) notes, for example, that shamanism (denoting the complex of ritual practices described by ethnographers in circumpolar regions) was treated as "the very type of 'magic'" (p. 218) in most late nineteenth- and early twentieth-century works, and yet in the second half of the twentieth century it "has been transferred to the 'religious'" category. So, different communities make different judgements over time regarding what is magic and what is not. One person's religion can be another person's magic—after all, there are clear aspects of sympathetic magic in operation in traditional Christian practices, and religious ritual makes much use of illocutionary and perlocutionary speech acts. As we have seen Smith (2004) pointing out, magic is often used as a *contrast term* in academic discourse and this will inevitably mean that its boundaries and definition will change as the concepts and practices against which it is contrasted change with academic understanding, emphases, and fashion. These are problems that constantly accompany the use of the word "magic" in what Smith (2004) calls "second-order, theoretical, academic discourse" (p. 218). However, although he would wish for its simple abandonment in such discourse due to its constantly fluctuating nature, it is at the same time undeniable that "magic" also has "cross-culturally, a native, first-order category occurring in ordinary usage which has deeply influenced the evaluative language of the scholar" (p. 219). Magic is a word that is not just used by historians of religion, ethnographers, and anthropologists. All societies seem to label some sort of ritual practice as deviant, evil, discomforting, harmful, or dangerous, no matter what they might call it. This word, or collection of terms, is then used often to literally (or perhaps metaphorically) describe practices or artefacts or people that are somehow possessed of supernormal, extraordinary power or significance. In other words, the shifting, oppositional understandings of magic that are reflected in Western scholarship must always be set beside the first-order ways in which societies use the concept. It is to two of those first-order uses of the term that I will now turn.

References

Agrippa, C. ([1651] 1898). *Three Books of Occult Philosophy or Magic—Book One—Natural Magic* (trans. J. Freake; Ed. By W. Whitehead). Chicago: Hahn & Whitehead.

Albas, D., and Albas, C. (1989). Modern Magic: The Case of Examinations. *The Sociological Quarterly*, 30(4), 603–613.

Arbatel. ([1655, trans. Robert Turner] 1978). *Of Magic*. London: Askin.

Austin, J. (1962). *How to Do Things With Words*. Oxford: Clarendon Press.

Bailey, M. (2006). The Meanings of Magic. *Magic, Ritual, and Witchcraft*, 1(1), 1–23.

Bremmer, J. N. (1999). The Birth of the Term 'Magic'. *Zeitschrift Für Papyrologie Und Epigraphik*, 126, 1–12.

Chlup, R. (2007). The Ritualization of Language in the *Hermetica*. *Aries*, 7(2), 133–159.

Collins, D. (2003). Nature, Cause, and Agency in Greek Magic. *Transactions of the American Philological Association*, 133(1), 17–49.

Evans-Pritchard, E. (1929). The Morphology and Function of Magic. *American Anthropologist*, 31, 619–641.

Frazer, J. (1894). *The Golden Bough: A Study in Comparative Religion*. First Edition. New York: Macmillan (Digital Archive Version). https://archive.org/details/goldenboughstudy01fraz [Accessed August 2, 2017].

Frazer, J. (1920). *The Golden Bough: A Study in Magic and Religion*. Part 1, Vol. 1. Third Edition. London: Macmillan (Digital Archive Version). https://archive.org/details/TheGoldenBough-Part1-TheMagicArtAndTheEvolutionOfKingsVol.1 [Accessed August 20, 2017].

Geertz, H. (1975). An Anthropology of Religion and Magic, I. *The Journal of Interdisciplinary History*, 6(1), 71–89.

Greenwood, S. (2000). *Magic, Witchcraft and the Otherworld: An Anthropology*. Oxford: Berg Oxford.

Hammond, D. (1970). Magic: A Problem in Semantics. *American Anthropologist*, 72(6), 1349–1356.

Lehrich, C. (2007). *The Occult Mind: Magic in Theory and Practice*. Ithaca: Cornell University Press.

Malinowski, B. (1935). *Coral Gardens and Their Magic*. New York, NY: American Book Co.

Smith, J. (2004). *Relating Religion: Essays in the Study of Religion*. Chicago: University of Chicago Press.

Stark, R. (2001). Reconceptualizing Religion, Magic, and Science. *Review of Religious Research*, 43(2), 101–120.

Tambiah, S. (1968). The Magical Power of Words. *Man*, 3(2), 175–208.

Tambiah, S. (1979). A Performative Approach to Ritual. *Proceedings of the British Academy*, 65, 113–169.

Tonks, D. (2002). Marketing as Cooking: The Return of the Sophists. *Journal of Marketing Management*, 18(7–8), 803–822.

Wax, M., and Wax, R. (1963). The Notion of Magic. *Current Anthropology*, 4(5), 495–518.

Yates, F. (2003). *The Occult Philosophy in the Elizabethan Age*. London: Routledge.

7 The Magical Roots of Rhetoric

As we saw towards the end of the last chapter, there can often seem to be some very powerful similarities between magical practice and some understandings of the rhetorical situation. A number of modern scholars of rhetoric have noted this resemblance. Kenneth Burke (1969), for example, argues that early anthropology had failed to recognize the relationship between rhetoric and magic. The scientism implicit in the discipline had insisted on interpreting magic as primitive, misguided (and therefore 'bad') science. In reducing the interpretive field down to a simple dichotomy of 'good science' and 'bad science', Burke maintained that anthropology before Malinowski had denied rhetoric any "systematic location" (p. 41). Instead of seeing magic as an early failed science, however, Burke suggests that it would make more sense to see magic as a "primitive rhetoric" (p. 43). He argues that magic is a "mistaken transference of a proper linguistic function to an area for which it was not fit" (p. 42). The "realistic" function of language is "as a symbolic means of inducing cooperation in beings that by nature respond to symbols" (p. 43). Magic, however, is a "faulty derivation" from this realistic, rhetorical function of language, "being an attempt to produce linguistic responses in kinds of beings not accessible to the linguistic motive" (ibid.). Burke's perspective is prompted by a desire to properly place rhetoric within considerations of social anthropology and social evolution. While he still insists on seeing magic as fundamentally mistaken or "misapplied" (in a very similar way to Frazer, for example) he attempts to shift the grounds of this misapplication away from the proto-scientific realm and into the rhetorical. He is also careful to note that, though magic might be rooted in a "mistaken transference", this does not deny its rhetorical role in contributing "variously to social cohesion" (p. 44). For unlike the unforgiving binary valence of a scientific perspective ("primitive" magic is incorrect, modern science is correct), a rhetorical framing of magic allows us to detect the 'unrealistic' nature of magic while at the same time recognising the power it has to create social cohesion.

Burke's discussion of magic and rhetoric is important to us for a number of reasons. It derails longstanding debates around science and magic by insisting that magic is a form of misapplied rhetoric—the question of magic's relationship to science is therefore largely bypassed. Magical thinking as enshrined in the laws of similarity and contact might be scientifically 'false', but that does not stop magic from having a powerful social role. This might also provide us with further food for thought when reflecting upon the marketing as 'art' or 'science' controversy—perhaps it is neither, perhaps it is simply rhetoric? Precisely due to Burke's rather sketch-like development of his thesis here, he also goads us into thinking more closely about the relationship between magic and rhetoric. As we shall see, this relationship has, indeed, been pursued by some scholars attracted to the Sophistic tradition and for good reasons. However, before we venture back into Classical waters, we can prepare ourselves by considering the work of another modern rhetorical scholar who has argued for an even clearer connection between magic and rhetoric.

Covino (1992, 1994), writing from the perspective of a scholar of composition, takes as his cue the work of O'Keefe (1983) who proposed a "social theory of magic". Covino (1992) therefore starts from the assumption that "magic is not the instant and arhetorical product of an otherworldly incantation; it is the process of inducing belief and creating community with reference to the dynamics of a rhetorical situation" (p. 349). Conceiving of magic in such terms then allows us to interrogate the power matrices within rhetoric, to "analyze and critique the powers at work within the 'plain rhetoric' that mesmerizes audiences with its seeming clarity and simplicity". For Covino, modern rhetoric has been stripped of its magical power and converted into a "plain style" of "discourse prepared for mass consumption" (ibid.). This is an evolutionary consequence of the sort of exorcism of rhetorical high style that we have already talked about in connection with the Royal Society's campaign for plain style, as described by Stark (2009). Covino sees this as a reflection of "changing concepts of 'phantasy' and the limits of imagination" over time that have discouraged a "fertile, dynamic and fluctuant imagination". He (1992) argues that before the Enlightenment "distinctions between literal and figurative identity are impossible to maintain because everything is both actual and symbolic: a talisman or a word signifies magic power and *is* that power" (p. 352). This was a conception shared by "sophistic, hermetic, gnostic, cabalistic, and patristic philosophers from antiquity forward" (p. 351). Of course, this is the "mistaken transference" identified by Burke, the idea that "minds exists *in* matter and language *affects* matter" (Covino, 1992, p. 352). Covino makes much use of Vickers' (1986) distinction between the occult and the scientific traditions in Renaissance philosophy. Vickers contends that in the scientific tradition "a clear distinction is made between words and things and between literal and metaphorical language", whereas in the occult tradition "words are treated as if they are equivalent to things and can be substituted for them" (Vickers, 1986, p. 95). Vickers traces a line of scientific mistrust of the magical/occult identification of word and thing that goes all the way back to Plato. He shows how the "Platonic-Aristotelian tradition of language as conventional and arbitrary" (p. 104) found its flowering in the Renaissance philosophers of the new sciences (Bacon, Hobbes, Galileo) and culminates with the anti-rhetorical campaign of the Royal Society and Locke's description of what should constitute scientific language. While the Renaissance also saw a resurgence in the "occult tradition" of language, with figures such as Agrippa, Ficino, and Pico della Mirandola offering systematisations of the universe based upon sympathy, contagion, and the identity of word and thing, this was but a short-lived revival. By the end of the Enlightenment, the "scientific tradition" and its clear understanding of the separation between language and the natural world had become the dominant paradigm in Western intellectual thought. Covino (1992) adopts Vickers' narrative and extends it by noting the Romantic poets' efforts to "reconstitute magic/rhetoric in the Western imagination" by appealing to "the 'witchery' of language" and aiming "to reform the public imagination by defining writing as a liberatory force that can construct alternate realities" (p. 355). He then further suggests that even though the Romantic project 'lost' to the "sterile and non-magical rhetoric of 'public business'" (ibid.) it would not be correct to conclude that the connection between magic and rhetoric has been irrevocably sundered. Instead, Covino returns to O'Keefe's and Burke's argument that magical rhetoric exists in the, admittedly, "diminished cosmology" of language altering the "social situation". Citing Austin's thinking on the performative function of language, Covino (1992) goes on to state that "in the event that any of us employ powerful words to change a situation, or are ourselves changed by what we read or hear, we participate in a magical transactive transformation" (p. 355). Covino's ultimate objective is to not persuade us that rhetoric is magical, for he regards this as clearly the case, but rather to convince us that there are two broad types of magical rhetoric, one which is "repressive" and "limits the possibilities for action" (ibid.) and one which is "liberatory", "re-ordering discourse and reality" (p. 356) to create rather than restrict. Repressive rhetoric magically mesmerises the masses, lulls them into an unquestioning state of acceptance, and is characterised by a robbing of energy. Liberatory rhetoric, on the other hand, infuses an excess of energy, a creatively destructive level of energy, which feeds phantasies of possibility and serves to undercut established, rigid positions and perspectives.

For both Burke and Covino, the magical essence of rhetoric is to be found in the illocutionary and perlocutionary force that words can have upon social situations. Rhetoric can 'magically' command—in the sense that the uttering of words can function as a means of control. Covino (1992) remarks that nowhere is this more obvious than in advertising, which displays the "magic of authoritarian, simplistic incantations" (p. 356). This attitude towards the magical rhetoric of advertising will be more closely examined later in this chapter. It is worth noting for now, however, the way that Covino distinguishes between a simplistic, commanding magic and the far more positive, liberatory magic which can be generated through the undercutting of established discourse. In this he is reproducing the sort of good/bad, science/ magic, rhetorical style/plain style dichotomies that we have been meeting throughout this chapter only this time we have the dichotomy *within* rhetoric itself.

In closing this section, I wish to now return to the beginnings of rhetoric and examine the way in which the very earliest rhetorical theorists, the Sophists, connected magic and rhetoric. In earlier parts of this book, I have used the Sophists (and their reception) to examine the deep roots of marketing—once again, I will return to the Sophists to explore the early connections between rhetoric and magic. For it is with Gorgias' famous piece of display rhetoric, the *Encomium for Helen*, that we have the first clear attempts to present a relationship between these two topics.

Gorgias' aim in the *Encomium* is to "demonstrate the all-conquering power of persuasive speech" (Dylan and Gergel, 2003, p. 76). As Wardy (2005) argues, the *Encomium* "crosses genres" (p. 28)—it is at once a *forensic* defence of the figure of Helen and at the same time an *epideictic* celebration of *logos*. The core of the piece is a consideration of the what might have made Helen elope with Paris and so cause the Trojan war—as Gorgias says, "I shall set forth the causes which made it likely that Helen's voyage to Troy should take place" (Dylan and Gergel, 2003, p. 78). There are a number of options to consider—perhaps the events were controlled by Fate, or the Gods, or perhaps Helen was taken by force, or persuaded by words, or possessed by love. Gorgias considers each possibility. If the Gods or Fate swayed Helen's mind, then she is without blame as such forces are always "a stronger force than man in might and wit and on other ways" (p. 79) and cannot be resisted. If she was forced to elope with Paris, then it is clearly Paris who is to blame, for "it is plain that the rapist, as the outrager did the wronging, and the raped, as the outraged, did the suffering" (ibid.). Then Gorgias moves on to consider the possible role of speech in Helen's actions, his real motivation for the entire *Encomium*. Gorgias first describes speech as "a powerful lord, who with the finest and most invisible body achieves the most divine works: it can stop fear and banish grief and create joy and nurture pity" (ibid.). As proof of this, Gorgias considers a few different types of speech. First, there is poetry, which is just "speech possessing metre" (p. 80). Poetry can induce strong physical effects in its listeners, "fearful shuddering", "tearful pity", and "grievous longing" because "through the agency of words the soul experiences suffering of its own" (ibid.). Of course, while poetry, *per se*, is not something that modern marketers might spend much time considering as a persuasive force, what Gorgias is talking about here is the powerful effect of the artfully turned phrase in bringing to life any narrative in a way that has an emotional effect upon an audience. The next form of speech that Gorgias considers brings us finally to the subject of this section of the book, magic. He reminds us that "inspired incantations conveyed through words become bearers of pleasure and banishers of pain" (ibid.) and they do this by 'beguiling' and 'persuading' the "opinion in the soul".

Furthermore, Gorgias states that the "twin arts" of "witchcraft and magic" rely upon the "the errors of the soul and deceptions of opinion". Gorgias' understanding of what magic is and how it works is extremely rhetorical in approach. Indeed, he then moves directly on from stating that magic takes advantage of a "deception of opinion" to discussing persuasive speech in general in the same terms. As we are unable to remember the past in perfect clarity, "consider the present" or "divine the future" we always find ourselves relying upon our opinion when making decisions. Opinion, though, is "slippery and insecure" and can be taken advantage of by those seeking to influence and persuade us. We hardly ever know the truth of a matter and so use our opinions to guide us, and that is reasonable because that is what we, as mortals, have access to. But, in relying upon opinion, we let ourselves open to the poetic, magical and persuasive forces of speech that can constrain the soul. If Helen were influenced, "against her will", by the power of Paris' speech, she would have been overpowered "just as if ravished by the force of pirates" (p. 81). There is no difference, Gorgias is arguing, between the constraint imposed by physical rape and that imposed by the influence of language. In either case, Helen is innocent of blame. Finally, Gorgias compares the power of speech over the soul with the power of drugs over the body. Some drugs can act for good and heal the body by getting rid of harmful secretions and are able to cure disease, while others can have quite the opposite effect and be used to end life. So it is with the power of speech, which can be used to "delight" or "embolden" the soul or to "distress" it, to "drug and bewitch the soul with a kind of evil persuasion" (p. 81). Speech as drug (*pharmakon*), speech as poetry, speech as magic, speech as persuasion—in the *Encomium*, Gorgias is, as Wardy (2005) observes, "at work on systematically obliterating distinctions between logoi" (p. 41). All speech that seeks to influence an audience (whether this is an audience who has elected to view a drama, someone who seeks out a witch or magician to effect a goal, the voters of an assembly, or the customers of a retailer) are manipulated through the power of speech to affect the soul through opinion. And through the soul, one affects the body. In praising the power of speech (while ostensibly seeking to shift blame from Helen), Gorgias, of course, is giving the more specific message that it is the rhetor who wields this power in society. Indeed, the conclusion of the speech makes it clear that the speech itself serves to demonstrate the power of rhetoric. Gorgias states that "I have through speech removed ill fame from a woman"—and this is not just any woman but one who had become a by-word in his society for treachery. The success of his rhetorical argumentation in favour of Helen works as *proof* of the remarkable, bewitching power of speech. As Wardy (2005) cogently summarises it—"when we ourselves are made to pity Helen and execrate Paris, are persuaded (perhaps) that persuasion is manipulation, enjoy the deception with which Gorgias amuses us even as we discern it, we feel in our own souls the seduction of rhetoric" (p. 51). The *Encomium* is an exercise in magico-rhetorical persuasion, a demonstration of how our souls can be led by the manipulation of opinion, bewitched by language.

De Romilly (1975), in her influential treatise on the links between magic and rhetoric in ancient Greece, has written convincingly of the way in which Gorgias' own style reflects liturgical or magical incantation. She traces a line of development in which poets began to use the style of religious chant and magical incantation in their verses in order to produce a magical effect. From the example of the poets, then, the early rhetors began to use the same techniques in order to spellbind their audiences and achieve their rhetorical goals. De Romilly (1975) notes that Gorgias was the pupil of Empedocles, a philosopher who was renowned both as a magician and as a poet, and who chose to convey his philosophical teaching in poetry of the "inspired style" (p. 14). Indeed, some authors have argued that Empedocles is more correctly understood as a magical, shamanistic figure rather than as a philosopher at all (Kingsley, 1996). Furthermore, in Gorgias' culture there was much fluidity between the concepts and practices surrounding of poetry, drama, sacred ritual, and magic. As de Romilly (1975) points out, one of the Greek words used by Gorgias for magic, ψυχαγωγειν, was "first used for the magical ritual of summoning the dead" (p. 15), but it also came to be used to describe tragic poetry, a form which "possesses and beguiles the listener's soul" (ibid.). Later still, she notes, Plato uses the word to define rhetoric when he has Socrates ask in the *Phaedrus*, "isn't the rhetorical art, taken as a whole, a way of directing the soul by means of speech, not only in the lawcourts and on other public occasions but also in private?" (261a)—the word is here translated by Nehamas and Woodruff as "directing the soul". It seems reasonable to let this fluidity of meaning point to some fundamental similarities of understanding regarding the relationship between magic, poetry and rhetoric.

But what characterises this magical style of language? If poetry, tragedy, magic, and rhetoric can all display similar effects (direction of the soul) what is the nature of the language that they use to do it? De Romilly (1975), through a comparison of poetry and tragic verse that was designed to imitate magical incantation as well as ancient Greek sacred liturgy and Gorgias' own rhetorical style, outlines "the means of magic" (p. 16). In listing them we find a startling similarity to those figures examined by the advertising researchers we have discussed above. There is the "haunting repetition of words" (p. 17), the "play on similar forms of words, equal in length and structure", "obstinate" rhythmic patterns, alliteration, rhyme. De Romilly notes that Gorgias' originality of rhetorical style was to be found in his use of just these devices, which "were meant to subdue the audience and produce in the listeners' souls such and such a feeling" and which "derived from the wonderful power that they had in magic song and that some poets had already imitated with a thrilling and impressive effect" (p. 19).

Importantly, it must be understood that de Romilly (1975) is not claiming that Gorgias' use of magical language means that his *rhetoric is magic*. Rather than this simple identification, she argues that Gorgias, "while emulating the magician" sought to change "magic into something rational" (p. 20) precisely by making it an art, a *techne*, something to be taught and to be used in public (and commercial life). In other words, rhetoric is an evolved, rational, practical instantiation of the magical power of speech. Gorgias, argues de Romilly, seeks to elevate this power of speech away from its dark, inspired, irrational roots, into a systematic, teachable, secularised technique—a technique that will allow its possessor to persuade and constrain the soul of the audience. Yet, in attempting to make use of the magical patterns of language while loosening it from the influence of the irrational, inspired essence of magic, de Romilly (1975) argues that Gorgias originated the separation that was to so obsess philosophers from Plato on—the division between the irrational or the magical and the rational or empirical— between science and magic. In admitting that "the very principle of the art of speech was to deceive" (p. 25), Gorgias, the epitome of the rhetorical magus, thus sows the seeds of Plato's critique of rhetoric and magic (as well as poetry and tragedy) as practices that threaten to hide the truth rather than expose it, a critique which goes on to become fundamentally embedded in the Western intellectual enterprise.

This division, as we have already seen, has been tremendously powerful over the millennia since Gorgias' death. Modern science was in many ways born from attempts to expunge magical rhetorical style from natural philosophy. It defined itself in opposition to philosophy couched in the 'high' style that made use of metaphor, metonymy, incantatory patternings, and matrices of symbolism. The Royal Society's promotion of a plain style for scientific discourse is an attempt to ground intellectual exploration in concrete certainties, to move it on from the spiritual, and magical, systems of contagion and sympathy that had come to dominate it in the Renaissance. Language had to be stripped of its magical power if it was to be used to describe the world as it actually was. It is, then, clear that while Gorgias might have inadvertently instantiated this central split in the Western understanding of how we see and explain the world, and while Plato might have then set out the battle lines in the clearest way possible, the division between science and magic has been continuing back and forth ever since. It was not won with Plato, it was not won with the Royal Society, it was not won with Logical Positivism, and it most certainly was not won with Shelby Hunt.

Indeed, when we consider the division by looking all the way back to Gorgias, perhaps it is no longer surprising that marketing has been so obsessed with it. In Gorgias we see the attempt to marry magic and rationality in the service of a flexible, practical, public persuasion. Marketing, as I have been arguing, is the true heir to this system of persuasion. But it is also heir to the inherent tension between rationality and irrationality, between empirical systematisation and bewitching ritual, between science and art, between sober prescriptivism and inspired improvisation, that lies at the heart of Gorgias' enterprise. I would therefore suggest that marketing will never be able to resolve this tension and still do the job of marketing. The tension is implicit within its nature. It was, perhaps, the case that Gorgias himself understood these tensions and was comfortable with them. His teacher, Empedocles, after all, saw the universe as subject to the two opposing forces of Love and Strife which in their interchange form "a ceaseless round, sure and unmoving in the style of a circle" (trans. Lombardo, 2010, p. 36). The broader Sophist pedagogical approach rested upon the use of contradiction and shifting reversals as embodied in the *dissoi logoi* and the *kata-ballontes* of Protagoras (Cassin, 2014). The dichotomy between seeing words as tools of magical inspiration, on the one hand, and the means for plain empirical description, on the other, is not a dichotomy for the Gorgian tradition because they are both at the service of the persuasive power of communication.

Aristotle attempts to re-write Socratic rhetoric as a pure *techne* without recourse to magical inspiration or bewitching seduction of the irrational— a one-sided rhetoric, as it were. De Romilly argues that such purgative attempts are never entirely successful, that there remains a resistant line of magical rhetoric that longs "for things that Aristotle cast away (1975, p. 77). The struggle between the two trends can be discerned "in all literatures and at all times" (p. 85), though, notes de Romilly, none of those movements standing as alternatives to the Aristotelian paradigm ever tried to return entirely to the *pre*-Gorgian state of language, "counting only on magic and on inspiration" (p. ibid.). Well, none until "our present time". For, de Romilly is convinced that, with the early years of the twentieth century, (manifesting initially in Symbolist poetry and then in the Surrealists) some movements appeared that attempted to do just that—treat language as if it were entirely magical. She suggests that this resurgence came from the "most irrational of all sources" (p. 86), the unconscious self expressing itself in "spontaneous language" via automatic processes, such as Breton's 'magic dictation' and Dali's 'paranoiac critical' method. The punning that was such a feature of Gorgias' style becomes endemic across the Surrealists and those influenced by their paradigm. Structuralists and postmodernists abandon the pretence that language is objective and transparent and instead celebrate the infinite, shifting diversity of interpretation and connotation.

Heady stuff, and fascinating to muse upon. However, as we shall see, some writers anchor this return of the magical rather earlier and in a more, shall we say, prosaic *milieu*—the marketing and advertising that evolves with the industrial revolution. For them, advertising *is* magic and they mean it in a most distinctively pejorative way. Before we move on to deliberate upon the reasons these critics have for linking the two so strongly, it is worth thinking about the way that magic and rhetoric are linked to control.

Magic, Control, and Rhetoric

In his examination of de Romilly's thesis, Ward (1988) focuses upon the way in which the 'oscillating pendulum' of our view of language manifested itself in medieval and Renaissance cultures. Centrally, he argues that in the Renaissance we can discern an "association between rhetoric/*techne* and 'control,' and on the other side, an association between rhetoric/magic and 'emotional power'" (p. 66). In other words, the Aristotelian tradition (as de Romilly sees it) of constructing rhetoric as a technique cleansed of subjectivity and irrationality is supported by, adopted by, promoted by, and rewarded by the forces of authority and governance. This, in turn, "implies restriction of persuasive rhetorical capacities to approved channels" (ibid.). The rhetoric of "emotional power", on the other hand, is a disruptive force anchored in the "incantatory, metaphoric, poetic mode" and represents a challenge to official forces of governance and prescription, particularly, Ward argues, because it tends to "traffic with occult systems" marginalised by those forces. Those employing the rhetoric of 'emotional power' are inevitably to be found in somewhat insecure vocational and socio-economic positions, reliant upon the vicissitudes of court patronage, rather than in institutional appointments. Importantly, rhetoric as an instrument of 'control' is a *response* to the unpredictable, ungovernable 'emotional power' of rhetoric. For Ward (1988) the medieval and Renaissance "clerical attack on sorcery, demonology, and witchcraft" is motivated by the threat that such practices "imply for the clerical establishment's control of the supernatural" (p. 67). This is the same motivation for the establishment's 'demonising' of the practitioner of rhetoric of 'emotional power', the "free rhetor". The supernatural, the irrational, the ungovernable, or that beyond governance—these are all different faces of the same thing for both the rhetor of control/*techne* and the free rhetor. For there are inevitably 'leaky boundaries' between the two, loci of convergence and interaction. Most significantly, as Ward states, "an interest in rhetoric as magic stimulates an interest in rhetoric as *techne*, in rhetoric as mode of control, and the interaction serves to focus attention on the irrational on the part of both practitioners and controllers" (ibid.). Those on the margins of court society, seeking influence (and so security) in precarious positions might seek to control aspects of their fortune through magic and through free rhetoric. At the same time, those in positions of control and authority will be attentive to just the same things for the threat that they pose—efforts at regulation and prescription will be focused upon the bounding and cleansing of the irrational, the magical, the inspired. Rhetoric as control/*techne*, therefore, becomes an effort to redirect and restrict attention away from something that many in precarious positions in society find themselves drawn to. One cannot help but be reminded of those passages in Plato's *Laws* that sought to prescribe the interface of the good citizens of Magnetes with the corrupting, unbalancing, irrational forces of the market.

These two different rhetorics—magical and official, inspired and prescribed, irrational and rational—are united in the matter of control, but see it from quite different perspectives. The outsider sees instruments of control as ways to break in, to reverse fortune, to slip the shackles of authority in order to share in authority. Magic is something that can help one achieve political or commercial influence when one doesn't have it, disempower those that you believe are holding your cause back, uncover those who plot against you, make you valuable in the eyes of others, heal you of ailments without doubtful recourse to the medical profession, aid in returning stolen things to you, and even make you invisible (*vide* the *Clavicula Salomonis* and *Le Grimoire du Pape Honorius*). It can make your gun always shoot on target, allow you to travel at twice or three times normal speed (vide *Le Grande Grimoire*), and it can impart the knowledge of all the sciences and arts to you without study, expense or discomfort (*vide* the *Ars Notoria*). And, of course, it can make someone fall in love with you (*vide* virtually every book of magic ever printed). Such diverse objectives reflect a common sense of insecurity. Other people, institutions, fate, conspire against the practitioner of magic—their ritual actions are designed to redress the balance, ease their passage through an uncertain society in which they do not have the status or wealth to function in the way that they would wish to. Other people have vast learning, that is why they are successful, so I should use magic to invoke in myself such learning; other people have access to great money in order to make their way in the world, so I can use magic to find some buried treasure and I will be their equal; others have great influence, knowing the right people and able to put the right word in the right ear, so if I am invisible perhaps I will also be able to hear the right secrets to give myself an advantage. Reading through the European grimoires is an exercise in opening oneself up to a vast dissatisfaction and anxiety with the way the human world works. It is also difficult to not study these texts without realising how much marketing has acted as a substitute for the value propositions of the magicians.

The other rhetoric is the rhetoric of *techne*, of rational, prescribing officialdom. Control here is more clearly concerned with exorcising the irrational, the unusual, the poetic, the inspired. It is this form of control that concerns court and government bureaucracy; it is the institutional attempt to keep discourse within sober, measured stylings that reflect the certainty and groundedness of evidenced procedures. This is the plain style of the Royal Society, the first person plural posture of academic writing, and the logical argumentation of 'reasoned' dialogue. As Ward (1988) argues, this form of rhetoric is ironically also obsessed with magic and the rhapsodic—but as the Other which it exists in order to bar the door to.

Ward's (1988) distinctions, themselves inspired by de Romilly's (1975) depiction of the oscillating nature of Gorgian and Aristotelian perspectives through the centuries, are echoed slightly differently in Cole's (1995) thesis regarding the origins of rhetoric in ancient Greece. Despite the common portrait of rhetoric's unbroken, though subtly transforming, historical evolution, Cole starkly contends that rhetoric (as conceived of by the ancient Greeks) has become non-existent in the academy. Authors such as Kenneth Burke, Ch. Perelman, I. A. Richards, Wayne Boothe, and the countless scholars who have participated in the many disciplinary 'rhetorical turns' over the past century are instead characterised as "neorhetoricians" or "antirhetoricians" (Cole, 1995, p. 20) who have fundamentally misunderstood what rhetoric is. They have sought to turn rhetoric into "an art of practical reasoning concerned not simply with mastering, as need arises, premises drawn from ethics, politics, psychology, or wherever, but making significant additions on its own to the total store of wisdom" (ibid.). The modern approach to rhetoric has resulted in a discipline "aggrandized beyond recognition" with only a "superficial resemblance" to ancient rhetoric. While, naturally, most scholars involved in rhetorical studies today might see Cole's position as highly contentious, it is interesting to place it alongside Ward's (1988) arguments and wonder whether "neorhetoric" is, in fact, another example of the rational, bureaucratic *techne* rather than the rhapsodic, inspired magic of rhetoric. Perhaps there is a danger that rhetoric as taught from the perspective of the neorhetoricians becomes a controlling, prescriptive force designed to place strict bounds upon what should be encouraged in 'civil discourse'. After all, is it not the job of first-year composition to instil a largely uniform, approved set of argumentation skills in the student body? And while a student (a good one) might be able to *identify* the Gorgian style, would they feel encouraged to *use* it in their university discourse?

Although Cole (1995) is quite adamant that the academy is not the place to look for genuine rhetoric anymore, he does suggest that the spirit of ancient rhetoric lives on it two modern arenas. He notes that "virtually the only areas where rhetoric is still vigorously practiced are those of propaganda and advertising, and the low esteem in which those arts are generally held, even by their practitioners, is yet another testimony to the antirhetorical character of our times" (p. 22). From this perspective, the reluctance of the rhetorical studies establishment to engage with marketing, which I have discussed above, might therefore be unsurprising if marketing is a re-instantiation of the Sophistic, the Gorgian, approach to the power of the word/*logos* as opposed to the Platonic and Aristotelian, bureaucratic orientation towards rhetoric as prescribed civil discourse.

Cassin (2014) also talks of a similar sort of dichotomy between Sophism and the Platonic/Aristotelian construction of rhetoric. She claims that "rhetoric is a philosophical invention, an attempt to tame *logos*, in particular the Sophist's *logos* and its effects" (p. 76). Gorgias himself, in his words that have come down to us, never uses the word rhetoric. He talks of magic, he talks of persuasion, he talks of speech—but his focus is *logos*, the power of words. It is only with Plato, in *Gorgias*, that the term rhetoric/*rhêtorikê* arises (Schiappa, 1990) and when it does it is presented so cunningly and skilfully by Plato "that the word, and the thing, seem to have been there long before Gorgias" (Cassin, 2014, p. 77). For Cassin, Plato's creation of 'rhetoric' is designed to take control over what is allowed and what should be kept outside. It is about boundaries, again—those strictures and structures that, as we have seen, so obsess Plato. His strategy in *Gorgias* is to control the Sophistic power of *logos* by creating a term, 'rhetoric'/*rhêtorikê* which he can then define into two clear disciplines. First is the rhetoric of the Sophists, which Plato "discards, devalues, annihilates, phantomatizes" (p. 79). Then, in the *Phaedrus*, Plato offers up a vision of what proper rhetoric should be, which is the philosophical pursuit of dialectic. In this way, Cassin argues, "philosophy may take possession of rhetoric" (p. 80) yet at the same time manages to destroy it—"rhetoric vanishes as rhetoric [. . .] two rhetorics, one good, and one bad, make zero rhetoric" (ibid.).

For Cassin (2014), Plato's fundamental motivation in this aggressive, destructive 're-branding' of Sophistic *logos* is to excise the performative power of language from influence in public life. The fact that "logos does things outside the subject, in the world" (p. 78) is not acceptable to Plato. Sophistic *logos* provides language with "the upper hand with respect to the object" (p. 79), it "crafts the objects" of attention. In the political arena this leads us to "manipulating evidence in order not to deal with preexistent proofs but to contrive new types of obviousness" (ibid.). It is this prospect that "Plato had to tame and to challenge with philosophy" (ibid.).

It is also this power that connects so clearly into the realm of magic, that affords *logos* the ability to create and manipulate reality. That allows words to 'add value' to the objects *out there* by changing the way we understand them, think of them, place them in our thoughts. This is clearly the realm of marketing communication, of branding, of marketing strategy, the whole marketing enterprise. A realm which is considered of too little esteem (to use Cole's term) for rhetoric scholars to concern themselves with, focused as they are upon the arena of the political (broadly defined), yet which has slowly but surely 'leaked' into civic discourse, passed into its very core, suffused it entirely so that to speak of marketing and politics as separate is to make a wilful category mistake. The political realm that had to be kept pure from the performative power of Sophistic logos has entirely succumbed to the masked Sophism of marketing.

In the next chapter, we shall examine a number of key texts that have sought to argue that marketing is, indeed, magical. Some of these texts are deeply Platonic in their attitude towards what Moore (2014) has memorably called "representational legerdemain" (p. 124), and most of them use the identification of marketing and magic in a pejorative way, but all of them can be read as essentially conflating their accusations of magic with accusations of Sophistic rhetorical practice.

References

Burke, K. (1969). *A Rhetoric of Motives*. Berkeley, CA: University of California Press.

Cassin, B. (2014). *Sophistical Practice: Towards a Consistent Relativism*. Oxford: Oxford University Press.

Cole, T. (1995). *The Origins of Rhetoric in Ancient Greece*. Baltimore: John Hopkins University Press.

Covino, W. A. (1992). Magic And/As Rhetoric: Outlines of a History of Phantasy. *Journal of Advanced Composition*, 12(2), 349–358.

Covino, W. A. (1994). *Magic, Rhetoric, and Literacy: An Eccentric History of the Composing Imagination*. Albany, NY: State University of New York Press.

de Romilly, J. (1975). *Magic and Rhetoric in Ancient Greece*. Cambridge, MA: Harvard University Press.

Dylan, J., and Gergel, T. (2003). *The Greek Sophists*. London: Penguin.

Kingsley, P. (1996). *Ancient Philosophy, Mystery, and Magic: Empedocles and Pythagorean Tradition*. Oxford: Oxford University Press.

Lombardo, S. (trans.). (2010). *Parmenides and Empedocles: The Fragments in Verse Translation*. Eugene, OR: Wipf & Stock.

Moore, K. R. (2014). Plato's Puppets of the Gods: Representing the Magical, the Mystical and the Metaphysical. *Arion*, 22(2), 37–72.

O'Keefe, D. (1983). *Stolen Lightning: The Social Theory of Magic*. New York: Vintage.

Schiappa, E. (1990). Did Plato Coin Rhetorike? *American Journal of Philology*, 111(4), 457–470.

Stark, R. (2009). *Rhetoric, Science, and Magic in Seventeenth-Century England*. Washington, DC: Catholic University of America Press.

Vickers, B. (1986). Analogy Versus Identity: The Rejection of Occult Symbolism, 1580–1680. In B. Vickers (Ed.), *Occult and Scientific Mentalities in the Renaissance*. Cambridge: Cambridge University Press, 95–163.

Ward, J. O. (1988). Magic and Rhetoric From Antiquity to the Renaissance: Some Ruminations. *Rhetorica*, 6(1), 57–118.

Wardy, R. (2005). *The Birth of Rhetoric: Gorgias, Plato and Their Successors*. London: Routledge.

8 Magical Persuasion and Marketing

The identification of marketing (or the communicative aspects of it, if one chooses to make such a distinction) with magic is one that has been promoted by a number of scholars. Sometimes this conflation is argued for pejorative reasons and adopts stereotypes regarding magic, witchcraft, and sorcery that have clear origins in the Western Enlightenment project—if marketing is magic then it is fakery, delusion, 'primitive' in some sense, irrational. Sometimes we find scholars identifying aspects of marketing and consumption with magic from a more ethnographic perspective, focused on trying to delineate the ways in which traditional or folkloric magic practices live on within, or have been adopted by, the modern marketing system. Occasionally, we find scholars who throw all caution to the wind and argue that the profession of marketing truly is the modern version of magic and practitioners and scholars would all be the better for it if they accepted the reality of their status as magicians. In this section, I shall explore these various scholarly traditions and argue that they all share an understanding of magic which is tightly bound to Gorgias' elision of speech magic and persuasion and, while some might be motivated by suspicion and others by the spirit of celebration, they all nevertheless help to underline the strong connection between magic, Sophistic rhetoric, and marketing.

Before starting an analysis of the scholarly tradition of identifying magic and marketing it is worth acknowledging that phrases such as "advertising magic" and "marketing magic" have been in use since at least the early 1900s. A Google Ngram search of "advertising magic", for example, reveals that writers in the early trade press such as *Advertising & Selling* were occasionally complaining that clients and the public talked unreasonably about "advertising magic". At the same time, advertising and sales authors have not been beyond using the comparison to drum up enthusiasm themselves—L. Daniel Shields' book *The Magic of Creative Selling* (1961) is a typical example of this hyperbolic genre, in which every sales technique presented by the author is promised to work "like magic" for (or should that be 'upon'?) the reader. And let us not forget Steve Jobs' "works like magic" keynote for the original iPhone (as well as the 'magic mouse', magic keyboard', and 'magic trackpad' still on sale for Apple). In other words, magic has been a common point of comparison, a frequently used metaphor and simile, within the post-industrialised *consumptionscape*.

At the same time, a Google Ngram search for the phrase 'like magic' will quickly disabuse us of the notion that magic and the marketplace are *uniquely* linked in the popular imagination. 'Magic' is commonly used as a comparator whenever something occurs which evades rational explanation or exceeds expectation whether in the realms of engineering, sales, hockey, horse riding, or hotels. However, there is an important difference between describing something as being 'like magic' and accusing people of practicing magic. Allegations of witchcraft, sorcery, and magic have been common in most cultures throughout history precisely because most cultures have tended to marginalise and outlaw those who are suspected of causing *malificium*, or harm through magic. A UNHCR report (Schnoebelen, 2009) on witchcraft allegations and human rights makes it clear that such claims are still very much a part of everyday life in many parts of the world. They are often connected to periods of "rapid cultural or social change" (p. 4) and can "profoundly impact" (p. 2) individuals, families, and communities. The "period of 'witch-hunting'" in Europe, roughly between the 1450s and 1750s, was a time that "saw the high point not only of witchcraft as a criminal offence but also of magic as a serious intellectual pursuit" (Ankerloo and Clark, 2002, p. vii). Yet even those (normally, male and educated) who studied 'magic' as an intellectual pursuit needed to be careful of accusations of practicing witchcraft and sorcery which could get them thrown out of universities, or result in their losing valuable patronages. Figures such as John Dee and Cornelius Agrippa, highly visible authors involved in the publishing of work on the 'occult sciences', had to constantly dodge such accusations throughout their lives. The motivations for accusations of magic and witchcraft have been widely explored in the literature, and there are clearly cultural differences that can affect the details. Mainland European witch trials, for example, particularly those in France and Spain, often concerned themselves with a construction of witchcraft that focused around heresy and the devil's pact, while witch trials in England generally centred upon the harm that a witch was said to have done to others (Thomas, 1991). In general, however, when someone accuses someone else of engaging in magic or witchcraft, it carries with it a clear sense of transgression, of crossing boundaries either in terms of what is acceptable from a dominant spiritual/religious paradigm or from what is considered socially acceptable behaviour. The witch, the magician, is always 'outside', and an accusation serves to formally identify the accused as an outsider.

It is important to remember the longstanding link between the legal/social act of accusation and the tradition of magic, sorcery, and witchcraft. As we have already seen, the 'shadow' tradition of magical, rhapsodic, inspired Gorgian rhetoric has often found itself at odds with the bureaucratic force of dialectical plain-speaking. Part of the history of that constant tension is the way in which the institutions of order, of standardisation, of administration attempt to marginalise the persuasive force of Gorgian/Sophistic rhetoric by accusing it of links to magic and the irrational. The first set of scholars that I will be looking at in this section can be characterised as 'accusers'—they are accusing advertising and marketing of being magic in a manner that makes it very clear that they mean this pejoratively. Advertising, according to these thinkers, has crossed important boundaries, it has transgressed, and while there is no call for capital punishment, the implication is that it, and the system that breeds it, should be shunned by society.

Raymond Williams—Advertising as Magic

Raymond Williams' (1980) essay 'Advertising: the magic system' is an often reproduced and well-cited example of the way in which magic can be used as a pejorative rhetorical comparison for the marketing enterprise. Indeed, it demonstrates a clearly disparaging attitude towards magic, advertising, and rhetoric. All of these things are examples of transgressions—against reality, against truth, against humanity, and against good taste. Williams is a foundational figure in UK cultural studies and the paradigm that he brings to his discussion of advertising (and magic) is that of Marxism. For him, "modern advertising" is formed in response to "certain characteristics of the new 'monopoly' (corporate) capitalism" (p. 177) that emerged in the last decades of the nineteenth century. Williams argues that the Great Depression made industrialists fearful of the downward effect on prices of productive capacity. As a result of that fear, industries began to behave a lot more conservatively, reorganizing "ownership into larger units and combines" and seeking to control as far as possible the market via such tools as tariffs, price-fixing, cartels, and advertising. For it is at this point in history, Williams contends, that advertising begins to switch from being a relatively small industry focused predominantly on serving the press (by selling space in newspapers and periodicals) to a vastly more powerful sector working for the manufacturers. So, modern advertising, as Williams puts it, "belongs to the system of market-control" and was soon recast as a "necessary part of the economy" (p. 178) rather than a disreputable profession with its roots in mountebanks and patent medicine quackery.

The real significance of advertising becomes realised, however, only during the First World War. Williams states that it was in the war environment, when "not a market but a nation had to be controlled and organized, yet in democratic conditions and without some of the older compulsions, that new kinds of persuasion were developed and applied" (p. 180). Most importantly, these new forms of persuasion revolved around the "entry into basic personal relationships and anxieties". After the war, the advertising industry integrated the "old methods of the quack and the new methods of psychological warfare". Although this evolution in market control was noted by social commentators and intellectuals of the time, producing a fair amount of criticism and alarm, Williams notes that the response of the advertising agencies was to simply develop "a knowing, sophisticated, humorous advertising" which served to forestall the critical voice by making its claims "either casual and offhand or so ludicrously exaggerated" (p. 181) that to take them too seriously would be to invite ridicule upon oneself. By the time that Williams was originally writing his essay in the 1960s, advertising had become not just an aspect of the market but an "organized extending system, at the centre of our public lives", the financial heart of modern media organizations, a "teacher of social and personal values", the "official art of modern capitalist society", and employed "perhaps the largest organized body of writers and artists, with their attendant managers and advisers, in the whole society" (p. 184). Having established this portrait of advertising's fundamental presence throughout the modern world, Williams begins his argument regarding the magical nature of the advertising system.

Instead of reasoning that advertising promotes a damagingly materialist understanding of life, Williams adopts a quite different tack, beginning with the conviction that "our society is quite evidently not materialist enough" (p. 185). Advertising has a power over us only because modern capitalist society's focus on consumption has left us with many aspects of our lives which do not satisfy us. Consumption cannot satisfy many of our social needs such as respect, friendship, quiet to reflect, etc. For Williams, advertising "operates to preserve the consumption ideal from the criticism inexorably made of it by experience" (p. 188), by magically associating the consumption of a product with "human desires to which it has no real reference" (p. 189). Advertising persuasion is focused on making magical associations—drink this beer and you will have these sorts of friends, drive this car and you will experience this sort of satisfaction with your life, etc. If we were not enchanted into thinking of ourselves as consumers and seeing everything around us as a consumption opportunity, we would be able to engage with the real material aspect of our environment and our place within it. We would appreciate beer for what it does for us physically rather than for what advertisers have persuaded it can do for us in terms of our social needs. Advertising magic "obscures the real sources of general satisfaction" because these undermine the workings of modern capital society. If we really understood what provides the sorts of social needs that advertising claims the consumption of products and services does then we would no longer perform (or be content to think of ourselves) as consumers. Advertising (and the general marketing industry that directs it) is designed to obscure the truth from people using a combination of traditional rhetorical trickery and modern psychological warfare to reach into the personal lives of the population and weave spells of consumption as eternal satisfaction.

Williams' accusation of magical practice here is being used metaphorically, we might argue. It is not that he considers advertising to be actual magic, but rather that he is using the term as way of explaining the sort of glamourising effect that advertising has upon the populace, hiding reality from them. However, that is precisely what Williams would consider magic to be, anyway. He is comparing the way that advertising functions in his society with the function served by "magical systems in simpler societies" (p. 185). For Williams, magic as identified by anthropologists and magic as identified by him in advertising are "functionally very similar", revolving around "magical inducements and satisfactions" as a means of control. Yet, Williams' own rhetoric is far from the attempted objective, non-judgemental observation of anthropological description. It is quite clear to any reader that the identification of advertising and magic is designed to damn the former via the latter's associations with trickery, illusion, pariahship, and, perhaps, even the resonant implications of the devil's pact. Of course, from Williams' point of view the magic of advertising is being used by the dominant bureaucracy of modern capitalism to generate, maintain, and control consumer culture. Williams' accusation of magic therefore appears almost entirely opposite in its framing to Ward's (1988) narrative of the 'plain rhetoric' of the control-obsessed bureaucracy attempting to outlaw the rhapsodic, magical rhetoric of the Gorgian/Sophist margin-dweller. Rather, Williams is the plain-speaking critical voice speaking out against the dominating enchanted/ enchanting magical rhetoric of the modern market—a quite Platonic voice, then. This is underlined by the way in which he links the more Gorgian side of rhetoric with the traditional quackery of advertising. He comments on the "commercial purple", "puff", and "hack verses" (p. 174) used by the advertising writers of the nineteenth century and then uses "puffing" (p. 183) as a general term to describe the techniques of twentieth-century agencies such as motivational research and market study. Like magic, puffing metaphorically resonates with the techniques of trickery, of blowing air into something to make it seem larger, fresher, more impressive. Williams early on describes the creation of "puffment" as the intense use of "all the traditional forms of persuasion, and of cheating and lying" (p. 172), making use of a despairing diary entry by Johnson from 1758 in which the writer noted the "sublime and sometimes pathetik" eloquence that advertisers had perfected for their copy. The figure of the plain-speaking, educated, sensible man railing against the dubious rhetoric of an army of persuaders who revel in the overheated sublime and the hyperbolic promise is an interesting trope. And it is, of course, a trope—we have seen many times now how those speaking against the persuasive rhapsodies of rhetoric and the enchanting subversions of magic are using their own carefully crafted rhetorical spells. What is important, here, is the way in which Williams characterises the practice of rhetorical and psychologically informed persuasion as magic in order to tar it with the brush of illusion and enchantment. Magic is bad and used for control—so, if advertising is a form of magic then it too is bad and being used for control. In the afterword to the essay (dated 1969), Williams notes that while many people complain that advertising is "vulgar or superficial, that it is unreliable, that it is intrusive", such criticism has only a marginal effect and is of a nature that the industry can "take in its stride" (p. 193). The implication is that only when people begin to realise the truth of his own position, that advertising exists to respond "to the gap between expectation and control by a kind of organized fantasy", will a significant mass of opinion begin to have a chance in combatting the veil of illusion that marketing has spread over the world in the service of capital's relentless need for control of the market.

Williams' (1980) essay obtains much of its (rhetorical) persuasiveness from the historical narrative that he constructs around advertising's evolution. He makes it clear to us at the start that he is doing "the real business of the historian of advertising" (p. 170), hunting down the objective facts in a practical manner which ironically uses the metaphor of commerce to promote a sense of empirical, grounded *work*. The story that he goes on to present frames advertising proper (as opposed to simple "notices") as arising from the "enthusiastic announcements" used to hawk "remedies and specifics" (p. 171) and freak shows. In other words, advertising is born in the margins of commercial life, with peddlers, mountebanks, and carnies, where fantasy and magic have always had an important place. Travelling sellers of cure-all pills and tonics are just a step away from the wandering magi, after all. As Williams notes, the "most extravagant early extensions" of the language of recommendation came early on from those selling medicines, which we should not forget is the traditional preserve of the magical φαρμακον (drugs) and φιλτρον (potions). Indeed, Gorgias' comparison of the power of words over the mind with the power of drugs over the body is so strongly embedded into the latter part of the *Encomium* that Wardy (2005, p. 46) describes it as an 'assimilation' of logos to the realm of "irresistible" drugs. We have also seen in Plato's *Gorgias* how the Sophist is depicted as enthralled with the power that his words have in the persuasion of patients. Of course, Williams (1980) has no intention of impugning the solidly empirical Western medical tradition. Once again, we can interpret him as a child of Plato, careful to "insist on a sharp distinction between healing doctor and amoral wizard" and denying "that the rhetorician deserves comparison with the doctor *properly* understood" (Wardy, 2005, p. 46). The 'extended' language used to persuasively promote cure-alls and patent medicines is, instead, the province of the "quack", whose only real ability is, as with Gorgias, an understanding of the power of *logos* and how to use it to connect to people's minds.

Born in the shadier, more magical, margins of pseudo-medical salesmanship, then, advertising is slippery and liminal from its inception. It seems to attach itself almost parasitically to the rise of modern capitalism in Williams' (1980) narrative. It is the perfect complement to industrialised production's increasing need for market control—so much so, indeed, that one almost begins to wonder whether it is advertising that is using capitalism. Perhaps what Williams is unknowingly describing is the revenge of the marginalised Gorgian rhapsodic rhetoric, a sort of survival instinct of the Sophistic paradigm, which sees an opportunity in early advertising to achieve the sort of social dominance that has eluded its since its early days in Athens. Certainly, there is an interesting memetic perspective here behind the anthropomorphism; one which might also be read, though using rather different terms, in Laufer and Paradeise's (2016) reading of the relationship between Sophism and marketing. I will return to this question in later chapters, but for now it is sufficient to underline the way in which Williams (1980) anchors his narrative of magical advertising in the pejorative depiction of the Gorgian, 'extended language' of the unsanctioned, marginal dealer in the φαρμακον.

Judith Williamson—Advertising as Totem

Although originally published two years earlier than Williams' (1980) essay, Williamson's ([1978] 2002) book on "decoding" advertising also adopted a Marxist approach to the consideration of advertising and also made much use of comparisons with witchcraft and magic. The aim of Williamson's study was to "analyse the way ads work" through a "dismantling of their mechanisms, to how they convey meanings to their products" (2002, p. vi). In order to do this she brings semiotic and psychoanalytical techniques and a Marxist perspective to bear upon the advertising executions of the 1970s. While Williams' Marxist lens is never overt, Williamson (2002) adopts terminology and arguments directly from *Capital* and the *Grundrisse*. Accordingly, although she ends up making many of the same points as Williams (1980) her discourse is far more theoretically elaborated. So, for example, she describes how

> in our society, while the real distinctions between people are created by their role in the process of production, as workers, it is the products of their own work that are used, in the false categories invoked by advertising, to obscure the real structure of society by replacing class with the distinctions made by consumption of particular goods.
>
> (Williamson, 2002, p. 13)

So, there is much similarity here to Williams' rhetoric of advertising as a tool that cloaks or hides reality, but it is delivered in more obviously Marxist terminology. Williamson's (2002) text also shares some of the rather eschatological tone that can be found in the latter part of Williams' (1980) essay. She finishes her introduction section, for example, with the observation that "the need for relationship and human meaning appropriated by advertising is one that, if only it was not diverted, could radically change the society we live in" (p. 14), though this does contrast quite noticeably with Williams' (1980) far more downbeat sign-off regarding the needs of corporations, where he warns that "unless they are driven back now, there will be no easy second chance".

Williamson (2002) uses comparisons from magic and religion in a number of ways in her analysis. Firstly, she describes the way that advertising makes us identify with the things we buy as "a kind of totemism" (p. 46). While totemism in tribal cultures is often suffused with spiritual and magical aspects, however, this is not the side of its practice that Williamson wishes to draw a comparison with. Instead, she works from Levi-Strauss' (1973) definition that sees totemism as a way in which human groups seek to differentiate each other by aligning themselves with differences between animals in the natural world. Williamson's point is that, in advertising, "the objects used to differentiate between us—No. 6 smokers, or Gauloise smokers, Mini drivers or Rolls Royce drivers—the objects that create these 'totemic' groups are *not* natural, and not naturally different, although these differences are given a 'natural' status" (p. 46). In other words, advertising is a manqué totemism based upon false, unnatural differentiation. This produces "two sets of false differences: between products, and between people, each perpetually redefining the other, through an exchange of meaning in the ad, and an exchange of money in the shop" (p. 47). One detects a certain underlying nostalgia or appeal to the noble savage mythos here—totemism is based upon natural differentiation and is therefore not false, while advertising is doubly false because it seeks to arbitrarily differentiate between people using unnatural 'products' which are not in themselves different. Williamson critiques advertising on the basis of its falsity and its unnaturalness—advertising manipulates us into defining/ identifying ourselves around consumption totems whose terms of differentiation are artificial and paradoxical. After all, she reasons, "one group is differentiated from another only at the price of a sameness within them" (p. 48) and so, in a beautiful phrase that demonstrates her own rhetorical magic, "we become the same, in each being made 'different' in the same way". Williamson uses the idea of totemism, then, in order to contrast the paradoxical, self-contradictory, constantly shifting way in which modern consumer society synthesises ad hoc social groupings around consumption acts with the simpler, more basic, more natural acts of group differentiation described by anthropologists. Both are totemic in the sense that they share the dynamic of using something to cohere a group around and signal analogous difference. But Williamson frames her comparison within the binary relations of natural/unnatural, real/false—terms that are fundamental to the weave of her work. As with Williams (1980), advertising is presented as fundamentally a practice of deceit. As with Williams, it is not difficult to discern the heavily Platonic origins of Williamson's (2002) perspective.

Totemism is not being used by Williamson (2002) as a way of identifying advertising with 'magical' practices or tropes, although its discussion is contributing to a general argument of deceitful, manipulative strategies that is familiar from the legacy of anti-Sophist thinking. However, Williamson (2002) does devote a whole chapter to the relationship between magic and advertising. Magic is "a kind of pivot around which misrepresentation can be produced" (p. 140). Advertising uses the suggestion of magic in order to 'short-circuit' "a multiplicity of transformations, productions, and actions". It is an "organising mythology" which advertising harnesses in order to provide a non-explanation for its fantastical narratives and assertions—because the "explanation *is* that it's *magic*". Importantly, this works only because the population already has a clear sense of what magic is. It is the existence of the trope of magic in our minds that allows an advertiser to use it. As Williamson (2002) points out, so much of the modern production process does really seem to work like magic—"consumer products and modern technology provide us with everything ready-made", so that the only thing actually left for us to do is to "buy the product or incant its name". The tiny amount of effort needed by us to consume something "inevitably creates a 'magical spell' element". In this way, Williamson (2002) concludes, "all consumer products offer magic, and all advertisements are spells" (p. 141). Furthermore, the magical nature of the products and the depiction of the transformations they can accomplish are paramount in forestalling any objections on the grounds of irrationality and hyperbole that consumers might have; "the more amazing results advertisements offer us, the more these come within the non-explanatory system of 'magic', and the less amazing they thus seem, because it is *not* amazing for *magic* to be amazing". The existence of magic as a concept in consumers' minds is accordingly framed as a weakness—it opens them up to manipulation by advertisers as it can be used "to misrepresent any system of production". Williamson does not attempt to locate the origins of our assumptions about magic—while she alludes to tropes from the Arabian Nights (p. 149), fairy stories that "every child" knows (p. 142), "common nursery knowledge" (p. 144), alchemy (p. 146), religious "sects" (p. 150), as well as "crystal balls" and "magic circles", there is no grounding of these elements within a larger argument of what magic means, and how it comes to have meaning, to a modern audience (and no discussion either of what type of audience we might be talking about). The general impression, though, is certainly that advertising is relying upon a childhood familiarity with folk and fairy tale depictions of magic and witchcraft in order to create these sorts of powerful effects. Products are seen to 'magically' appear in our lives (divorced from any sort of production process) and then are depicted as having powerful "material effects" (p. 141) upon those lives. The "space and time of production" can thus be powerfully elided, which in turn allows the consumer to become the 'magical' producer, creating the effects simply by buying the product.

Williamson (2002) argues that advertising executions contain a whole host of tropes and paraphernalia from the "common nursery knowledge" of magic such as "genies in lamps and bottles, rites and spells, sudden growth or miniaturisation, turning things to gold, magic wands and implements, and a vast number of other things" which construct the "iconography of magic". While Williams (1980) did not explicitly note the same patterns, his examples of quack cures and patent pills as well as the focus on "early commercial purple" and 'extended' language can be seen as covering some similar ground. Williamson (2002), though, makes a convincing case through her illustrated trawl across the iconography of magic in advertising that sorcery is an important allusion in much advertising work. Her explanation of the larger significance of magic for advertising therefore seems to be dependent upon the way in which childhood understandings of the place of magic in the world work against us in making advertising's elisions and transformations acceptable. So much of the modern capitalist world seems to function 'as if by magic'; indeed, so much of it is constructed so as to erase the traces of production. Tropical fruit magically appears in our supermarkets throughout the year, a constantly evolving parade of consumer electronic devices materialise in the market, from where we are never quite sure, and so many of our products contain no user serviceable parts, almost as if were we to open them up (if we could find the appropriate proprietary screwdriver) we would inadvertently let the sorcery out that makes them work. This is an 'acceptable' state of affairs to consumers, Williams appears to be arguing, because we are first 'softened up' in childhood by exposure to the "common nursery knowledge" of magic and then advertising executions directly and indirectly resonate with this knowledge in their use of the "iconography of magic". Magic, in both its fairy tale and marketing guises, is something that enchants us, sets a glamour (in its original *and* modern senses) over us so that we cannot see the *reality* of the world and can be cheated and manipulated by the forces of capitalism. Advertising's spell casts us back to a naïve, childlike way of thinking—it takes away our common sense, our learning, and our embeddedness in the social world.

On a *meta* level, Williamson's (2002) work is essentially a study in the rhetoric of advertising. She analyses advertisements as persuasive texts, breaking them down in terms of their verbal and visual symbology, patternings, allusions, and misdirections. While her apparent sources for such an interpretive focus are semiotics, Lacanian psychoanalysis, and Foucauldian discourse analysis, this is simply because (as I have already argued) these are the more fashionable extensions of rhetorical work in the second half of the twentieth century. Williamson's (2002) communicative model is entirely rhetorical—a rhetor (the advertiser) constructs a text (the advertisement) that plays upon the common assumptions of the target audience and uses verbal and visual elements to lead that audience to think about products and their relationship to those products in certain ways. Advertising is rhetoric (persuasive communication) and rhetoric both uses magic (as a rhetorical resource) and is magic (in its effect). And this is clearly to the detriment of society in general. Although we might come to it in a rather more involved and evidenced manner, the conclusion is similar to that of Williams (1980).

Sut Jhally—Advertising as Fetish Religion

The general thesis of Williams (1980) and Williamson (2002) has been developed and maintained by Sut Jhally across a number of works (Jhally, 1989, 1990; Leiss et al., 1997) where he has argued that advertising integrates "people and things within a magical and supernatural sphere" (Jhally, 1989, p. 225). Jhally uses magic in a noticeably less pejorative sense than either Williams (1980) or Williamson (2002). This is because, although he approaches the issue from a Marxist perspective, he acknowledges the limitations that Marx's views of symbolism and religion can have on a nuanced understanding of the functions that religion (and magic) can play in people's lives. Jhally (1990) starts from Marx's concept of commodity fetishism in which goods are "a unity of what is revealed and what is concealed in the processes of production and consumption", revealing to us "their capacities both as satisfiers of particular wants and as communicators of behavioural codes", while at the same time drawing a "veil across their own origins" (p. 49) and so masking "the story of who fashioned them, and under what conditions" (p. 50). The fetishism of commodities means that commodities are first emptied of meaning, hiding "the real social relations objectified in them through human labour, to make it possible for the imaginary/symbolic social relations to be injected into the construction of meaning at a secondary level" (p. 51). This is summarised in Jhally's memorable (and rhetorically powerful) slogan: "Production empties. Advertising fills" (p. 51). In contrast to Williamson (2002), Jhally is generally careful to avoid centring his discussion around real/false binaries. From his perspective, advertising cannot be providing false meanings precisely because, by the time that advertising and marketing enter the production process, the commodity has no meaning left whatsoever.

Jhally (1990) spends some time unpacking the word fetishism. This is the word that Marx's thought on the subject has supplied him with, so the way that he understands it and (re-)defines it is vitally important in his careful recasting of the Marxist perspective on advertising. He notes that Marx himself "derived the term from the early anthropological writings" (p. 53) and that its use to describe religious or magical practices seems to have originally started with Portuguese sailors who used their word *feitiço* (for a charm or amulet) to refer to the objects they saw native Africans worshipping. Jhally (1990) describes how the term gained currency in early sociological and anthropological theories, particularly those delineating evolutionary stages of social or religious order but also notes the increasingly "fuzzy and confused" (p. 54) understanding of the word that grew as more writers adopted it for their own particular purposes. Consequently, Jhally attempts to chart some common ground across this confusing landscape. Firstly, he points out that fetishism is "not a *total* spiritual belief" but always exists as part of a much wider spiritual system. Such a system might well include the belief in a supreme being, but fetishism assumes that such a being, or beings, have little relevance "as regards the conduct of everyday life" (p. 55). Instead, the fetish has power because it is the abode of a lesser spirit, something which can be made to care about the day to day concerns of the worshipper. Jhally (1990) summarises that the fetish works at the "short term and immediate" level and its use is focused on the "practical welfare of its possessors" (p. 56). It might protect a worshipper from evil spirits, poison, attack by animals, or thieves, or it might confer help in fishing, the affairs of the heart, or the earning of money. The fetish is something that affords a sense of security in an arbitrary world, it uses objects as (vehicles for) intermediaries which can help ameliorate daily anxieties and risks. As well as the anthropological and ethnographic literature, the concept of the fetish has been adopted, via Freud, into clinical psychoanalysis, where it is "regarded as a 'perversion'" (p. 58) manifested in adult males by the childhood "trauma of seeing the female genitals and is an attempt to ease the castration anxiety this causes" (p. 60). The fetish object that might be perversely fixated upon represents "the *imaginary* penis of the mother" and possession of it allows the fetishist to overcome castration anxiety. As Jhally points out, this means that the fetish is itself without actual power, "it merely completes the scene" though "without it there can be no action" (p. 61). The fetish object becomes a way of maintaining "the woman as a phallic woman, and thus denying her natural sexual definition"—it therefore aids in "distorting reality". In all of these understandings, the fetish is a vehicle—meaningless in and of itself, significant only in so far as it contains or stands for something else. So it is with the fetishisation of commodities. Products have been stripped of meaning by the production process—they are as empty as any tribal or sexual fetish before the spirits make them their home or the sexual fetishist interprets them as the imaginary maternal penis.

In Jhally's (1990) view, advertising is not responsible for the original emptying of meaning from commodities and neither it is to be blamed for its filling of products with meaning. Advertising derives its power "not from the ingenuity of advertisers but from the need for meaning" and "if it is manipulative, it is manipulative with respect to a real need: our need to know the world and to make sense of it, our need to know ourselves" (p. 197). In non-capitalist society, the institution that performs this meaning-giving function is religion. But earlier Marxist scholars "tended to see religion as having been superseded, as a thing of the past" (p. 197) and therefore did not appreciate the fact that advertising was stepping into the void left by a dormant or receding religious influence in capitalist society. People, naturally, will continue to search for meaning in their lives even if religion is no longer felt to be relevant them. Advertising offers up a magical religion, often couched in an irrational blind faith in the power of technology, "'where anything is possible', where anything can be 'fixed', where science can bestow miracles" (p. 199). Technology, in other words, is conflated with "magical feats of enchantment and transformation" (p. 198) in this "new religion of modern life" (p. 200). Jhally (1990), proceeds to construct a developmental history of "the different forms in which the commodity life has been cloaked through this century", positing four "distinct chronological stages" which can be interpreted as "different religious frameworks for the commodity-form" (p. 201). The first stage, from the 1980s to the 1920s, Jhally calls the era of idolatry, in which consumers "venerated, almost worshipped" products and advertising celebrated them as harbingers of "the new age" in a spirit of discovery and exploration. In the second stage, running from the

1920s to the 1940s and dubbed the period of iconology, advertising focuses on the meanings of products "within a special social context". Although this heralds a move towards constructing meaning in terms of the consumer, the abstract qualities attached to commodities "were still bound very tightly to the things themselves", contributing to the construction of a "twilight world of abstract significance that is neither wholly thing-based or person-based". The next stage, between the 1940s and 1960s, is the one that Jhally explicitly describes as the period of fetishism. The move towards locating the qualities of a commodity within the person and the act of consumption becomes absolute—"the product puts its power at the disposal of the individual and consumers are encouraged to consider what the product can do for them" (p. 202). The power of the product is evinced "largely through 'black magic' where persons undergo sudden transformations or where the commodity has power over other people as well". The final stage, which Jhally judges to be between the 1960s and 1980s (i.e. up to the 'present' of the writing of his text), is that of totemism, echoing Williamson's (2002) arguments regarding products as differentiators. Jhally argues that this last phase "draws together and synthesises" the other stages, with "utility, symbolisation, and personalisation" being "mixed and remixed under the sign of the *group*" (Jhally, 1990, p. 202).

So, although Jhally (1990) finally understands advertising "as a religion" (p. 203) it is a religion of distinctly magical elements, of idolatry, iconography, fetish and totem, where objects come to have the power of transformation and binding. Advertising has stepped in to fill the void that capitalist production (and the withering away of religion) has left in people—in a "world without meaning wherein people search for meaning arises the religion of use-value, the religion of advertising" (p. 203). Jhally's explanation makes of advertising an inevitable outcome of the human need for meaning—he rhetorically disempowers the makers of advertising by asserting that it works not because of anything that advertisers do, *per se*, but rather because we are so desperately searching for meaning that even the "trivialities" (p. 52) of advertising will do when we can find nothing else. Our celebration of the ingenuity of advertising (in terms of the cunning that we afford it and the creativity that we so often reward it for) is entirely misplaced. Modern capitalism has ensured that consumption has "replaced community, class and religion as the defining feature of social life" (p. 192) and, as a consequence, the need for meaning can be looked for only within the structures of consumption. Advertising has evolved to feed that need and has grown by reflecting the fundamental nature of the object-human relationship that capitalist production dictates—the object world "performs magical feats of transformation and bewitchment, brings instant happiness and gratification, captures the forces of nature, and holds within itself the essence of important social relationships (p. 172).

Jhally's (1990) identification of advertising and magic reflects a larger understanding of the inevitable relationship between commodities and humans in modern capitalism. It is still grounded in the narrative of an almost Lapsarian elision of the truth of production—as Jhally (1989) puts it, capitalism creates a world of goods where "true meaning has been stolen" (p. 225). In that sense, 'consumer society', the modern marketplace, marketing, etc., are all based upon an initial act of theft. All meaning that comes after that theft is false, but at the same time necessary. We cannot do without meaning and, as all that is left to us is the consumption of commodities, we look for meaning there. And advertising is able to provide it for us. Tragic, rather than mendacious, the magic of advertising is an unavoidably false, and inexorably weak and frivolous, construction. The accusation of witchcraft rhetorically serves to damn capitalism through fetishism's links with sexual perversion and with a small, practically minded, quotidian subset of religious practice that has by necessity become inflated into a poor substitute for a complete religion's propensity to answer the human need for meaning. Jhally's argumentation is rhetorically based upon a *bathos* figure. This is what we have been reduced to by capitalism—searching for meaning in the low magic of detergent ads and alcohol promotions.

Tricia Sheffield—Advertising as Not-Magic

Taking Jhally's (1989, 1990) as a starting point, Sheffield (2006) argues that advertising "is not after all, a religion, as Jhally states, but advertising has religious dimensions that reflect a totemic discourse" (p. xiii). This conclusion, perhaps, might be expected from a scholar who argues from a "perspective configured by an engagement with the religious practices of the Christian theological tradition" (p. 1). Sheffield's (2006) main bone of contention with Jhally is that, rather than seeing advertising as a "fetish religion", she sees it as "not a religion at all," but rather as "having religious, or totemic dimensions" (p. 6). In this she is far closer to Williamson's (2002) initial focus on totemism, though she does rather downplay the fact that Jhally (1990), as we have seen, also argues that the current phase of the "religious framework for the commodity-form" (p. 201) is one of totemism which draws together all the other stages "under the sign of the group" (p. 202). Sheffield seems to find the linking of fetishism with a definition of religion uncomfortable. Indeed, we can be a bit more specific in saying that the way in which Jhally connects advertising, religion, and magical practice is what unnerves Sheffield. She notes that "for many theologians, Jhally's implied definition of religion would be problematic" because "he seems to be relating black cats, ghosts, and ouija boards to God" (p. 23). Of course, what is really at issue is the fact that Jhally sees all manifestations of religion from a Marxist perspective—religion serves to satisfy humanity's 'need for meaning' and that goes for those parts of it which might be defined as magical practice as well as those more grander aspects involving a Supreme Being. Sheffield (2006) points out that Jhally's understanding of religion would not make much sense to theologians—but then it seems unlikely that this is whom he is writing for. That said, much of Sheffield's critique of Jhally's use of the concept of fetishism does hit home. In particular, she argues that "if as Jhally notes, one of the main aspects of religion is to give answers to humanity's search for meaning, his definition of fetishism as a religion does not comply with this standard" (p. 28). He has, after all, described fetishism as a basic, everyday, practical sort of thing, concerned with securing food, warding off harm, and attracting love. A fetish religion, therefore, would not seem to be attempting "to address ultimate concerns" (ibid.) but would instead give "temporary satisfaction in the realm of the magical" (ibid.). Quite how this is in accordance with the deep 'need for meaning' that Jhally writes of is indeed difficult to see. Certainly, we can see in Sheffield a sense that magic and fetishism do not constitute real religion. Indeed, Sheffield's (2006) reading of Durkheim, whom she relies upon in her construction of the larger argument that advertising has totemic dimensions, allows her to remind us that magic "does not have the moral community of the Church" and, because "magic does not have a community, it cannot be a religion" (p. 39). According to Durkheim, recounts Sheffield, magic is performed individually or for clientele who might have no knowledge of each other. Sheffield concedes that magic has some connection to advertising, but this is only in so far as magical devices are occasionally used in the content of advertising executions when "normally inanimate objects come alive and speak to the consumer" (p. 27)—that old rhetorical figure of anthropomorphism, in other words. Despite this, fundamentally, "magic is not the culture created and sustained by advertising". Instead, it is the clan creating, totemic aspect of advertising which can be seen as the driving power of advertising and supplies the religious "dimension" of marketing communication, even though it does not reach to the heights of religion proper.

Ultimately, Sheffield's (2006) study is a repositioning of Williamsons' (2002) argument from the perspective of theological scholarship. It is interesting because of the way that it explicitly dismisses magic as a term of comparison for advertising, attempting to erase it from Jhally's argumentation. It is tempting to wonder whether the reason behind this is that magic is such a disturbing practice to have connected to both religion and advertising. Certainly, there are clearly dismissive rhetorical strategies employed by Sheffield (2006) to frame magic as something both unreligious and lacking power. Though the explicit identification of anthropomorphism and magic is also telling for its faint echoing of the legacy of Gorgian, rhapsodic rhetoric.

Linda Dégh—Advertising as Magic Folk Tale

The final author in my review of thinkers *outside* marketing who have identified aspects of marketing communication with magic is folklore scholar Linda Dégh. In two substantial chapters in her work on American folklore and the mass media (Dégh, 1994), she argues for a reading of television advertising which sees it as resurrecting the magical story traditions of the Märchen, "the classical oral prose narrative of Old World peasantry" (p. 34). Dégh notes that the Märchen tradition fell out of use with the advent of industrialisation, when its "entertaining function depending on primary communication, became dispensable, often unnecessary, and in most cases impossible" (ibid.). Instead, it lived on in a severely weakened form in children's stories, often adopted for educational rather than entertainment purposes. Dégh argues, however, that the Märchen found a new home on television, a technology that "terminated the occasions for traditional storytelling" but which nevertheless helped the "Märchen to survive on the basis of entirely new traditions" (p. 43).

Dégh (1994) maintains that the presence of folklore magic in advertising is the result of the advertising industry reacting to the desires of their target audiences. She notes that marketing communication "never loses touch with the masses" (p. 42) and "in all its moves, it consults public opinion, which sensitively and immediately reacts to advertising strategies". If we see the Märchen in television advertising, then, that "would seem to indicate that Märchen-like enchantment is in fashion, that magic is in demand" (p. 43). America, she reasons, is "eager to welcome" the "salesperson's substitute: the fairy and goblin impersonators" into its homes. Mirroring Williamson's (2002) focus on the way that advertising magic achieves its resonance from the stories of childhood, Dégh (1994) explains that modern America has a rather limited knowledge of the variegated Märchen forms and is restricted to selections from the Grimm Brothers, Hans Christian Andersen, and Andrew Lang" and consequently their "frame of reference is rather narrow" (ibid.). Indeed, the elements from these limited childhood sources are then further fragmented within the world of advertising—they become disseminated "in the form of disintegrated, atomized units and enter the bloodstream of communication and 'manipulated communication' in disjointed particles". The fairy princesses and genies that populate advertising belong to the "Märchen world" but are disconnected from the specifics of their stories, serving only to conjure up the possibilities of magical enchantment rather than function as specific figures from specific tales.

Dégh's (1994) explanation for the utility of Märchen magic in advertising revolves around a firmly rhetorical understanding of their persuasive nature (though she does not use the word itself). She begins by pointing out that the traditional Märchen "is not meant to be believed by its audience" (p. 44). Everything about the way that it is styled and structured suggests "that, in the everyday sense of the word, it is not true". Instead, "what the tale demands and stimulates" is the "temporary suspension of disbelief on the part of the audience" for "artistic enjoyment" (ibid.). The magical metaphors brought over from the "Märchen world" are mean to be resolved by the audience, not taken at face value, Dégh reminds us. The "advertisement-Märchen neither needs nor tolerates belief" (ibid.) because its "enchantment is converted into features of artistic narration, figurative speech, symbols, and metaphors" (p. 48). Interestingly, Dégh is arguing that, in reception by an audience, advertising magic collapses down into obvious, identifiable, rhetoric and so loses its irrational side—it becomes, simply, recognisable persuasion (at which point we "leave the world of the Märchen behind us", p. 49). This is not to say that the irrational is not to be found in advertising, however. Dégh (1994) suggests that "under the Märchen layer" (p. 50) there is another stratum, that of legend, which is the realm of "irrational" magic that cannot be so easily transformed into the product of persuasive patternings. In the legend layer of advertising, "magic appears, even if only latently, as a real power in real life" (p. 53). It provides a hidden message which "suggests that certain everyday situations represent intolerable and maybe ruinous deficiencies, beside which everything else shrinks into insignificance, and which can be remedied exclusively by one single solution" (ibid.).

So, the folk tale magic, the "Märchen-simulating" (p. 53) aspects, of advertisements are rational because they allow us to easily understand that they are working upon us as formal persuasive devices. In that sense, Dégh also argues, they have little actual power over us—because we recognise them as rhetorical techniques, "we viewers feel free to make our own choice" (p. 48). Yet, the layer of legend in advertising, which hides beneath the clearly fictional stratum of the Märchen, is quite the opposite—it is here that magic and the irrational are tightly bound together and (very tellingly from a Gorgian perspective) when energised by the "synergism of innumerable repetitions" (p. 53) can achieve a sort of terrible fascination upon the viewer. It "shrinks the complex problematics" of the world "to a single isolated problem" that can be solved with "a single magic trick". Dégh describes the result as a sort of "messianic worldview", a cargo-cult that "makes believe that the sought-after goods have already arrived and stand at cult members' disposal" (p. 53). She then identifies this "ideology" with the same "kind of irrationality" that makes people give over their judgement to horoscopes, join religious cults, "chase monsters in the woods, summon spirits, exorcise demons, search for UFOs in the sky, and become well-versed in the legendary of such activities" (ibid.). This layer of hidden magic turns consumers into irrational 'fanatics' because it magically compresses all the problems of life into one point, promoting a single act of consumption as the cure for all ills. What Dégh (1994) is describing here is the enthymematic (and fallacious) nature of advertising argumentation. Rhetorical argumentation relies upon compressed structures of argumentation in comparison to dialectic's careful steps through the syllogistic format. Instead of 'if x, and if y, then therefore z', the enthymeme presents the audience with a simple 'if x, then z'—a far more ambiguous, slippery patterning that is ideal for taking advantage of the audience's existing assumptions, prejudices, uncertainties, and fears.

Dégh (1994) goes on to examine the marketing of actual magical paraphernalia and services in modern America, making it clear that the explicit selling of magical objects (the commodification of magic) is reliant upon the same need for magic, and taps into the same irrationalism, that she identifies in the population at large when talking about advertisements for household products. For her, the 'occult explosion' of the 1970s and 80s, which saw a vast surge of interest in new age mysticism, ceremonial magic, and pagan and neo-pagan beliefs, is not a sign that "urban mass society has become more 'superstitious', only that mass communication and social stratification have made supernatural belief more visible, more normalized and adaptable" (p. 54). She further argues that "the exploitation of magic to market products" has been going on since the industrial revolution", locating its origins in the "rough and aggressive Yankee peddling and boosterism" (p. 55) that was initially "repulsive" to the sensibilities of Old Europe but which was eventually "adopted by most industrial nations" in the decades after World War II. This is a telling reversal to Williams' (1980) narrative where the use of miraculous and magical descriptors for patent medicines was well entrenched in Samuel Johnson's eighteenth-century England. Once again, though, we have an origin tale which conflates magic, rhapsodic rhetoric of the high style (highly inappropriate for commercial discourse, of course), the irrational, and marketing.

Dégh (1994) is quite clearly not 'accusing' marketing of witchcraft or magic—instead, marketers are responding to the desire for magic that consumers have always had (even before they were consumers). There is a close relationship between the way that marketers use magic and the rhetorical nature of advertising in Dégh's analysis. Magic works rhetorically in advertising at the level of figuration, metaphor, anthropomorphism, etc., but it also works at deeper levels by rhetorical strategies of compressed, enthymematic argumentation and repetition that can bind with human irrationality to produce cult-like adherence to consumption practices and choices. So, while Dégh mostly displays a detached folklorist's perspective her analysis manifests a real sense of disturbance at the way in which the combination of marketing and magic can invoke the irrational in a consumer audience.

Marketing Academics and Identifications of Magic

Identification of magic with marketing from inside marketing scholarship is rare but does have a significant history. Perhaps the earliest example is to be found in the occasional scholarship of US advertising legend Howard Luck Gossage.[1] Gossage's (1967) essay, originally published in 1961 in *Harper's Magazine* and slyly entitled 'The Gilded Bough: Magic and Advertising', adopts Frazer's anthropological perspective (including his categorisations of imitative and contagious) in order to claim that modern advertising was an example of "the most common denominator of all, magic" (p. 364). Gossage's piece is mostly an early iteration through the sorts of magical content in advertising that Williamson (2002) and Dégh (1994) identify. However, it has been cited by Pollay (1986) as an example of the anthropological interpretation of advertising and, although Gossage is not usually thought of as an advertising *scholar*, he is an example of a careful, insightful thinker about advertising from within the industry. It is certainly a significant point of departure for a review of how marketing scholars link their discipline and the practice of magic. When given the opportunity to contribute to a collection of essays regarding current perspectives on communication and reflect upon his own profession, Gossage chooses to frame it squarely within the practice of magic as described by Frazer. It is also satisfying to note that Gossage's essay is situated in a section entitled "The Modern Persuasion: The Rhetorics of Mass Society" (p. 333). Perhaps the most insightful element of Gossage's (1967) piece is his argument that magic "is the most adaptable of creatures". Magic continually blends into the background and "so thoroughly identifies with its surroundings as to be unnoticed by the inhabitants" (p. 363). Gossage then artfully explains that this propensity is why "such now obvious performances of magical thinking as the Inquisition, the Dutch tulip craze of the seventeenth century, the stock-market boom of the late twenties, Couéism, McCarthyism, and chain letters escaped recognition at the time" (ibid.). For Gossage, then, magic is always with us and advertising just makes it "more apparent" (p. 369). There might be different degrees of magical thinking present in different types of advertising, but "whatever its form, advertising's magic is relatively lucid in that it never confuses the main issue, what it has to sell" (p. 370)—in other areas of life, in politics and the running of the larger economies that advertising serves, Gossage implies that this is not so much the case. Advertising magic is, comparatively, straightforward in its motivations. It should be noted, though, that Gossage blames the extremes of unsubtle magical thinking in advertising on the audience; "if some advertising is more blatantly guilty of magical thinking than others, it is because some audiences are more simple-minded" (ibid.). Now, while this highly condescending attitude smacks of 1960s mores, it is significant for the way in which it implies that advertising uses magical thinking because audiences are simple-minded enough to respond to it. The consumer is a dupe, then. As we shall see, this position is seriously challenged in later marketing and consumer research that invokes magic.

The next instance of ascribing magical significance to marketing practices comes in Rook (1987). This chapter in Umiker-Sebeok's (1987) edited collection on marketing and semiotics examines what Rook calls "modern hex-signs", namely, the "stake signs and stickers which announce that a home has been professionally secured" (p. 239). The hex-signs that Rook is alluding to are protective talismans affixed to buildings in order to "ward off harmful or evil forces". He makes a reference to the "colorful geometric designs nineteenth century Pennsylvania Amish farmers" used to mount on their barns but otherwise does not provide much historical or anthropological detail. Indeed, beyond the initial setting up of the comparison, Rook (1987) does not really engage in depth with the connection to magic. Instead, he treats both hex-signs and security signs as symbolic ways to project strength, preparedness, and commitment to the seriousness of property protection. Having said that, there is no trace of embarrassment or a 'need to explain' the use of comparisons with witchcraft—although this is probably to do with the fact that the comparison is being used as a quick way to attract attention to the research on security signs rather than as a serious proposition of identity. It might also have to do with the fact that Rook had already published work from his PhD thesis that argued for a careful consideration of the ritual aspect of consumption practices (Rook, 1985). Rook sees hex-signs as evidence of protection rituals in the same way that the display of aggressive security signs threatening physical violence and legal retribution are part of modern protection rituals. What is important is the ritual nature of the displays rather than their connection to magic *per se*. This is an important point because it is typical of much marketing scholarship which touches on aspects of magic. Ritual is interpreted largely from a *sociological* or *socio-anthropological* perspective rather than a spiritual or religious one. Even when comparisons are made to religious, spiritual, or magical practice the frame such comparisons are made within is a sociological one. So, Rook (1985) sees rituals as "dramatic enactments" (p. 253), "expressive, symbolic" (p. 252) activities which are "constructed of multiple behaviours that occur in a fixed, episodic sequence" and tend "to be repeated over time". His emphasis on dramatic scripting underlines his grounding in Goffman's ([1957] 1990) theory of interaction rituals and there is certainly a sense in which we can interpret Goffman's focus on performance in terms of rhetorical persuasion (Harré, 1985). Furthermore, Rook (1985) makes much use of Erikson's (1982) approach to rituals in terms of stages of psychological development, particularly his focus on smaller, everyday ritualised behaviour such as grooming rituals. The Eriksonian perspective affords ritual significance to practices and habits that have traditionally been overlooked, and this means that Rook (1985) is able to identify consumption rituals that have "magical components' to them. In his exploration of male grooming rituals, he finds that "not infrequently, the subjects described various grooming effects that can be characterized as ritual magic" (p. 261), in that they produce dramatic transformations in their users. It must be emphasised that the magical effects that Rook's respondents are talking about here are not those depicted in advertising—rather they are reporting the effects that the grooming rituals have upon themselves. So, some of the ways in which these rituals would cause magical changes would be that "a tired drone is transformed into an energetic dynamo; an elixir makes Plain Jane look glamorous; one of the guys becomes a Romeo" (ibid.). Additionally, Rook notes that a grooming ritual might often be described as a "psychic energizer" in order to combat introversion. It is no coincidence that many of Rook's respondents' descriptions of the magical effects of their rituals follow quite closely "the plots of many grooming product commercials" (ibid.). Marketing communication has primed consumers to look upon consumption as a magical process that can confer extra luck, extra charisma, extra attraction upon them. And this is how they come to then incorporate their rituals involving such products into their self-narration.

There is a significant strand of literature in consumption research that has looked at the way that consumers use products as fetishes empowered with magical, transformative capabilities. Distinct from the line of scholarship I have already delineated, this research sees the fetishising of consumption as something that originates from within the consumer and has had little time for explaining it as a function of capitalist production. Instead, work by Belk (1988, 1991), Arnould and Price (1993), Arnould et al. (1999), Gmelch (2012), Newman et al. (2011), Fernandez and Lastovicka (2011) has explored the ways in which consumers bring products into their inner lives, using them to construct their identities and transform themselves in ways that display magical or fetishistic thinking. Such scholarship, of course, can be viewed as essentially supporting the points that Williams (1980), Williamson (2002), and Jhally (1990) make regarding capitalism's presentation of products as fetish objects which have a meaning entirely separated from their original meaning erased by the process of production. In this reading, the consumer (and the researcher) are 'dupes' (Slater, 1997), simply adopting the meanings of the products that are projected to them by marketing communications in the service of capitalism. Their magical thinking is foisted on to them by advertising—when they fetishise a product to help in the construction of their identity they are playing into the hands of a system which desires them to define themselves in terms of their consumption. Much consumer culture theory scholarship has instead sought to investigate consumers as 'postmodern identity-seekers' or even 'crafters' (Campbell, 2005, p. 23) who are largely expressing their own agency in their magical consumption rituals—not exactly 'sovereign' but certainly proactive and with power to interpret and shape their own understandings.

Belk et al. (1989) uses magic as a descriptor for the way that consumers interact with product and consumption rituals that they consider to be "sacred" (p. 11). The authors use ethnographic and anthropological research to point out similarities between the ways that believers interact with sacred objects in their religion and the ways that consumers can interact with objects that have special, sacred significance for them. Consumption of marketed products, in other words, can play the same part in people's lives as interaction with sacred objects can in the lives of those believers in magic described in anthropological accounts. Belk (1988), in his more elaborated discussion of the ways in which consumers make objects an (extended) part of their selves, uses a number of direct comparisons to Frazerian magical theory. Although he makes reference to Marx's commodity fetishism, Belk is much more comfortable with Frazer's terminology of sympathetic and contagious magic particularly as they enable him to consider the ways that consumers build relationships with objects. Owning objects that might have belonged to a famous or historical person, for example, is described as a "desire to bask in the glory of the past in the hope that some of it will magically rub off—a form of positive contamination", and "just as we seek to extend ourselves by incorporating or owning certain objects, we may still seek the sympathetic magic (contagion) of possessions that retain a part of the extended self of valued others" (p. 149). Belk is offering a magical explanation for the reasons that consumers might seek out objects owned by people they admire and also goes on to note that many purchases can function in the same way "as magical amulets and totemic emblems in more traditional societies" (p. 153), helping to make someone feel that luck is on their side or that they have more chance to become part of an aspirational grouping. In Belk's (1988) work, the consumer is the active magician—they are performing the rites, making the magic. They are rarely portrayed as responding to marketing propositions; instead, consumers are framed as imaginative symbolic manipulators of objects. Magic, here, is a positive, empowering force, helping the consumer to get the meaning that they want. It cannot be called 'marketing magic' because there is little sense of marketing going on—this is *consumer* magic.

In his slightly later paper on the "ineluctable mysteries of possessions", Belk (1991) argues that the ways in which scholarship has traditionally seen consumption is to try to reduce it to a "hedonic calculus" which is "bound to fail" and risks supporting an impoverished conception of the consumer as a "rational information-processor or human-as-computer" (p. 17). Instead, we must "recognize, reestablish, and reclaim" the magic of our possessions. Humans "court magic in a plethora of material loci" (p. 18) and any realistic theory of consumption must acknowledge this. The entire paper is a stance against the prevailing assumptions of human rationality that drive analytic paradigms such as economics and social psychology. These disciplines tend to ignore the fact that in many of our relationships with possessions, "there is more magic than reason involved" (p. 19). Much of the reasoning here is familiar from the earlier (1988) paper but Belk (1991) bolsters much of that earlier argumentation with a wider range through different product types and possession relationships. All of the "theoretical alternatives" (p. 37) that Belk (1991) brings to bear upon our possession relationships, such as fetishism, the concept of sacredness, and self-extension, portray the consumer as an active identity constructor, using possessions to further their lives or themselves. Once again, marketers as agents are almost entirely off-stage. Rather magic is something that inhabits the relationships that consumers create with their possessions.

In their exploration of the 'fire of consumer desire', Belk et al. (2003) do attempt to describe more fully the exact magical relationship between the marketer and the consumer. They explain that consumers are mesmerized by the promise of "goods not yet possessed" as if they promised "magical meaning in life" (p. 327). One source of this magic are the "advertisers, retailers, peddlers, and other merchants of mystique". However, they are quick to claim that these agents of the marketing system are not the only elements "at work in bewitching us". Consumers themselves "willingly act as sorcerers' apprentices" (p. 327) and take on a "more proactive role [. . .] than prior research has typically envisioned" (p. 328). In the end, Belk et al.

(2003) conclude that consumer desire is not *magical consumption* (which we will come to below) but rather a *search for magic*, the imaginative aspiration to be transformed magically by the desired for object. Similarly to Dégh (1994), then, Belk et al. (2003) imply a general propensity for magic in the population. However, they emphasise the way in which the consumer participates, via the power of their imagination, in the evocation of magical significance for the product. Marketers are brought into the equation as sorcerers, but the real focus of the authors' scholarly attention is directed towards the creative part played by consumers.

Arnould and Price (1993) explore the consumer experience of white water rafting adventures, an experience that is often described by those involved as "magical" (p. 25). They note the ways in which river guides act as narrative designers of an "interactive gestalt orchestrated [. . .] over several days' journey into the unknown" (ibid.). They help to produce an experience that can lead to a profound sense of transformation in the customer, a sense of having known "river magic". It is clear that while much of the experience is crafted by the narratives of the river guides, who provide framing language and prime customers for their experience, the actual magic that is produced is a function of the "romantic cultural scripts" (p. 41) that "evolve over the course of the experience" and which require the interaction (and imagination) of both guide and customer. Arnould and Price (1993) use the word 'magic' in their analysis because that is the word that the guides and customers use to describe the "sense of reverence and mystery" (p. 24) that accompanies the transformative power of the rafting experience. The term is not particularly analysed—it is taken for granted as something that comes from their respondents. Certainly, there is no effort by the authors to try to link "river magic" with any other type of magic. However, this changes substantially in Arnould et al. (1999), where the same experience (white water rafting) is interpreted by the authors in terms of its similarities to magical rituals in other societies. They describe magic as a "moral practice that concerns itself with establishing proper modes of living in relation to others", and that also "concerns itself with the relationship between human beings and the natural world", and often involves the "activation of certain indefinable 'latent virtues' in the immaterial world" (p. 36). Importantly, they also note that "unlike Cartesian science, magical thinking and action is straightforwardly rhetorical, based in metaphor and simile" (p. 37). In terms of its motivation, Arnould et al. (1999) assert that magic "is a non-Cartesian strategy for resolving intractable social problems" (p. 37). White water rafting, then, becomes a "magical consumption system" (p. 38) that "mirrors traditional magical systems in intent and effect" (p. 38). Their descriptions of the way that the river guides prepare and guide their customers through the magical transformative experience makes them *consumption shamans*, saying the right words, providing the right atmosphere, invoking the spirits of the river so that the magic will be manifest. "Central to the rite" (p. 48) are the rhetorical narratives that the guides use to prime and prepare their charges for the dangerous but exhilarating experience they have ahead. Such narratives also are important for the way in which they reproduce the magic of the experience long after it is over, providing stories that can spread to others the magic a customer has experienced (as well as recreating powerful feelings in the storytellers themselves). Arnould et al. (1999) also identify the power of formalised/formulaic utterances, or "magical language" (p. 56) in the rafting rituals, noting the presence of verbal taboos (which help to engender a sense of power around the word/thing elided) and other "innovative, locally situated rhetoric" (p. 54) devices that are "designed to elicit cooperation from symbolic forces" (p. 52).

Arnould et al. (1999) paint a convincing portrait of the magical nature of the rafting consumer experience. At the centre of that picture, too, is rhetoric functioning as a magical, performative force. The guides are marketers, of course, though the authors are careful not to cast them in quite such terms. Yet, despite the fact that much of the magic that is experienced by the customers is generated as a result of the guides' careful preparation, priming, and nurturing of the customers' understanding and interpretation of events, there is never a sense in the article that customers are being manipulated, tricked, lied to, or duped. Indeed, Arnould et al. (1999) conclude their article by stating that "at least some customers are indeed in search of encounters such as Stoller's struggle with the sorceress Dunguri cited in the epigraph" (p. 59). Customers are active seekers, not passive receptors. They willingly "lend their bodies to the process, both consuming creatively and aesthetically" (ibid.). Further, the authors ask whether modern Western consumers, perhaps, "need magic [. . .] to reconstitute their life worlds and intentionality in postmodernity" (p. 63)? Again, this is a very different perspective from Williams (1980), Williamson (2002), and Jhally (1990). For Arnould et al. (1999), magic is something that people might need, actively seek out, and benefit from. They contribute to the creation of magic through their immersion in the consumption process.

While it is encouraging to see magic treated as a natural part of the consumption process and, also, to see magic and rhetoric so fully entwined in their analysis, Arnould et al. (1999) nevertheless perform an important piece of rhetorical magic themselves that is typical of much consumer culture theory. As noted above, the guides are not called marketers, they are not even really framed as marketers—they are framed as providers of a service but not one that is described in marketing terms. It is almost as if the authors are more comfortable portraying a river guide as a shaman or sorcerer than they are with referring to them as a marketing agent. Granted, the focus of the research is on the consumer experience, but when so much of that consumer experience is guided, directed, suggested, *midwifed*, by the guides and their ritual it is very curious that there is so little overt consideration of the guides as marketers for the experience. When so much of the language in the paper supports an interpretation of the consumer as an active creator, one wonders why there was not more discussion of the problematic question of how much one can be creating when others script the experience for you? I would suggest that the impression of the rafting consumers as active is heavily influenced by the fact that the guides are not framed as marketing agents. Indeed, it might even be said that the adoption of magic as a comparator term (and the casting of guides as shamans) allows Arnould et al. (1999) to downplay the controlling, directing nature of the experience in order to celebrate the consumer empowering aspects more clearly.

As in the case of Belk's work, Arnould et al.'s (1999) framing of magic is certainly positive. It provides a transformative experience that aids the consumer in their self-construction. It is not associated with practices that are duplicitous or malevolent but rather is linked to the elective creation (or, at least, co-creation) of rewarding encounters with the power of nature. This is world's away from the framing that magic is given in the work of Williams (1980), Williamson (2002) and Jhally (1990). However, we should be careful to remember that Arnould et al. (1999) are not implying that all service encounters are suffused with magic. The white water rafting adventure is dangerous, carried out in the midst of nature, and comparatively prolonged—it shares little with, say, cashing a check at our bank. 'River magic' is not being investigated for what it can tell us about all marketing encounters or consumer experiences. Indeed, it is because of rafting's unusual nature, or 'river magic's' *extra*ordinary status as a consumption experience, that it becomes worthy of investigation. While Dégh (1994) talks about how the "masses" (p. 42) seeming to have a need for magic, Arnould et al. (1999) are content to point to "at least some" consumers (p. 59) who can be identified as craving the transformative power that it can provide. Perhaps, though, Arnould et al. (1999) are simply reflecting something of the conservatism that they describe as existing in "post-Enlightenment scholarship", where "magic is virtually taboo" and even "ethnographies that take magic seriously" can "evoke controversy" (p. 63). It might well be the case, then, that Arnould et al. (1999) are using 'river magic' to carefully introduce their concepts into the marketing and/or consumer research scholarly arena—using a small, unusual case to subtly suggest its ramifications for the larger discipline. Certainly, some of the phrasings towards the end of the article can be interpreted in this way, particularly when they wonder whether "western consumers" (ibid.) might need magic to "reconstitute their lifeworlds and intentionality in postmodernity". The final sentence of the piece, it should be noted, hopes that their "work inspires further reconsideration of the role of magical practice in Western social life" (p. 64).

This hope certainly seems to have had some performative power. Muñiz and Schau's (2005) influential investigation of religiosity in the Apple Newton community contains much discussion of the presence of "magical motifs" in the narratives constructed by community embers around the object of their affection. They link these motifs directly to the "consumer magic" described by Arnould et al. (1999) and they note that "our findings suggest that "consumer magic need not be limited to such intense experiences as white-water river rafting but can also manifest in the mundane world of everyday technological goods" (p. 740). They use as an example the way in which, in responding to the disparaging comments from outsiders regarding the Newton's abilities, they fervently demonstrate its features, asserting that the community members "are using technopagan magic to demonstrate the Newton's powers" (ibid.). They also note that much of the magic around the narratives constructed by such communities is dependent upon the "suspension of rational disbelief" (p. 741) when consuming them. Once again, we see that consumers are complicit in co-creating the magic around the product—their willingness to be part of a magical experience is central to the strength of the magic that is produced. This magic helps to sustain members of the Newton community through tough times, disparagement, anxiety around the continued viability of their devices, abandonment by the parent brand, etc. The magic is useful, valuable to them. And it helps to galvanise the community: "through the invocation of magico-religious narratives and complex consumer sacralization rituals, this community is renewing and reinforcing beliefs about the brand, the relationship to the market it implies, and their support of it" (p. 745). Muñiz and Schau (2005) conclude that "a common aspect of brand communities could be the potential for transcendent and magico-religious experiences" (p. 746). Again, we seem to be coming back to Dégh's (1994) observation that consumers have a deep need for magic—and brand communities are just one of many reflections of this.

A number of recent articles in the *Journal of Consumer Research* have continued to mine the seam of consumer magic. Fernandez and Lastovicka (2011) investigate the way that consumers turn products into fetishes, which they define as "a magical object of extraordinary empowerment and influence" (p. 278). Their particular focus is upon "replica-fetishes", objects which achieve their fetish status due to their designed similarity with a famous object, such as a "rock star's personal instrument or a warrior's battle shield" (ibid.). They note that there has been little research of the way such objects offer "the promise of magical meaning" that consumers believe will 'alter their state of being'. The key to explaining such beliefs is *magical thinking*, "the attribution of meaningful connections to correlated actions/ events and/or objects" (p. 280). Fernandez and Lastovicka (2011) argue that "consumers can utilize magical thinking to imbue objects with cues that then signify that magical thinking has occurred" (ibid.). Replica objects use semiotic cues that can strengthen the link to the replicated object, the original. This 'tangibilizing' helps to trigger magical thinking in the consumer, making them think that, if the replica is this much like the original, then perhaps it contains some of the magic of its pseudo-original-owner. They note that this is a form of "imitative magic" (echoing Frazer's original categorisations). Contagion magic then becomes manifest when the consumer feels that, by physically handling the replica, using it, wearing it, coming into contact with it, the power of the pseudo-original famous owner will be transferred to them.

The examples that Fernandez and Lastovicka (2011) use demonstrate the ways in which artists, marketing agents, and consumers come together to co-create a magical experience based upon the marketing and consumption of replica objects (guitars, in the case of the extended case used in the paper). The marketing agents here are true intermediaries, taking the original guitars and distilling their essence down into a replica which can then be packaged with paraphernalia, documentation, and all sorts of "indexical cues" (using the Peircean term the authors adopt) that serve to heighten the imitative magic. Consumers are then able to 'activate' this magic through their imagination, and their willingness to experience magic, or their need for it, serves as the foundation for the marketing interaction. The marketer uses the consumers' need for magic (and the ease with which they apply magical thinking patterns) in order to weave their own magic.

Newman et al. (2011) also examine the contagion magic that works in the market for celebrity-owned objects. They frame it, also, as a form of magical thinking on behalf of the consumer, glossing it as a belief "that a person's immaterial qualities or essence can be transferred to an object through physical contact" (p. 217). While only a small point in their general exploration of the celebrity collectibles market, it is nevertheless a measure of the level of acceptance in consumer research that magical thinking and consumer fetishising of products has achieved that they can be easily presented as part of a wider explanation of consumer thinking around certain product categories.

St. James et al. (2011) seek to give magical thinking a fundamental place in modern society. They note that, although the "Western intellectual tradition" has treated magic with "suspicion, fear, and ridicule" (p. 632), magical thinking is something that has always had a presence in our civilisations and continues to play a vital part in our "contemporary, technology-based culture of consumption". For St. James et al. (2011), magical thinking is typified by "creating or invoking extraordinary connections—symbolic relationships founded on a belief or intuition in the presence of mystical forces in the world—in order to understand, predict, or influence events" (ibid.). They contend that it becomes particularly important when people are faced with "loss or the inability to attain a desired outcome". Importantly, St. James et al. (2011) point out that magical thinking is often characterised in the anthropological, psychological, and marketing literature as "irrational" and depicted as an indication of an inability to apply logical thought, or properly understand cause-effect relationships. They argue that this characterises the consumer as "helpless and misguided" (p. 633). As a result magic is often seen as a way of dealing with a lack of hope, in that it provides a sense of control and certainty. However, in their research with consumers, St. James et al. (2011) find that in their "informants' coping efforts uncertainty becomes a source of hope since it transforms impossibilities into possibilities" (p. 647). Magical thinking for consumers in the sorts of difficult personal circumstances experienced by the authors' respondents provides a creative way of dealing with uncertainty. This further leads St. James et al.

(2011) to suggest that the fundamental difference between magical thinking and 'scientific thinking' does not lie in the area of ontology (fantasy versus reality) but instead "in a different position towards the possible" (p. 647). Science "seeks to empirically validate or invalidate possibilities to classify them as reality or fantasy", whereas magical thinking "maintains ambiguity around what is possible in order to provide meaning and sustain hope in the context of stressful situations" (ibid.). The cultivation of uncertainty and ambiguity around a situation means that its outcome is still in flux, can still be effected, can be transformed. Consumers use the "creative persuasion" of magical thinking upon themselves (a form of self-persuasion, or what Nienkamp, 2001, calls "internal rhetoric"). In this way, they are displaying what the authors call "chimerical agency", wherein the "consumer invokes, alters, and constructs the dual strands of reality and fantasy to create a realm of possibility that is a hybrid of the two" (ibid.). As St. James et al. (2011) assert, such an interpretation of magical thinking and the agency it brings to consumers is very different from more traditional views of magical thinking which have seen those who use it as "irrational dupes, unable or unwilling to understand causal relationships" (ibid.). However, as we have seen above, consumer-oriented research has been largely celebratory of consumer agency since the early 1980s. The problem, indeed, has been that consumer research has tended to divorce consideration of consumer magical thinking from the influence of marketing agents. While this has the benefit of redressing the imbalance generated by years of 'consumer as dupe' woolly thinking, it does rather throw the baby out with the bathwater, producing a scholarly landscape wherein exploration of consumer magical thinking rarely acknowledges the existence of marketing communication which seeks to work magically (let alone rhetorically). While consumers might well "creatively forge meanings to claim agency over marketer-determined practices and solutions" (ibid.), they are also subjected to, targeted by, exposed to, a myriad of marketing communication efforts that also harness magical thinking (and Gorgian as well as Aristotelian rhetorical techniques). "Celebratory" examinations of how consumers think magically are fascinating and useful but surely touch upon only half the story. How does magical thinking employed by marketing agents interact with the magical thinking employed by consumers? According to Dégh (1994), the advertising industry is highly sensitive to the ways in which consumers desire magic and employ magical thinking—might it not make sense to wonder if marketing magic and consumer magic are far more symbiotic than the consumer research scholarship above might lead us (or wish us) to believe?

To finish this examination of the way in which marketing scholars have engaged with the idea of magic, I will move on to Brown's (2009) article on "the equivocal magic of marketing". This paper might also be described as celebratory in nature, but it is not directed at the celebration of consumer agency as expressed in their repurposing of magical thinking. Instead, Brown (2009) wishes to celebrate the magical nature of marketing. As we have seen in previous chapters, Brown has been involved with the great science versus art debate in marketing scholarship for some time. In his 2009 article, he takes the contentious stance that marketing's ills and "scholarly shortcomings" cannot be improved by the vain attempt to become more scientific but can be countered only by adopting an "essentially magical" worldview which is "much closer to what managers actually do on a day-to-day basis" (p. 163). Brown (2009) begins by noting the dire position of marketing in general public opinion that sees it as "a term of abuse, a synonym for charlatanry, a word freighted with negative connotations" (p. 164). This, despite so many decades of marketing scholars declaring to anyone who will listen that "marketing is a force for the good, that customer wellbeing is our calling's raison d'être, that the marketing philosophy must permeate every organisation, for-profit or otherwise" (ibid.). Yet, when marketing academia is faced with the evidence of its failings, its inability to effectively market the profession to everyone else, it falls back to blaming those "bad apples" amongst practitioners, who let the side down by falling into cheating, manipulation, and deceit. In other words, marketing has a bad reputation because people don't market in the way that we tell them to. As Brown (2009) perceptively argues, this is just "blaming the customer" (p. 165), the customer here being the marketing professionals who have failed to understand and implement scholarly marketing advice correctly—"the people who buy our concepts and ideas and scholarly insights are at fault because they don't listen, they don't do as they're told, they don't take their marketing medicine as instructed" (ibid.). And marketing should be the last discipline that falls back on blaming the customer.

In Brown's (2009) opinion, the main problem that marketing has as a discipline is its reliance upon the "marketing science mentality that pervades our discipline", and he further notes (with what seems like a battle-weary sigh) that "the belief system is so deeply internalised that criticism only makes science stronger" (p. 165). The result is a discipline that is "increasingly arid, barren, contaminated, diseased" (ibid., fn. 4). However, Brown (2009) declares that, despite its almost complete dominance of the discipline, marketing science is not the "the only life support system that's available to us" (p. 166). Instead, he suggests, we would be well served by remembering Sir James Frazer's anthropological distinction between the religious, the scientific, and the magical worldview. While Frazer originally saw these paradigms as evolutionary stages, with magic being associated with an earlier stage of social development than religion and science finally capping them both, Brown is quick to note that "no one subscribes to such views today". Instead, we recognise that "worldviews co-exist", and even in the West the "old ways, the allegedly abandoned ways, have never really gone away" (ibid.). So it is with marketing itself—magic is "clearly discernible in the practice of marketers themselves" (p. 166) and consumers also "consistently refer to marketplace practices in magical terms" (p. 167). As a way of giving a sense of just how fundamentally magical marketing is, Brown then proceeds to sketch out "ten salient themes" which link marketing with magic. So, we read that marketing works with magical incantations and spells in the form of straplines and slogans which, if they are repeated enough times (so "managers believe") will "bestow great wealth and fortune on the organisation or brand responsible" (p. 167). The "primal magical urge" (p. 168) of animism can be found in marketing's 'incessant exploitation' of anthropomorphic imagery, while the spirit of alchemy is alive and well in marketing's own presentation of itself as a "corporate philosopher's stone" (p. 168) that "turns the base metal of production orientation into the 22-carat gold of customer-facing marketing orientation" (p. 168–9). Brown also includes the theme of "shamanism", comparing the power that marketing management gurus have over organisations with the "extraordinary power and immense prestige" (p. 169) that traditional shamans have in their societies. The practice of marketing segmentation, so fundamental to the strategic identity of the profession, is compared to the way that astrology divides all of humanity into the twelve different personality types of the Western star signs—both are also calculated "through occult statistical procedures" (ibid.). The Frazerian categorisation of imitative and contagious magic is invoked in order to explain the power of celebrity endorsement as a marketing technique where "in return for immodest remuneration, [celebrities] graciously transfer a modicum of their personal magic onto the supplicant product or service" (ibid.). Finally, marketing's obsession with resurrecting old brands, products, and promises is declared a form of necromancy.

Brown (2009) is not concerned with providing exhaustive argumentation or empirical data for his set of analogies. The thrust of his argument does not require it, for "just as marketing can be imagined as a science, so too it can be re-imagined as magic" (p. 170). Although marketing scientists might quarrel with every comparison he makes, Brown (2009) is confident that the "ever-widening gulf between the ivory tower and the oak-paneled boardroom" undercuts the relevance of such naysayers. The solutions that *they* are coming up with, solutions such as Vargo and Lusch's (2004) Service-Dominant logic, are simply more of the same scientism. Brown argues that we would be far better off presenting ourselves as "management magi" (ibid.) who "mysteriously sprinkle magic dust on otherwise unremarkable new products, promotional campaigns, strategic plans, you name it" (p. 170–71).

While arguing that what marketers really do is perform magic, Brown (2009) also adapts for his examination the popular distinction between 'white' and 'black' magic. "White marketing" is "socially responsible" marketing which acts to support consumer choice, achieve socially desirable aims such as fair trade, healthy eating, waste recycling", etc., while "black marketing" is the sort of reprehensible consumer manipulation designed to persuade people to buy goods which are "unnecessary or unsafe or exploitative or wasteful", or "the invention of non-existent ailments or anxieties or concerns" (p. 171). While this sort of distinction might make sense for those marketers who wish to create a clear 'us' and 'them' dichotomy (usually in order to then perpetrate some form of 'no true Scotsman' fallacy), Brown (2009) remarks that it is a misrepresentation of both magic and marketing. You can't have the 'black' without the 'white'; they are "intertwined, inter-dependent, inseparable" (ibid.). Marketing, we have to recognise, is "at least partially responsible for the iniquities that we're accused of". Even when a marketing campaign might appear to be tremendously successful in creat-ing money, jobs, entertainment, and 'culture' it will most likely also have a "dark side" (p. 172). Brown (2009) uses the Harry Potter phenomenon as an example. Despite the Harry Potter brand being "enormously impressive for a cultural product" and having an "incredible economic impact on the cultural industries" as well as giving a vaunted boost to "teenage reading habits" and even "boarding school enrolments", the Harry Potter books have also had a seriously debilitating effect upon the book trade. In par-ticular, the "ever-steeper discounting" that the phenomenon triggered "has proved ruinous for traditional independent booksellers" (ibid.). Brown's point is that "even a feel good brand like Harry Potter can have negative marketing consequences" (ibid.). So, marketing, like real magic, needs both the white and the black. We cannot pretend that *correct* marketing is a force for social good while only *incorrect, faux* marketing is responsible for social problems and abuses. Not only does this tend to naturally pitch academics (the source of marketing purity and correctness) against marketing practi-tioners (the source of misunderstanding, poor implementation, and venal-ity) but it also strips the discipline of any real connection to human truth. Brown (2009) places this sort of attitude firmly at the feet of the manage-ment science movement that resulted from the Ford and Carnegie reports and which is "at least partly responsible for the catastrophic mess that capi-talism now wallows in" (p. 73). A marketing based around the pose of sci-ence has not, in Brown's view, helped practitioners, who "look elsewhere for insight and guidance" and it has also left critique to "crusading journalists like Naomi Klein and Michael Moore" (ibid.). Instead, marketing scholar-ship has become a "dry-as-dust desert of unreadable articles and tiresome textbooks" that has succeeded in banishing the "superabundant supernatu-ralism of the marketplace". The war against magic has been a truly Pyrrhic victory, consigning the academic discipline to irrelevance, disconnection, and posturing.

Brown (2009) does not offer a clear way out—he ends the paper with a momentary glimpse of a future where "students are sated, practitioners are appreciative and academics have stopped scraping the barrel of science" (p. 173) but it shimmers like a mirage and offers little to buttress hopes of a magical marketing renaissance.

A Way Forward

We can see that there are a number of different motivations for marketing and non-marketing academics to identify marketing with magic. For some, particularly those outside the discipline, accusing marketing of being a magical system is a way of explaining how marketing is used to support modern capitalism through a form of enchantment, pulling the wool over human eyes, leading them to lives centred around satisfying their desires as consumers rather than social beings. Here, the magic of marketing is designed to mask the emptiness that industrialised production generates and it is quite clear that this is meant to be understood as something undesirable, unfair, manipulative, foolish, and wrong.

At the same time, within and without marketing there are voices that situate the magic of marketing first and foremost within the consumer. These scholars mostly focus upon the incredible resonance that magic and magical figurations appear to have for general populations. Magic is seen as something that people need and which they can find, or construct, in the act of consumption. These perspectives treat magical thinking as something we should not be ashamed of. Instead, they frame consumption magic as celebratory and liberatory, helping the consumer to approach the future positively or construct their identity in empowering ways. Yet, whilst the power of magic is acknowledged and explored, the place of marketing in the generation, direction, and navigation of that magic is artificially suppressed. In trying to move away from a construction of the consumer as a dupe, in focusing on interpreting the consumer as an agent in full control of their own identity, the marketplace is presented as something which is only tangentially connected to marketing—marketers are ghosts in much of the consumer culture research on magic, they flicker vaguely on the margins of awareness, with little consequence.

What we have, then, is a literature of extremes. Both poles embody truths but neither can ever hope to tell the whole story, or even present narratives that stand up to much scrutiny. The 'marketing is magic designed to keep us under control' perspective ignores the ways in which consumers use magical thinking to engineer their identity and facilitate their path through life. The 'consumer magic' discourse stream chooses to ignore the tremendous power of marketing to dictate the magical paradigms adopted by consumers, to influence their imagination and symbology. It refuses to engage with the necessary, constant interface between marketing magic and consumer magic.

A magico-rhetorical approach to marketing, rooted in the tradition of Gorgian Sophism, provides a far more nuanced 'third way'. Across all of the different perspectives and motivations we have explored in this chapter, the importance of rhetoric has been clear. Of course, rhetoric has been present in the way all of these scholars have been using the identification of marketing with magic in one way or another as a part of a larger rhetorical strategy, a persuasive gambit to serve a higher argumentative purpose. More fundamentally, however, it is clear that rhetoric is a central part of magic in all of these perspectives. Metaphors of transformation, verbal and visual patternings that entice and play with audience expectations and which echo sacred language and ritual speech, figurations which reach deep into the emotions of the audience and resonate across their desires, exaggerations which conjure worlds of magical relations and effects, webs of words and imagery which snare attention and enchant thinking—rhetorical techniques, magical techniques, marketing techniques.

Yet, we must not miss the lessons of *consumer magic*—marketers do not simply *do* magic *to* consumers. Consumers are witting, enthusiastic, co-creators of magical enchantment—so much so that when left to their own devices (as in the case of Muñiz and Schau's [2005] community of Newton fans) they can make just as much magic as marketers. However, given the ubiquity of marketing and the long historical links with the magical side of rhetoric that scholars such as Williams (1980) (inadvertently) pick up on in the evolution of advertising and marketing communications, it is surely the case that in most instances the magic of the marketplace is going to be a product (to some degree) of marketing agents. It is does not even make much sense to say that marketing agents *take advantage* of the consumer propensity for magical thinking—instead, perhaps it would be more truthful to say that both marketers and their audiences live within the same imaginative realm. Certainly, Brown (2009) seems to be suggesting that the scientism of marketing scholarship entirely misses the magical reality of marketing practice. As he notes, it is not just marketers who exhibit the "magical perspective", but "consumers too, I've discovered, consistently refer to marketplace phenomenon in magical terms" (p. 167), "incessantly" employing "supernatural language" when discussing the relationships they have with brands, shopping, and the consumer experience. Marketing scientists have exorcised the magical from their discourse and so ensured that their scholarship is similarly exorcised of relevance. Such statements must surely remind us of the many variations of the Gorgian versus Platonic/ Aristotelian narrative that we came across in the previous chapter. Marketing scholarship, in adopting the discourse of scientism, embodies the Platonic, bureaucratic conception of rhetoric as the dialectical establishment of administrative truth and knowledge boundaries. Marketing practice, on the other hand, is still far more strongly attached to the Sophistic, Gorgian obsession with the performative, magical power of language, with crafting the object of attention (Cassin, 2014), with crossing boundaries, or dissolving them. As so many of the scholars we have discussed in this chapter have intimated, consumers are far more attracted by the Gorgian, by the magical, by the transformative, and by the rhapsodic. And they are not just attracted to it as audiences—but also as creators, as "sorcerer's apprentices". For the academic discipline of marketing to be able to engage with this magical community of practitioners and consumers, it must re-found itself on a recognition of its liminality, its awkward, almost ritual, middle position, and on an understanding that the Sophistic celebration of the performative nature of language sits at the core of all marketing practice.

In the final chapter of this monograph, I will attempt to lay out the elements I consider to be necessary for such a re-founding.

Note

1. Sidney's Levy's (1960) piece for *Art Direction* magazine (reprinted in Levy, 1999) entitled 'Symbols of Substance, Source, and Sorcery' might be argued to represent an even earlier example. However, Levy's description of symbols of sorcery is narrowly focused upon the way in which the medium of television uses magical transformations and does not concern marketing communication *per se* at all.

References

Ankerloo, B., and Clark, S. (Eds.). (2002). *Witchcraft and Magic in Europe: The Period of the Witch Trials*. London: The Athlone Press.

Arnould, E. J., and Price, L. L. (1993). River Magic: Extraordinary Experience and the Extended Service Encounter. *Journal of Consumer Research*, 20(1), 24–45.

Arnould, E. J., Price, L. L., and Otnes, C. (1999). Making (Consumption) Magic: A Study of White-Water River Rafting. *Journal of Contemporary Ethnography*, 28(1), 33–68.

Belk, R. (1988). Possessions and the Extended Self. *Journal of Consumer Research*, 15(2), 139.

Belk, R. (1991). The Ineluctable Mysteries of Possessions. *Journal of Social Behavior & Personality*, 6(6), 17–55.

Belk, R., Ger, G., and Askegaard, S. (2003). The Fire of Desire: A Multisited Inquiry Into Consumer Passion. *Journal of Consumer Research*, 30(December), 326–351.

Belk, R., Wallendorf, M., and Sherry Jr, J. (1989). The Sacred and the Profane in Consumer Behavior: Theodicy on the Odyssey. *Journal of Consumer Research*, 16(June), 1–38.

Brown, S. (2009). Double, Double Toil and Trouble: On the Equivocal Magic of Marketing. *Journal of Customer Behaviour*, 8(2), 163–175.

Campbell, C. (2005). The Craft Consumer. *Journal of Consumer Culture*, 5(1), 23–42.

Cassin, B. (2014). *Sophistical Practice: Towards a Consistent Relativism*. Oxford: Oxford University Press.

Dégh, L. (1994). *American Folklore and the Mass Media*. Bloomington: Indiana University Press.

Erikson, E. (1982). *The Life Cycle Completed*. New York: W.W. Norton.

Fernandez, K., and Lastovicka, J. (2011). Making Magic: Fetishes in Contemporary Consumption. *Journal of Consumer Research*, 38(2), 278–299.

Gmelch, G. (2012). Baseball Magic. In J. Spradley and D. McCurdy (Eds.), *Conformity and Conflict*. Upper Saddle River, NJ: Prentice-Hall, 266–274.

Goffman, E. (1990). *The Presentation of Self in Everyday Life*. London: Penguin.

Gossage, H. L. (1967). The Gilded Bough: Magic and Advertising. In F. Matson and A. Montagu (Eds.), *The Human Dialogue: Perspectives on Communication*. New York: Free Press, 363–370.

Harré, R. (1985). Situational Rhetoric and Self-Presentation. In J. P. Forgas (Ed.), *Language and Social Situations*. Springer Series in Social Psychology. New York, NY: Springer.

Jhally, S. (1989). Advertising as Religion: The Dialectic of Technology and Magic. In L. Angus and S. Jhally (Eds.), *Cultural Politics in Contemporary America*. New York: Routledge, 217–229.

Jhally, S. (1990). *The Codes of Advertising: Fetishism and the Political Economy of Meaning in the Consumer Society*. New York: Routledge.

Laufer, R., and Paradeise, C. ([1990] 2016). *Marketing Democracy: Public Opinion and Media Formation in Democratic Societies*. New Brunswick, NJ: Transaction Publishers.

Leiss, W., Kline, S., and Jhally, S. (1997). *Social Communication in Advertising: Persons, Products, & Images of Well-Being*. London: Routledge.

Levi-Strauss, C. (1973). *Totemism*. London: Penguin University Books.

Levy, S. J. (1999). *Brands, Consumers, Symbols, and Research: Sidney J. Levy on Marketing*. Thousand Oaks, CA: Sage.

Muñiz Jr, A., and Schau, H. (2005). Religiosity in the Abandoned Apple Newton Brand Community. *Journal of Consumer Research*, 31(4), 737–747.

Newman, G., Diesendruck, G., and Bloom, P. (2011). Celebrity Contagion and the Value of Objects. *Journal of Consumer Research*, 38(2), 215–228.

Nienkamp, J. (2001). *Internal Rhetorics: Towards a History and Theory of Self-Persuasion*. Carbondale and Edwardsville: Southern Illinois University Press.

Pollay, R. W. (1986). The Distorted Mirror: Reflections on the Unintended Consequences of Advertising. *Journal of Marketing*, 50(2), 18–36.

Rook, D. W. (1985). The Ritual Dimension of Consumer Behavior. *Journal of Consumer Research*, 12(3), 251–264.

Rook, D. W. (1987). Modern Hex Signs and Symbols of Security. In J. Umiker-Sebeok (Ed.), *Marketing and Semiotics: New Directions in the Study of Signs for Sale*. Berlin: Mouton de Gruyter, 239–246.

Schnoebelen, J. (2009). Witchcraft Allegations, Refugee Protection and Human Rights: A Review of the Evidence. *New Issues in Refugee Research*, Paper 169. Geneva: UNHCR.

Sheffield, T. (2006). *The Religious Dimensions of Advertising*. New York: Palgrave Macmillan.

Slater, D. (1997). *Consumer Culture and Modernity*. Cambridge: Polity Press.

St. James, Y., Handelman, J. M., and Taylor, S. F. (2011). Magical Thinking and Consumer Coping. *Journal of Consumer Research*, 38(4), 632–649.

Thomas, K. (1991). *Religion and the Decline of Magic*. London: Penguin.

Umiker-Sebeok, J. (Ed.). (1987). *Marketing and Semiotics: New Directions in the Study of Signs for Sale*. Berlin: Mouton de Gruyter.

Vargo, S. L., and Lusch, R. F. (2004). Evolving to a New Dominant Logic for Marketing. *Journal of Marketing*, 68(1), 1–17.

Ward, J. O. (1988). Magic and Rhetoric From Antiquity to the Renaissance: Some Ruminations. *Rhetorica*, 6(1), 57–118.

Wardy, R. (2005). *The Birth of Rhetoric: Gorgias, Plato and Their Successors*. London: Routledge.

Williams, R. (1980). *Problems in Materialism and Culture*. London: Verso.

Williamson, J. ([1978] 2002). *Decoding Advertisements: Ideology and Meaning in Advertising*. London: Marion Boyars.

9 A Sophistic Marketing

In Chapter 4, I presented a tentative definition of marketing based upon my exploration of the middle position of the marketer. This definition stated that:

> *Marketing is the provision of intermediary services that facilitate the continuing exchange of attention between firm and stakeholders.*

In this chapter, I would like to improve and deepen this definition by framing it clearly within a Sophistic understanding of rhetoric, an understanding which combines particular perspectives on relativism, the performative/magical power of language, competition, and the place of irrationalism in the 'business' of persuasion.

First, I will return to the subject of control that we have seen to be an important motivation in the practices of marketing, rhetoric, and magic. Then I will move on to a discussion of the way in which competition, framed in terms of the Sophistic approach to *agon*, is at the heart of the marketing project. This will allow us to arrive at a nuanced understanding of the relationship between marketer/rhetor, audience/consumer, and client. I will then demonstrate how magic and rhetoric are integrated in a Gorgian manner in marketing practice. Finally, I will return to the middle position of the marketer/Sophist in order to draw a complete picture of what marketers do and how they do it.

Marketing Control Redux

As I have argued in earlier chapters, marketing is a discipline built upon the need for meta-control—it has sought to integrate under central control practices that are motivated by the desire to control production, distribution and consumption. Even in a definition that is focused around marketing as a service for facilitating the exchange of attention, control is implicit—marketing is helping to control the flow of attention, to make sure it is directed in the ways that strategically make the most sense. Similarly, rhetoric is concerned with control. The rhetor seeks to control the attention of the audience, control their regard, their understanding, and the behaviour that is born from understanding. Magic, too, is always motivated by the urge to control—the forces of nature, fate, luck, other people, or simply one's own life.

However, control, it would appear, must always be acquired and exercised at a cost. If the rhetor achieves control of an audience, then she has achieved it by the audience surrendering *their* control. If the marketer achieves control of a target audience, then they achieve it at the cost of the audience's control of their *own* need and desires (perhaps, of their *own understandings*). And if the magician seeks control over another human, then it would seem quite clear that this comes at the cost of the victim's own ability to control their destiny. Exerting control over something is an attempt to take control of that thing away from something or someone else—and, in the case of exerting control over entities with their own agency, that will often mean that control is being taken away from that entity. Here we can remember Gorgias' *Encomium on Helen*, where he states that "the speech which persuades the soul constrains that soul" (Dillon and Gergel, 2003, p. 81). It is this side of control, its violence, its theft of agency, which has made so many uneasy with it, so many suspicious of its presence and protesting at its force. Who likes to feel controlled, after all? Brehm's theory of "psychological reactance" (Brehm and Sensenig, 1966; Brehm and Cole, 1966) gives the scientific stamp of approval to something that rhetors have known for millennia, namely, that audiences don't like to feel like they are being forced into a choice. We want to believe that we have made choices from our own volition. Practices such as marketing, rhetoric, and magic are therefore bound to draw suspicion and raise hackles. Such reactions have been at the root of marketing scholarship's increasing unease with persuasive communication. The relationship and service perspectives that have grown to encompass much of marketing theory since the early 1980s have had a very critical attitude towards traditional 'manipulative' marketing communication. Varey's (2000) arguments are typical of this direction. He observes that the "conduit metaphor" (Reddy's [1979] term for the way in which we tend to think of 'sending' our thoughts to others by using the conduit of language) is "thoroughly taken for granted by institutional structures and everyday thinking" and supports "the dominant group [. . .] in accomplishing control over those they choose to subordinate" (Varey, 2000, p. 333). Management sees communication as a "conduit for the transmission or transportation of expressions of self-interest" (p. 336). Instead, Varey (2000) advises that management should adopt the "alternative participatory conception of communication" (ibid.) in which the organisation "does not inherently and covertly support the deployment of power over others". A manager should therefore be seen as a "steward of a responsive and responsible productive community". Theorists of the relationship and service marketing perspectives have constantly echoed Varey's call for marketing communication to move from "controlling to stewardship" (p. 337). Duncan and Moriarty (1998), in their examination of communication in marketing relationships, seek to de-emphasise the place of persuasion, which they gloss as "manipulative", and instead argue for an "interactive communication" approach in marketing where "*listening* is given as much importance as *saying*" (p. 2). This focus on interaction, which has been a significant function of both a turn towards the relational in marketing as well as the availability of communication tech-nologies that can facilitate it, has led to a valorisation of dialogue as the dominant marketing communication mode. For example, Vargo and Lusch (2004), in their foundational paper for the Service-Dominant logic, heavily cite Duncan and Moriarty (1998) and conclude that the "normative goal should not be communication to the market but developing ongoing com-munication processes, or dialogues, with micromarkets and ideally markets of one" (Vargo and Lusch, 2004, p. 14). Marketing promotion should be "characterized by dialogue, asking and answering questions" (p. 13) rather than persuasive monologues from the firm.

Marketing scholarship's enthusiasm for promoting a move away from monological, persuasive forms of communication towards interactive, sym-metrical dialogues with stakeholders is often framed as a simple reaction to the realities of the market. As Lindberg-Repo and Grönroos (2004) note, "service firms in the new environment can no longer create a com-petitive advantage by implementing only persuasive traditional marketing communication principles" (p. 238). In other words, customers and other stakeholders are no longer reacting well (or at all) to the "persuasive tradi-tional" techniques and so we have to find another approach. Even so, the path to dialogue is clearly a thorny one. Marketers seem to have a hard time getting it right. Grönroos (2000) admits that "frequently relationship marketing fails because marketers rely on relationship-like, but nevertheless manipulative, one-way communication" (p. 6). Similarly, Varey (2008) has further cautioned that paying lip service to the idea of marketing dialogue is not enough—true interaction with stakeholders cannot be based upon "mutually reactive or directive dyadic monologues of reciprocal manipula-tion" (p. 81). Dialogue must be understood as the "path to communion and the ground for self-discovery" (p. 90). The general consensus, then, is that marketing should be moving towards "mutually creative co-constructed dialogue" (Ballantyne et al., 2011, p. 208) and eschewing 'manipulative' persuasion based on 'traditional' 'one-way' models.

This movement in marketing scholarship is important for a few reasons. Firstly, in the repeated references throughout this literature to 'traditional' marketing communication there is a rhetorical attempt to construct a quite simplistic understanding of marketing communication history. Secondly, that history is built around the identification of persuasion with manipu-lation and control. This means that scholars promoting relationship and service perspectives are able to frame themselves as enlightened (rational) saviours of commercial communication, advancing an oppositional reading of 'traditional' marketing communication, which places co-created meanings and dialogue in clear distinction to persuasion. This assumes that dialogue, co-created understandings, or the process of "reasoning together to build up a common meaning" (Grönroos, 2000, p. 10) are in some sense free of persuasion and rhetorical strategies. Perhaps this stance stems from the persistent Platonic/Aristotelian bureaucratic rhetoric tradition that influences even scholars who are not overly enmired in the 'marketing science' paradigm and which promotes the idea of a discourse which 'benevolently' controls through process and exclusion (of irrationality, emotion, magical thinking, etc.)—'let's all sit down and talk sensibly about this . . .'.

The attempt to frame management as stewardship rather than control is a rhetorical feint. Dialogue, listening, and two-way communication are not aspects of communication that are impervious to practice of persuasion—indeed, they are very much essential to it. Full and continuous appreciation of the audience will be a central concern for any rhetor—the means of persuasion grow from a consideration of what a particular audience at a particular time will respond to. This is something that is embedded in Aristotelian rhetoric just as much as it is in Sophistic approaches. Furthermore, rhetoric can occur over mass media, in front of a large live audience, in a back office, a classroom, or in a one-to-one dialogue. *Listening* does not *prevent* rhetoric, it enables it, makes it more powerful and more likely to succeed. Listening provides the rhetor with the information that they need to understand the assumptions, prejudices, desires, beliefs, moods, and reasonings of their interlocutors. Without such information, any attempt at persuasion is always going to be based upon assumed lowest common denominators and therefore highly likely to produce failure or suboptimal results.

Having said this, the motivation behind the service and relationship marketing focus on dialogue seems clear. It is manipulation that is the real target. Traditional marketing communication is characterised as manipulative and it is manipulation that we must move away from. 'Tricking' customers, manipulating them into buying things they don't want for reasons that really don't make sense is not something that marketing should be doing anymore (the assumption being that this was indeed the way that marketing communication functioned 'traditionally'). The "traditional concept" of marketing communication is portrayed as something which is done to a "passive consumer" who is treated "as an object in the process" (Finne and Grönroos, 2009, p. 190), the target of a bag of "old and well tried tricks, upgraded by sophisticated scientific manipulation" (Gummesson, 2008, p. 326). In contrast, working with stakeholders to co-create shared meaning is depicted as power symmetrical and therefore non-manipulative—if we see the customer as an equal actor in the creation of shared meaning then it stands to reason that we would not be trying to persuade them of anything. Instead we would focus our marketing efforts on creating a "platform for communicative interaction" where "reciprocal value propositions" can be co-created to the mutual advantage of all stakeholders (Ballantyne et al., 2011, p. 208).

The opposition of dialogue and persuasion (control), is a false dichotomy, however. As we have seen in the literature on the presence of magical thinking in consumption experiences, stakeholders pursue consumption patterns which they feel might afford them control over their environment, their life, and their sense of identity—they adopt and adapt marketing communications, value propositions, cultural symbologies, tools and techniques to their own ends. Many of the discourse patterns that Muñiz and Schau (2005) find in Apple Newton communities, for example, are classic rhetorical attempts to persuade others that their choices are not as optimal as the choices that a Newton user has. Many of the dialogue or conversation forms that we are involved with day-to-day, whether as consumers, workers, stakeholders, friends, or family, are persuasive in their broad motivation, or at least have persuasion as a significant component. It, therefore, makes little sense to demonise persuasion in the hope that marketing can provide a platform for the sort of power-symmetrical, explorative, enriching dialogue which, when listening, does not try to "oppose or assimilate" (Pearce and Pearce, 2004, p. 45) but instead seeks to remain "in the tension between standing your own ground and being profoundly open to the other" (p. 46). Attempting to make marketing into an adjunct of something like Pearce and Pearce's (2004) "coordinated management of meaning" (p. 40) inspired Public Dialogue Consortium seems like a fundamental category error. Marketing, as both practice and discipline, is not suited in any way to a role as a public dialogue facilitator. Of course, it can be used to influence public discourse, and it can engage in public 'dialogue', but how can we envisage it as a 'neutral' platform for the advancement of mutual understanding? Surely, other practices, disciplines, and services are more credentialed to carry out such tasks? Is this, then, simply one more example of marketing's omnivorous nature? Are the service and relationship perspectives evidence of marketing scholars trying to slowly take over management of the public sphere as well as the commercial sphere under the guise of promoting reasonable, balanced, co-creating dialogue? This pattern, that we have already remarked upon when discussing the debates around the scope of marketing in Chapter 3, is just as much a part of the service and relationship perspectives as it has been of Kotlerian marketing management. Service-Dominant logic, for example, has been slowly extending itself since Vargo and Lusch's (2004) foundational article and most recently has been positioned as a logic "of human exchange systems that includes the economy and society and transcends academic disciplines" (Lusch and Vargo, 2014, p. 102). The logic's emphasis has moved outwards to social institutions in general, rather than simply firms (Vargo and Lusch, 2015). In an even more impressive example of how a scholarly perspective centred around symmetrical dialogue, co-creation, and transparency turns into a bid for relevance across the entire public sphere, Prahalad and Ramaswamy's (2004) explication of their DART model finishes with a description of how their perspective "may ultimately portend the emergence of a truly democratic global society in which human rights, needs, and values are predominant—not the demands of institutions" (p. 238). The marketing strategies behind Build-A-Bear Workshop and Lego Mindstorms, then, appear to be extensible across the whole of society, offering a more effective instantiation of democracy than any so far offered by the woefully short-sighted institutions of politics and ideology.

Such scholarship seeks to (rather ironically) persuade firms to surrender control and their reliance upon the "traditional" tools of persuasion and manipulation. Yet, as I have also argued elsewhere (Miles, 2010, 2014, 2016, 2017) such scholarship has a tendency to both misapprehend the extent to which it is enmired in existing control paradigms and also overstate the possibility (and, perhaps, desirability) of power-symmetrical marketing relationships. Marketers, after all, fundamentally *manage* marketing co-creation—if they *create* the co-creation space, then they inevitably set the terms and boundaries of dialogue, and if they join an existing stakeholder space then the financial power and communication skills that they bring to the forum inevitably mutate and overbalance it.

However, what if we were to see the whole of the market as a rhetorical space? Firms, suppliers, distributors, retailers, customers, media—everyone is involved in persuasion and self-persuasion attempts. If we begin to accept that human discourse is filled with persuasion and that the market environment is a particularly energetic nexus of persuasion then perhaps we can understand the marketing enterprise for what it is. Yet, as scholars such as Williams (1980), Williamson (2002), and Jhally (1989, 1990) prove, it is hardly just the preserve of progressive marketing scholars to pejoratively characterise 'traditional' marketing work as the magico-rhetorical manipulation of unwitting dupes. Furthermore, those marketing scholars oriented towards explorations of consumer culture are loath to engage positively with the magical 'control' aspects of marketing practice, even while celebrating the use of similar perspectives by consumers themselves. Such attitudes are also mirrored in much of the rhetoric scholarship of the twentieth century which, as we saw in earlier chapters, is intent on constructing the study of rhetoric as an antidote to the irrational in public discourse (and as such has carefully avoided investigating rhetoric's central place in the development and practice of marketing).

In the rest of this chapter, I will demonstrate how Sophistic rhetoric, or at least a re-constructed version of it, can provide us with a way of negotiating the place of control in the market place in way that does not flatly demonise persuasion, asymmetrical stakeholder relationships, and magical thinking, and also provides a strong platform from which to think about the evolution of the marketing enterprise. The following discussion naturally builds upon the work done in Chapters 4 and 5 outlining the similarities between marketing and the Sophistic tradition. I will begin with an explication of what the place of *agōn*, competition or struggle, in Sophistic performance can tell us about the function of marketing.

Marketing and the Sophistic Agōn

Competition was a crucial feature of Sophistic approaches to logos. Hawhee's (2004) exploration of the underlying relationship between athletics and rhetoric in ancient Greece begins with a remarkable discussion of early rhetoric's "agonism" (p. 25). She first notes that struggle, or strife, was an "idea that fascinated and drove the ancients", particularly the idea that struggle can be a positive, creative thing. Hesiod, she notes, speaks of two types of strife, destructive and productive, antagonism and agonism, and it is the latter which is the source of movement in the world. In the Greece of the Sophists, the *agon* of physical competition was an "occasion for the demonstration and hence production of virtue" (p. 27). Yet, we must not forget that while festivals of physical struggle held the constant attention of the Greeks, such events also included struggles of rhetoric. Indeed, Gorgias himself was famous for his declamations at such festivals, including the Olympics. In ancient Greece, competition was considered to be the most effective way of achieving and demonstrating virtue in sport, music, poetry, and the discursive art of rhetoric. As Hawhee (2004) explains, the preparation for, and participation in, competition embodied a "questing" ideal, a commitment to repetitive 'trying' after virtue in one's field through struggle and competition with others. While final victory was an important element of such festivals and the training for them, of far more importance was the generative nature of repetitive struggle itself, for it is in the struggle that virtue comes into being, not the victory. The Sophist approach to discourse was always agonistic. One of the clearest indications of this is the way in which metaphors drawn from combat sports like wrestling and boxing litter the descriptions of Sophistic debate by people like Plato as well as by Sophists themselves (Hawhee, 2004). Additionally, a Sophistic debate was a lively, interactive experience, where the two speakers sought to position each other and trick/trip each other up in a manner directly analogous to a wrestling match and where the audience would be just as vocal in their expressions of sentiment. This is a *very* different form of communication situation than that currently characterised as 'traditional marketing communication' by relationship and service perspective scholars, but it demonstrates a form of discourse which *can* be about persuasion, manipulation, and the irrational but which nevertheless can also be highly interactive and involving of many stakeholders.

How far can the concept of Sophistic agonism help us in a consideration of the rhetorical nature of marketing work? In abstract, one would have thought that a competitive environment is a natural one for marketing. Isn't marketing about finding strategies and tactics to help a firm succeed in a competitive environment? Branding, after all, is a response to cluttered competition spaces where it becomes important to be able to succinctly make a promise about a "unique and welcomed experience" (de Chernatony, 2009, p. 104). Most marketing strategies in the modern toolbox can be seen as responses to competitive landscapes. The service and relationship perspectives are themselves strategies designed to give a firm a competitive advantage (while cloaking themselves in the rhetoric of familial love and reciprocation). Even when the strategic response to competition is to search for a momentarily competition-free space (as in Ries and Trout's [2001] *creneau*) or a less competitive industry (as in applications of Porter's [1979] five forces) this is done with a view to being a struggling player in an overall competitive environment. Such strategies are akin to highly defensive wrestling positions, as we can quite appreciate from Porter's own language when concluding that "the key to growth—even survival—is to stake out a position that is less vulnerable to attack from head-to-head opponents" (p. 145). When going head-to-head doesn't make sense, then choose another line of attack, search for another point of competitive advantage, find a point of leverage or the best place to pivot—how can we ever pretend that marketing is not fundamentally agonistic? To adapt Porter's (1979) phrasing, competitive forces shape marketing in the same way that competition shapes Sophist rhetoric.

However, the exact way in which marketing fits into the competitive landscape is in need of some careful consideration. A Sophistic disputation took place between two speakers and in front of an audience. The audience, ultimately, judges the primacy of a Sophist even if there is a formal judge. The panhellenic festivals were places where rhetors would perform in contest in order to attract disciples (Tell, 2011). The audience is thus a group of consumers, or prospects, and the contest is a way of directing attention towards the speaker who has the most powerful grasp of *logos*. Sophist speakers could have an effect on such consumers that is entirely redolent of modern cult brands—Protagoras and Empedocles, for example, would have thousands of people meeting them at the entrance to a festival and exerted what Tell (2011, p. 120) calls an "Orphic attraction" on their audiences. In marketing terms, then, the rhetorical contest is a display of the competing Sophists' ability to attract and hold the attention of their consumers, the more effectively their words enchant, then the more customers they are likely to have (and the more their reputation will grow). The two competitors are trying to differentiate themselves before the eyes of the consumer. Another important part of the Sophist's presence at such festivals was that the audience also had the opportunity to engage the speakers directly when they made themselves available to answer any question that was posed to them. Here, the valuable Sophist technique of *kairos*, or improvisation, is able to be tested and displayed and it highlights once more the manner in which interactive, dialogical communication can be framed within a persuasive, competitive, marketing environment. Marketers should see interacting with customers as a persuasive mode—every dialogue touchpoint is an opportunity to persuade a prospect or existing customer of the firm's greater fitness to their purpose, of the fact that they offer a more attractive and desirable value proposition than the competition.

So, thinking about competitive Sophistic debate allows us to think about marketing's persuasive nature. Sophists at the games and festivals sought to differentiate themselves, to manage the audience's regard, through public competition—when they debated with their competitor their words were ostensibly directed at a fellow rhetor but were in fact composed (or improvised) for the consumption of the judges and the audience. In marketing, we rarely engage in such direct, 'head-to-head' (to use Porter's designation) communication—indeed, the ability to address market rivals by name is usually highly regulated—however, we are always communicating within a competitive situation, with one eye on the performance of our rivals, and this has a powerful effect upon the form and content of our discourse with consumers. So, while a Christmas TV campaign for a retailer such as John Lewis might look like a direct address to a consumer audience, it is also very much a piece of communication in Sophistic contest with the brand's rivals. Indeed, not just marketing communication performances, but all marketing strategy decisions are born out of contest and played out in front of (for the benefit of) consumers and other stakeholders targeted for influence. So, while contesting Sophists argued with *each other*, it was always the *audience* who were spellbound, enchanted, or charmed (Tell, 2011).

Rhetoric, persuasion, *logos*, magic—these are not things done to the audience. They are done *with* the audience, made *from* the audience. The enchantment that Protagoras and Empedocles could weave was something that the audience travelled many miles to experience. Their understanding of what makes a good argument, what form of words should make them feel in a particular way, what symbols they value the most deeply is just as important as the Sophists' understanding of these things about the audience. It also helps to make the audience into more self-aware users of *logos*—it demonstrates the many forms of rhetorical argumentation and the varieties of persuasive style.

We might baulk at describing marketing in such a way. 'Yes,' we might say, 'the words of greats like Empedocles and Gorgias, they can be admirable demonstrations of persuasion, argumentation and kairos, but marketing is just vulgar and manipulative and is simply crafted for commercial purposes'. And said this we have. Even marketing scholars, as we have seen, have largely been loath to stand up for the value of marketing's argumentation and persuasion—so much so now that we are trying to 'make it over' into some impossibly misguided model of civic discourse (rather like a curious 'my boyfriend does my makeup' video on YouTube). But marketers are not Aristotelians, not even Isocratians; they are Sophists in the highly competitive market for attention. We should be celebrating the profession's facility with *logos*, researching and evolving it, rather than hiding it behind scientism and appeals to rationality.

Wholeheartedly adopting Sophistic agonism into marketing scholarship does not necessarily mean that we have to stop talking about relationships, *per se*. However, rather than the central metaphors of marriages and family that tend to dominate current perspectives (O'Malley et al., 2008), we should explore relationship frames that are generated by situations of performance, contest, and competition far more fully. Understanding firms as performers in contests of rhetorical argumentation would mean that audience members are automatically empowered as the final arbiters of value and virtue. A performance succeeds as far as it convinces the audience, moves them, changes their attitude, and resonates with them—in other words, as far as it makes the performer and object of regard. And audience members are always potential performers themselves—the persuasion and attention manipulation that they employ in their own lives in so many different ways are terms of reference for their understanding and evaluation of the performance of brands.

The job of marketing is to provide a strategic and tactical service to win stakeholder regard in a competitive environment and, while the nature and extent of that competition might change, the struggle of competition is an essential driver for marketing.

Sophistic Relativism and Marketing Service

The agonistic nature of Sophism also illustrates one of the most disturbing characteristics of rhetoric for both the general public and philosophers of the rational and systematic—relativism. As implied in the story of great Sophist speakers opening themselves up to questions on any topic, Sophists drew great pride from their training's ability to allow them to discourse on any subject without being an expert. We have already seen in Chapter 5 how Gorgias delighted in being able to persuade patients of his doctor friends to undergo treatments that their actual doctors had not been able to convince them the worth of. This sort of practice is, of course, embodied in the *dissoi logoi* which were used as training aids for Sophists and which required the student to rehearse arguments for and against the same statement. Such Sophist techniques underline a view of truth that is relative—an argument can always find *a* truth. If the speaker has to convince an audience that the city should go to war, then the speaker should be able to find an argument to support such a proposition, and if they are required to promote the opposite then they should be able to do that as well. Finding appropriate arguments and working out how to best convince an audience are the valuable skills that Sophists 'sold' in their teaching and demonstrated in their public disputations. The marketer, too, should be able to pick up a brand, a product, a client and construct a convincing 'argument' for how to increase stakeholder regard. And should a rival brand, product, or client offer to pay them more or provide them with a more attractive future, then the marketer should be able to do exactly the same thing for them. A marketing agency can work for many different clients across many different industries as well as from the public sector, and it is expected that they will be able to produce creative, effective solutions for them all. The spirit of the *dissoi logoi* is absolutely embedded in marketing work. Marketing helps a firm to find its own truth, its value proposition—and that truth is generated in the light of the competitive environment within which the firm exists, and so is its essential point of differentiation in the contest for regard.

The scientification of marketing scholarship has worked against an understanding of the value proposition in these relativistic terms. Marketing science attempts to use empirical research using aggregated data that is statistically analysed in order to find patterns (in consumer behaviour, firm growth, market entry success, etc.)—and these patterns then become truths of the market that can be applied to those making related decisions in the future. The promise of marketing science is the promise of science— concrete, provable, reproducible truths that can be relied upon. Yet, if we see marketing as a Sophistic enterprise, such a chasing after scientific truth makes little sense. The truth depends upon the firm you work for, their stakeholders, their competitors, a myriad of shifting variables—how can there be *universal truths* in such *rhetorical* situations? Perhaps, indeed, the move towards a positioning of the firm around the value proposition in service perspectives such as S-D logic is an unconscious recognition of the rhetorical nature of the marketing endeavour?

An interesting question that arises from a consideration of the relationship marketing paradigm in this context is to what extent is the "part-time marketer" (Gummesson, 2002) involved in Sophistic practice? Gummesson (2002) defines full-time marketers (FTMs) as "those who are hired for working with marketing and sales tasks" and part-time marketers (PTMs) as "all others in the company and those in its environment that influence the company's marketing" (p. 77). He makes the sensible point that it is "legitimate and imperative for everyone [in the firm] to influence customer relationships" (p. 78)—indeed, if there are employees "who do not influence the relationship to customers full-time or part-time, directly or indirectly", then they are "redundant" (p. 82). Consequently, it makes perfect sense for any internal PTMs to be practiced in the *kairotic, agonistic* art of marketing rhetoric, to be mindful of the contest in which their firm is continually engaged and to be aware of their role in manipulating the regard of external stakeholders. Gummesson (2008) notes that those external stakeholders can also function as PTMs, and he argues that customers are the "most important marketers" (p. 80) outside the firm. I think that an understanding of marketing as a rhetorical practice would support Gummesson's views here. Rhetoric is not something just done by a single speaker getting up in front of an audience. The audience itself is involved in creating any rhetorical situation and in many instances there might well be no simple audience but instead a group of contending rhetors who function in shifting ways as rhetor and audience, judge and rival. Scholarship of consumer culture has demonstrated definitively that the consumer should be considered as a rhetor, too. Though that scholarship might well have tended to avoid the problem of how to understand the ways that consumer rhetors and marketer rhetors engage with each other, it has been vital in bringing to marketing's attention the fact that consumers are not the passive propaganda receivers of early communication theory myth. While the marketing department or marketing agency might be the site of full-time, professional rhetorical work, that does not mean that marketing rhetoric work is not continually carried out by everyone else. The marketing profession represents a powerful, systematised nexus of *logos workers*, but consumers, suppliers, and distributors (to name just three stakeholders) are also users of logos and will engage in rhetorical argumentation to manage regard to greater or lesser degrees. I would argue that a re-orientation of marketing around a recognition of its rhetorical nature would actually enable a far more powerful awareness of the power of logos across stakeholders and publics. This would also enable the efficient identification and training of PTMs by the marketing department in rhetorical skills which would be of benefit to the firm but also the employee (in terms of transferrable, empowering knowledge and experience).

A marketing practice conscious of its roots in Sophistic relativism might attract accusations of ambiguity, deception, and untrustworthiness—rather like the accusations that have accompanied marketing since it began. But an explicit, conscious owning of those roots would do a lot to contextualise the reasons for such mistrust. Ambiguity and deception are realities of many forms of human discourse and they can have positive, generative meanings. As Jarratt (1998) explains, when discussing Gorgias' theory of *logos*, "deception is a function of any discourse event", and the audience is always complicit, co-creating that deception—"their mental participation and, eventually, their assent is required for any discourse to have the force of knowledge" (p. 56). She notes that the early Sophists existed at a time when there were no hard boundaries between genres of discourse—poetry, tragedy, political declamation, religious ritual, magical charm, and competitive eristics were all one and the same. While we have delighted in building the existence of genres, sub-genres and micro-genres into our way of understanding human expression, we have done so at the cost of a great deal of flexibility in our thinking about the power of language and imagery.

Sophism sees relativism, ambiguity, and deception in a positive light. They make of discourse something that we should all be highly engaged with, moment-to-moment. Sophistic rhetoric is an argument for constant, mindful alertness—precisely because we are the measure of all things, we create our identities but also our realities through logos (and the imagery) we employ. If we are fooled, it is because we have allowed ourselves to be fooled—we have succumbed to opinion, to poetry, to magic, to an argument that feels right because it touches just the right emotions and prejudices in me. And this is the case not just for marketing arguments but for every argument we are exposed to. A marketing which embraces its Sophistic nature demands far more from its practitioners but also from its audiences—it holds them accountable for what they choose to submit to, what truths they choose to co-create. Consequently, it also reifies the agonistic nature of both marketing and non-marketing discourse. A Sophistic marketing understands every 'touchpoint' as an instance of contest, an opportunity to argue for the fitness of a value proposition—but in doing so it also promotes every touchpoint as an occasion for others to dispute, and for audiences to choose to succumb or not. Naturally, none of this denies the existence of scientific truth nor seeks to scorn the scientific project. However, it does rest upon the assumption that, for much of the time in our discourse as humans, we are not concerned with arriving at 'scientific truth' or the scientific process. Instead, we are concerned with promoting the 'truth' of our businesses, our relationships, our histories, our narratives, our selves. Sophistic marketing would see all of these as contested sites that require rhetorical argumentation to continually establish.

It is, at this point, worth pointing out that anyone who worries that a Sophistic marketing would open the floodgates of irrational public discourse simply needs to open their eyes and take a look around at what passes for public discourse in their society. The pretence that civic discourse, let alone commercial discourse, should be based upon logic, rationality, and measured dialogue is palpably failing us. I would argue that our loss of intellectual involvement with rhetoric as a practice, as something that we should all be involved in from an early age, has resulted in the currently impoverished state of civic discourse. A marketing which embraces the agonistic arena of Sophist rhetoric has the potential to draw our attention towards, and increase our regard for, the power of logos, enabling us not just to criticise its use in others (only ever half of the story) but also to invoke that power ourselves.

Magico-Rhetorical Relationships in Marketing

An understanding of marketing that sees it as an instantiation of Sophist practices of logos would accrue little advantage from ignoring the development of rhetorical scholarship from Socrates onwards. As we have seen, however, much of this development is positioned in opposition to Sophistic eristic practices and perspectives. The downgrading of style, the overemphasis of *logos* proofs at the expense of intellectual engagement with *ethos* and *pathos*, and the periodic merging of dialectic with rhetoric are all aspects of this oppositional historical development. As the chapters on the relationship between marketing, rhetoric, and magic suggest, though, there is a sense in which Sophistic approaches can be seen to have survived in our fascination with the magical and the performative power of words. Magic is continually referenced in advertising, both explicitly and figuratively, and as the consumer culture literature demonstrates, it also suffuses consumer relationships with products and services as well as their self-construction projects. How far can general marketing scholarship accept magic, though? Despite Brown's (2009) call for a re-casting of marketing as a branch of applied magic, such a position is intrinsically anathema to the majority of scholars who would identify as working within the discipline of 'marketing science'. One also wonders just how supportive those scholars of consumer culture who have helped to identify magical thinking in consumers would be of a marketing practice which chose to see itself as adapting to consumer magical thinking and consciously using it in their persuasive interaction with consumers? Should we co-create magical thinking? Or should we be more 'responsible'? One would assume that scholars who self-identify as rationalists and 'scientists' would baulk at such suggestions, even though consumer research might suggest that this is a powerful factor in the consumption experience.

A Sophistic understanding, a Gorgian perspective, might be helpful here. The Sophistic style is not all resonant sound, hypnotic patternings, and vivid metaphor. As a cursory study of Gorgias' *Encomium* shows, subtle, clever argument that engages the audience within their social, political, and religious contexts is also a vital part of how a Sophist practices the art of *logos*. The *Encomium* is described by Jarratt (1998) as a "performance piece" in which Gorgias "balances the disturbing recognition of linguistic indeterminacy with the familiarity of myth, both occurring within a clearly structured argument" (p. 57). The lesson here for us is that we should not turn away from magic, from the performative aspect of *logos*—we need to see it as co-existent with structure, rationality, cleverness, even the 'scientific'.

Consider the, by now, quite established marketing scholarship on the use of figurative language in persuasive communications that we explored in Chapter 2. How have we integrated the insights generated by this research into wider marketing scholarship? The answer is that we have not. Works written by marketing practitioners for other marketing practitioners, however, are quite a different matter. There is a long history of practical texts written by seasoned copywriters, for example, that speak enthusiastically about the importance of metaphors, language patternings, and other figurations in order to affect consumers viscerally as well as intellectually (some examples close to my desk would include Horberry and Lingwood, 2014; Shaw, 2015; Maslen, 2015; Sullivan, 2008). While *some* of these authors might have little familiarity with the rhetorical tradition and, indeed, might well transmit their wisdom under the mantle of 'what psychology can teach us about language', the truth is that much of their advice comes straight out of Sophist and Aristotelian rhetorical play-books. Integrating the rational and the irrational, the systematic with the rhapsodic, is not a problem that marketing practitioners have. Marketing scholarship, however, is still very far from having the tools or mindset to facilitate such a rapprochement. Yet our attention, our regard is affected by the irrational as well as the rational, the magical as well as the scientific or bureaucratic. We can make marketing decisions based upon magical thinking because, as we have seen, consumption is often based upon magical thinking. As scholars, we are also consumers/audiences—and we are as much influenced by magical thinking in our scholarly judgements and decisions as any other consumer might be. Integrating into marketing scholarship and education a nuanced understanding of the power of magico-rhetorical performative language and imagery, as well as the surreal logic of magical thinking, allows the discipline to function more effectively, and in far more subtle ways.

Kairos and Marketing Strategy

Perhaps one of the areas where Sophistic approaches to the control of attention and regard can have the most immediate effect in terms of aiding marketing practice is in the area of *kairos*. As Cassin (2014) states, improvisation is a "key element which sums up an entire series of features of sophistic *logos*" (p. 88). *Kairos* represents an enthusiasm for thinking on one's feet, judging the immediate context, the state of the audience, the resources at hand, to create a powerful argumentative line through the rhetorical encounter. It also, at a deeper level, conveys the truth that an argument is never finished, never completed, for "every argument turns into its own contrary as soon as it is enunciated because it has been enunciated" (p. 89). The Sophistic rhetor only ever pauses, never stops (in their persuasion, but also in their consideration of the audience, context, resources, etc.). Marketing also operates within this improvisatory dynamic, though there are also elements within marketing practice and education which work towards an agglutinating, or solidifying, of this flux due to the urge to institutionalise and bureaucratise marketing work. So, we have the tradition of the marketing plan (Cohen, 2006; McDonald, 2017; Kotler and Keller, 2015, etc.) which seeks to pull together all of the contextual information, objectives, tools, and financial and resource considerations in order to set out a logical, organised schema for any specific marketing campaign. The traditional divisions of the plan such as situational analysis, objectives, strategic decisions, tactical decisions, and measurement instruments make the marketing process highly structured and bureaucratic—a teachable, repeatable mechanism for the development of proficient marketing strategies. Rhetoric, of course, has its own equivalent planning tradition as we saw when reviewing the Classical legacy of Cicero and the *Rhetorica ad Herennium*. These structures are born from the Aristotelian systematisation of rhetorical practice and become more and more detailed over the centuries. Just like the marketing plan they solidify rhetorical practice to make it easy to teach, easy to reproduce, and easy to execute. A practiced speaker will not have to sit down and sweat over the choices of the five canons and the six parts of arrangement every time they need to persuade someone. The structure is designed to be internalised through practice so that it becomes something that can act as a scaffold for creativity and a true, *kairotic* reaction to the resources of the moment. The danger is, though, that rhetorical planning comes to dominate over the improvisatory. Frameworks become overly relied upon, transforming into ever more complex and inflexible structures that drain persuasive communication of creativity and a keen awareness of the flux in any situation. Improvisation, then, becomes the foe of the planning mind, a threat to the bureaucratic instinct and, accordingly, it becomes constructed oppositionally as something to be expelled from the profession/ discipline or dismissed as unteachable and unreliable.

A Sophistic marketing needs to re-assert improvisation as an essential part of the practice, and scholars aiming to support such a marketing must make concerted efforts to research, understand, and teach the manner in which kairos sits at the heart of Sophistic practice. Rhetorical improvisation is a real-time, resource-based, customer-focused practice. It embodies all of the traits that we expect of marketing but disengages it (by necessity) from the bureaucratic planning process. There are some similarities here to what has been dubbed "real-time marketing" (McKenna, 1995, 1997; Oliver et al., 1998), which is born from an appreciation of the general move towards mass customization and interactive communication technologies. Real-time marketing emphasises "creativity and flexibility" (Oliver et al., 1998 p. 36) and attempts to base the modern marketing process in a dialogue orientation (McKenna, 1995, 1997) that connects it intellectually to larger relationship and service perspectives. However, while the scholarly work on real-time marketing does concern itself with the necessity to react quickly and individually to rapid changes in customer requirements, it contains no engagement with the concept of improvisation that any form of dialogue-based relationship must contain. Instead, it falls to the marketing science urge to systematise, to bureaucratise the real-time. Technology is seen as a *substitute* for human improvisation rather than as an aid to its performance. If improvisation was acknowledged by, welcomed into, marketing as a desirable, teachable, essential skill, how much more effective and 'realistic' any dialogue/relationship orientation would be! Yet, there is a distinct sense in which improvisation might represent the thin end of the Sophist wedge. How could a marketing discipline obsessed with the structures of scientification admit improvisation into its heart? Even on one of the very few occasions that a marketing scholar has enthusiastically addressed the importance of improvisation (Holbrook, 2003), it has been done so within the rhetorically 'safe' scientific frame of an exploration of how chaos theory and the study of complex adaptive systems can have implications for marketing thought (though one charmingly leavened by Holbrook's characteristic humanistic valorisation of jazz). The rhetorical tradition, however, considers improvisation within the framing of persuasive address, disputation, and dialogue—just the sort of framing that marketing requires. The value of this tradition, particularly with respect to the construction of pedagogical modalities that could be effective in giving full-time and part-time marketers the abilities to function more effectively in stakeholder relationships and encounters can not be overstated. However, it is contained most firmly within a Humanities tradition of scholarship and enquiry and, like all other aspects of Sophistic marketing, it requires an internal re-ordering of the discipline towards a balanced understanding of how the Humanities and the Sciences can work with and support each other.

Finally, the importance of practiced, nuanced, and informed improvisatory approaches to marketing communication in an era of social media should not need to be pointed out. Contextual opportunities need to be seized, fleeting resources need to be effectively harnessed, and the *agonistic challenge* of real-time dialogue with a variety of stakeholders needs to be entered into professionally and a full understanding of its importance in generating and directing regard.

Marketing and Liminality

As argued earlier in this book, the liminal, middle position of marketing is something that it shares with rhetoric, particularly the Sophistic tradition. It is in the nature of this position to engender fear, suspicion, and hostility in others while at the same time attracting, fascinating and alluring. Indeed, the former is in many ways simply a function of the latter. The middle, intermediary position is so often a sacred one—intercessors, prophets, shamans, priests, and, of course, magicians, all stand in between the everyday world and the numinous, the dreamlike, the mysterious. The marketer is in between stakeholders and the firm, but also stands at the borders of rational and irrational, the customer's conscious deliberation and their unconscious desires, between the past of a brand and its future. As a result, it is often treated with scepticism, wariness, or disdain—by clients, the C-suite, non-marketing scholars and 'thinkers', journalists, and consumers. The accusations of magic and witchcraft made by Williams (2002) and Jhally (1989), for example, are reactions to their perceptions of marketing's intermediary services for capitalism that are perceived to construct a veil between the reality of production and the consumer. Yet neither marketing scholarship nor marketing practice have truly faced up to the consequences of marketing's liminal, middle position. And all the while the relevance of marketing scholarship to practice appears to be decreasing (AMA Task Force, 1988; McCole, 2004; Nyilasy and Reid, 2007; Reibstein et al., 2009; Lee and Greenley, 2010; Lehmann et al., 2011) and the reputation of marketing in practice seems to be waning (Hill et al., 2007; Nath and Mahajan, 2008; Verhoef and Leeflang, 2009; Clark et al., 2013; Park et al., 2012). Increasing the scientific rigour of marketing scholarship has not had any effect on this state of affairs, as cogently argued by Brown (2009). It is time for marketing to recognise its liminality—and to work with it. Instead of retreating further into the undergrowth of scientific discourse, marketing scholarship needs to provide marketing practice with the intellectual support that it deserves and this support is to be found in the traditions of persuasive communication and the direction of regard that have been developing for thousands of years. Marketing scholarship can do nothing but benefit from a resolve to celebrate and then strengthen the practice's position as an intermediary between realms. If we stop trying on lab coats perhaps clients, managers, and stakeholders will begin to recognise us for what we are—researchers and practitioners in the direction of regard. And perhaps then we can all recognise just how important it is for *all* of us to be able to engage in this contested realm.

In modern scholarship, as has been the case at many points in its development, the study of rhetoric is primarily focused upon its place in political discourse. The marketplace is ignored or marginalised as an arena for important rhetorical encounters. Perhaps much of the reason behind this is because politics has a longstanding tradition of being valorised intellectually within Western academic discourse, whereas the market is seen as an infecting, liminal space that threatens virtue, honour, and decency. And so the realm in which we spend most of our time immersed (even while we are 'doing politics'), the ever-flowing, ever-seeping sea of the *agora*, is blindly relegated to footnotes and marginalia. If marketing scholarship can begin to understand marketing's place at the end of a long and distinguished rhetorical tradition, perhaps rhetorical scholars will begin to engage reciprocally with marketing.

A Final Definition of a (Sophistic) Marketing

I now offer a slightly re-worded and glossed definition of what I see as a (Sophistic) marketing, a new understanding of what marketing does and should be doing and therefore what the object of marketing scholarship should be.

> *Marketing provides intermediary services to facilitate the continuing exchange of attention and regard between firm/client and stakeholders. It seeks to manage and direct this exchange through an appreciation of the changing rational and irrational motivations of the firm and stakeholders, using these as resources for the construction of both planned and improvised persuasive interactions in agonistic environments.*

References

AMA Task Force on the Development of Marketing Thought. (1988). Developing, Disseminating, and Utilizing Marketing Knowledge. *Journal of Marketing*, 52(October), 1–25.

Ballantyne, D., Frow, P., Varey, R., and Payne, A. (2011). Value Propositions as Communication Practice: Taking a Wider View. *Industrial Marketing Management*, 40(2), 202–210.

Brehm, J., and Cole, A. (1966). Effect of a Favor Which Reduces Freedom. *Journal of Personality and Social Psychology*, 3(4), 420–426.

Brehm, J., and Sensenig, J. (1966). Social Influence as a Function of Attempted and Implied Usurpation of Choice. *Journal of Personality and Social Psychology*, 4(6), 703–707.

Brown, S. (2009). Double, Double Toil and Trouble: On the Equivocal Magic of Marketing. *Journal of Customer Behaviour*, 8(2), 163–175.

Cassin, B. (2014). *Sophistical Practice: Towards a Consistent Relativism.* Oxford: Oxford University Press.

Clark, T., Key, T. M., Hodis, M., and Rajaratnam, D. (2013). The Intellectual Ecology of Mainstream Marketing Research: An Inquiry Into the Place of Marketing in the Family of Business Disciplines. *Journal of the Academy of Marketing Science*, 42(3), 223–241.

Cohen, W. (2006). *The Marketing Plan.* Hoboken, NJ: John Wiley & Sons.

de Chernatony, L. (2009). Towards the Holy Grail of Defining 'Brand'. *Marketing Theory*, 9(1), 101–105.

Dillon, J., and Gergel, T. (2003). *The Greek Sophists.* London: Penguin.

Duncan, T., and Moriarty, S. E. (1998). A Communication-Based Marketing Model for Managing Relationships. *Journal of Marketing*, 62(2), 1–13.

Finne, Å., and Grönroos, C. (2009). Rethinking Marketing Communication: From Integrated Marketing Communication to Relationship Communication. *Journal of Marketing Communications*, 15(2), 179–195.

Grönroos, C. (2000). Creating a Relationship Dialogue: Communication, Interaction and Value. *The Marketing Review*, 1(1), 5–14.

Gummesson, E. (2002). *Total Relationship Marketing.* Oxford: Butterworth-Heinemann.

Gummesson, E. (2008). Customer Centricity: Reality or a Wild Goose Chase? *European Business Review*, 20(4), 315–330.

Hawhee, D. (2004). *Bodily Arts: Rhetoric and Athletics in Ancient Greece.* Austin: University of Texas Press.

Hill, M. E., McGinnis, J., and Cromartie, J. (2007). A Marketing Paradox. *Marketing Intelligence & Planning*, 25(7), 652–661.

Holbrook, M. B. (2003). Adventures in Complexity: An Essay on Dynamic Open Complex Adaptive Systems, Butterfly Effects, Self-Organizing Order, Coevolution, the Ecological Perspective, Fitness Landscapes, Market Spaces, Emergent Beauty at the Edge of Chaos, and All that Jazz. *Academy of Marketing Science Review*, 2003(6).

Horberry, R., and Lingwood, G. (2014). *Read Me.* London: Laurence King.

Jarratt, S. (1998). *Rereading the Sophists: Classical Rhetoric Refigured.* Carbondale, IL: Southern Illinois University Press.

Jhally, S. (1989). Advertising as Religion: The Dialectic of Technology and Magic. In L. Angus and S. Jhally (Eds.), *Cultural Politics in Contemporary America.* New York: Routledge, 217–229.

Jhally, S. (1990). *The Codes of Advertising: Fetishism and the Political Economy of Meaning in the Consumer Society.* New York: Routledge.

Kotler, P., and Keller, K. L. (2015). *Marketing Management.* Boston: Pearson.

Lee, N., and Greenley, G. (2010). The Theory-Practice Divide: Thoughts From the Editors and Senior Advisory Board of EJM. *European Journal of Marketing*, 44(1/2), 5–20.

Lehmann, D., McAlister, L., and Staelin, R. (2011). Sophistication in Research in Marketing. *Journal of Marketing*, 75(July), 155–165.

Lindberg-Repo, K., and Grönroos, C. (2004). Conceptualising Communications Strategy From a Relational Perspective. *Industrial Marketing Management*, 33(3), 229–239.

Lusch, R. F., and Vargo, S. L. (2014). *Service-Dominant Logic: Premises, Perspectives, Possibilities.* Cambridge: Cambridge University Press.

Maslen, A. (2015). *Persuasive Copywriting: Using Psychology to Influence, Engage and Sell*. London: Kogan Page.

McCole, P. (2004). Refocusing Marketing to Reflect Practice: The Changing Role of Marketing for Business. *Marketing Intelligence & Planning*, 22(5), 531–539.

McDonald, M. (2017). *Malcolm McDonald on Marketing Planning: Understanding Marketing Plans and Strategy*. London: Kogan Page.

McKenna, R. (1995). Real Time Marketing. *Harvard Business Review*, July–August, 87–98.

McKenna, R. (1997). *Real Time: Preparing for the Age of the Never Satisfied Customer*. Boston: Harvard Business School Press.

Miles, C. (2010). *Interactive Marketing: Revolution or Rhetoric?* London: Routledge.

Miles, C. (2014). The Rhetoric of Managed Contagion: Metaphor and Agency in the Discourse of Viral Marketing. *Marketing Theory*, 14(1), 3–18.

Miles, C. (2016). Control and the Rhetoric of Interactivity in Contemporary Advertising Theory and Practice. In J. Hamilton, R. Bodle, and E. Korin (Eds.), *Explorations in Critical Studies of Advertising*. London: Routledge, 110–123.

Miles, C. (2017). The Rhetoric of Marketing Co-Creation. In G. Siegert and B. von Rimscha (Eds.), *Commercial Communication in the Digital Age—Information or Disinformation?* Berlin: De Gruyter.

Muñiz Jr, A., and Schau, H. (2005). Religiosity in the Abandoned Apple Newton Brand Community. *Journal of Consumer Research*, 31(4), 737–747.

Nath, P., and Mahajan, V. (2008). Chief Marketing Officers: A Study of Their Presence in Firms' Top Management Teams. *Journal of Marketing*, 72(January), 65–81.

Nyilasy, G., and Reid, L. (2007). The Academician-Practitioner Gap in Advertising. *International Journal of Advertising*, 26, 425–445.

Oliver, B., Rust, R., and Varki, S. (1998). Real-Time Marketing. *Marketing Management*, 7(4), 29–37.

O'Malley, L., Patterson, M., and Kelly-Holmes, H. (2008). Death of a Metaphor: Reviewing the 'Marketing as Relationships' Frame. *Marketing Theory*, 8(2), 167–187.

Park, H.-S., Auh, S., Maher, A., and Singhapakdi, A. (2012). Marketing's Accountability and Internal Legitimacy: Implications for Firm Performance. *Journal of Business Research*, 65(11), 1576–1582.

Pearce, W., and Pearce, K. (2004). Taking a Communication Perspective on Dialogue. In R. Anderson, L. Baxter, and K. Cissna (Eds.), *Dialogue: Theorizing Difference in Communication Studies*. Thousand Oaks, CA: Sage, 39–56.

Porter, M. (1979). How Competitive Forces Shape Strategy. *Harvard Business Review*, 57(2), 137–146.

Prahalad, C., and Ramaswamy, V. (2004). *The Future of Competition: Co-Creating Unique Value With Consumers*. Boston: Harvard Business School Press.

Reddy, M. (1979). The Conduit Metaphor: A Case of Frame Conflict in Our Language About Language. In A. Ortony (Ed.), *Metaphor and Thought*. Cambridge: Cambridge University Press, 284–324.

Reibstein, D., Day, G., and Wind, J. (2009). Is Marketing Academia Losing Its Way? *Journal of Marketing*, 73(July), 1–3.

Ries, A., and Trout, J. (2001). *Positioning: The Battle for Your Mind*. London: McGraw-Hill.

Shaw, M. (2015). *Copywriting: Successful Writing for Design, Advertising, and Marketing*. London: Laurence King.

Sullivan, L. (2008). *Hey Whipple, Squeeze This: A Guide to Creating Great Advertising*. Hoboken, NJ: John Wiley & Sons.

Tell, H. (2011). *Plato's Counterfeit Sophists*. Washington, DC: Center for Hellenic Studies.

Varey, R. J. (2000). A Critical Review of Conceptions of Communication Evident in Contemporary Business and Management Literature. *Journal of Communication Management*, 4(4), 328–340.

Varey, R. J. (2008). Marketing as an Interaction System. *Australasian Marketing Journal*, 27(1), 79–94.

Vargo, S. L., and Lusch, R. F. (2004). Evolving to a New Dominant Logic for Marketing. *Journal of Marketing*, 68(1), 1–17.

Vargo, S. L., and Lusch, R. F. (2015). Institutions and Axioms: An Extension and Update of Service-Dominant Logic. *Journal of the Academy of Marketing Science*, 1–19.

Verhoef, P. C., and Leeflang, P. S. H. (2009). Understanding the Marketing Department's Influence Within the Firm. *Journal of Marketing*, 73(2), 14–37.

Williams, R. (1980). *Problems in Materialism and Culture*. London: Verso.

Williamson, J. (2002). *Decoding Advertisements: Ideology and Meaning in Advertising*. London: Marion Boyars.

Index

For Product Safety Concerns and Information please contact our EU representative GPSR@taylorandfrancis.com Taylor & Francis Verlag GmbH, Kaufingerstraße 24, 80331 München, Germany

Printed and bound by CPI Group (UK) Ltd, Croydon, CR0 4YY
01/05/2025
01858416-0001